Intelligence-Driven Incident Response

Outwitting the Adversary

Scott J. Roberts and Rebekah Brown

Beijing · Boston · Farnham · Sebastopol · Tokyo

Intelligence-Driven Incident Response

by Scott J Roberts and Rebekah Brown

Published by O'Reilly Media, Inc., 1005 Gravenstein Highway North, Sebastopol, CA 95472.

O'Reilly books may be purchased for educational, business, or sales promotional use. Online editions are also available for most titles (*http://oreilly.com/safari*). For more information, contact our corporate/institutional sales department: 800-998-9938 or *corporate@oreilly.com*.

Editors: Courtney Allen and Virginia Wilson
Production Editor: Shiny Kalapurakkel
Copyeditor: Sharon Wilkey
Proofreader: Amanda Kersey

Indexer: Judith McConville
Interior Designer: David Futato
Cover Designer: Karen Montgomery
Illustrator: Rebecca Demarest

August 2017:   First Edition

Revision History for the First Edition
2017-08-21:   First Release

978-1-491-93494-4

[LSI]

Table of Contents

Foreword.. ix

Preface... xiii

Part I.   The Fundamentals

1. Introduction.. 1
Intelligence as Part of Incident Response   1
   History of Cyber Threat Intelligence   1
   Modern Cyber Threat Intelligence   2
   The Way Forward   3
Incident Response as a Part of Intelligence   4
What Is Intelligence-Driven Incident Response?   5
Why Intelligence-Driven Incident Response?   5
   Operation SMN   5
   Operation Aurora   6
Conclusion   7

2. Basics of Intelligence... 9
Data Versus Intelligence   10
Sources and Methods   11
Process Models   14
   OODA   14
   Intelligence Cycle   17
   Using the Intelligence Cycle   21
Qualities of Good Intelligence   23
Levels of Intelligence   24

Tactical Intelligence	24
Operational Intelligence	24
Strategic Intelligence	25
Confidence Levels	25
Conclusion	26

3. Basics of Incident Response. **27**

Incident-Response Cycle	28
Preparation	28
Identification	30
Containment	30
Eradication	31
Recovery	32
Lessons Learned	33
Kill Chain	35
Targeting	36
Reconnaissance	37
Weaponization	38
Delivery	42
Exploitation	43
Installation	43
Command and Control	44
Actions on Objective	45
Example Kill Chain	47
Diamond Model	49
Basic Model	49
Extending the Model	50
Active Defense	50
Deny	51
Disrupt	51
Degrade	52
Deceive	52
Destroy	52
F3EAD	53
Find	54
Fix	54
Finish	54
Exploit	55
Analyze	55
Disseminate	55
Using F3EAD	56
Picking the Right Model	57

Scenario: GLASS WIZARD   57
Conclusion   58

Part II.   Practical Application

4. Find. **61**
   Actor-Centric Targeting   62
     Starting with Known Information   63
     Useful Find Information   64
   Asset-Centric Targeting   70
     Using Asset-Centric Targeting   71
   News-Centric Targeting   71
   Targeting Based on Third-Party Notification   72
   Prioritizing Targeting   73
     Immediate Needs   74
     Past Incidents   74
     Criticality   74
   Organizing Targeting Activities   75
     Hard Leads   75
     Soft Leads   75
     Grouping Related Leads   75
     Lead Storage   76
   The Request for Information Process   77
   Conclusion   77

5. Fix. **79**
   Intrusion Detection   80
     Network Alerting   80
     System Alerting   85
     Fixing GLASS WIZARD   87
   Intrusion Investigation   89
     Network Analysis   89
     Live Response   96
     Memory Analysis   96
     Disk Analysis   97
     Malware Analysis   99
   Scoping   101
   Hunting   102
     Developing Leads   102
     Testing Leads   103
   Conclusion   103

6. Finish. **105**

Finishing Is *Not* Hacking Back   105

Stages of Finish   106

    Mitigate   107

    Remediate   109

    Rearchitect   112

Taking Action   113

    Deny   113

    Disrupt   114

    Degrade   115

    Deceive   115

    Destroy   116

Organizing Incident Data   116

    Tools for Tracking Actions   117

    Purpose-Built Tools   119

Assessing the Damage   120

Monitoring Life Cycle   121

Conclusion   122

7. Exploit. **123**

What to Exploit?   124

Gathering Information   125

Storing Threat Information   126

    Data Standards and Formats for Indicators   126

    Data Standards and Formats for Strategic Information   130

    Managing Information   132

    Threat-Intelligence Platforms   133

    Conclusion   135

8. Analyze. **137**

The Fundamentals of Analysis   137

What to Analyze?   139

Conducting the Analysis   141

    Enriching Your Data   142

    Developing Your Hypothesis   146

    Evaluating Key Assumptions   147

    Judgment and Conclusions   151

Analytic Processes and Methods   151

    Structured Analysis   151

    Target-Centric Analysis   154

    Analysis of Competing Hypotheses   156

    Graph Analysis   158

  Contrarian Techniques   159
  Conclusion   161

9. Disseminate. **163**
  Intelligence Consumer Goals   164
  Audience   164
    Executive/Leadership Consumer   165
    Internal Technical Consumers   167
    External Technical Consumers   169
    Developing Consumer Personas   170
  Authors   173
  Actionability   174
  The Writing Process   176
    Plan   176
    Draft   177
    Edit   178
  Intelligence Product Formats   180
    Short-Form Products   180
    Long-Form Products   184
    The RFI Process   193
    Automated Consumption Products   197
  Establishing a Rhythm   202
    Distribution   202
    Feedback   203
    Regular Products   203
  Conclusion   204

Part III. The Way Forward

10. Strategic Intelligence. **207**
  What Is Strategic Intelligence?   208
    Developing Target Models   209
  The Strategic Intelligence Cycle   212
    Setting Strategic Requirements   212
    Collection   213
    Analysis   216
    Dissemination   220
  Conclusion   220

11. Building an Intelligence Program. **223**
  Are You Ready?   223

Planning the Program   225
  Defining Stakeholders   226
  Defining Goals   227
    Defining Success Criteria   228
    Identifying Requirements and Constraints 228
    Defining Metrics   230
Stakeholder Personas   230
Tactical Use Cases   231
  SOC Support   232
  Indicator Management   232
Operational Use Cases   234
  Campaign Tracking   234
Strategic Use Cases   235
  Architecture Support   235
  Risk Assessment/Strategic Situational Awareness   236
Strategic to Tactical or Tactical to Strategic?   237
Hiring an Intelligence Team   238
Demonstrating Intelligence Program Value   238
Conclusion   239

A. Intelligence Products. 241

Index. 251

Foreword

Over 20 years ago, I was involved in my first large scale intrusion by a nation state actor from Russia called Moonlight Maze. My job for the Air Force Office of Special Investigations was to aid in data collection, interception, and analysis of adversary activity that occurred on the network and compromised systems. We learned through analyzing multiple attacks across many targets that this adversary was not going away by only "pulling the plug" from the back of the hacked systems. The enemy was extremely patient. Once they detected our response measures, they would persist in not reaccessing the same target for weeks. The attackers would ensure survival by hitting more than one target across the network and leave back doors on many systems. Across multiple intrusions by the same attackers, the task force started to put together a playbook on who this adversary was, how they operated, and what they were after. This playbook helped inform the defenses of many DoD locations worldwide. What was one of the outcomes of the Moonlight Maze intrusion? The scope and urgency of the attacks led to the formation of the Joint Task Force–Computer Network Defense (JTF-CND) that later became the gestation of U.S. Cyber Command.

We learned a lot from these advanced attacks in the late '90s. First and foremost, we learned that to detect the adversary, we had to learn from the enemy. Early on we discovered tools and practices that would allow us to pinpoint the same adversary on other networks. The information that helped inform our defenses and detect specific attackers became the formation of, likely, the most significant information security development since the intrusion detection system and the firewall: cyber-threat intelligence.

Having responded to hundreds of incidents through my career in the DoD, US Government, Mandiant, and my own company, the one thing we always rely on is that incident responders' primary objective is to use the opportunity to learn about the adversaries attacking you. With this information, we can observe another network and assess if the same enemy compromised them. This intelligence lays the bedrock for our approach to proper information security and defensive posturing against these specific threats. Organizations aren't likely to be hit by any hacker, they are likely part of a group, and they have your organization's name on a hit list. Without cyber-threat intelligence as the primary consumer of incident-response data, the security defenses could never improve and reduce the dwell time for the adversaries inside the networks they're compromising.

Threat intelligence was vital to intrusions over 20 years ago, starting with the story told in the *Cuckoo's Egg*, written by Cliff Stoll, and has been ever since. But somehow, most organizations are still learning to adopt the same principles. Part of the reason is the failure of proper resources that groups can follow. Another factor is bad advice from security vendors. Lucky for us, this book now exists and steps the reader through proper threat-intelligence concepts, strategy, and capabilities that an organization can adopt to evolve their security practice. After reading this book, your operations can grow to become an intelligence-driven operation that is much more efficient than ever in detecting and reducing the possible impact of breaches that will occur.

As the SANS Institute's Digital Forensics and Incident Response Curriculum Director and Lead, I have been discussing the importance of proper threat assessment and intelligence for many years. Many argued that it was a "nice to have" and "not as important" as stopping the adversary until analysts started to learn there was little they could do to eliminate an adversary without it.

I have advised many executives over the years that money would be better spent on developing proper threat intelligence than on vendor hardware that will likely not detect the next intrusion without being fed indicators learned and extracted as a part of the threat-intelligence analytical process. Part of that advice came from listening to conversations with the authors of this book, Scott and Rebekah.

Scott and I worked together at Mandiant and have remained friends ever since. I regularly follow up with him over the years and am an avid reader of his papers and articles. Scott is currently one of our instructors for the SANS Institute's Cyber Threat Intelligence course (FOR578). Listening to Scott present on this topic for many years is always a breath of wisdom that is equivalent to hearing Warren Buffet give financial advice. I can hear Scott's voice in my head as I read his thoughts pouring off the pages in this book.

Similar to my background, Rebekah is former military and worked across the board in cyber operations. She is formerly the Cyber Unity Operations Chief for the U.S. Marine Corp. She was also a cyber-operation exercise planner in the DoD, a network warfare analyst while at the NSA, and worked to create threat intelligence in Fortune 500 companies and across information security vendors. Rebekah's knowledge is on point and intuitive. She knows and understands this space like no other, having lived it by working inside and outside the DoD (both Intel and cyber communities) and across many companies. Rebekah has provided cyber-threat intelligence briefs at the

White House, based on her theories of coordinated defensive and offensive cyber operations. Getting to know Rebekah has been amazing and enlightening, especially as I continue to learn how traditional intelligence methods are applied to cyber-operations analysis. I am also proud to highlight that Rebekah is also a course author and instructor for the SANS Institute's Course in Cyber Threat Intelligence (FOR578).

Together, Scott and Rebekah have put together their thoughts on paper in one of the most informed cyber-operations strategy guides you could ever pick up. You should consider making this book mandatory reading for all cyber analysts in your organization. This book is at the top of my recommended reading list for any cyber security analysts old and new. The ideas expressed in this book don't solve technical challenges, hacking tactics, or configuring security defenses, but instead, focuses on concepts, strategy, and approaches that indeed work at improving the posture, detection, and response inside the security operations of your organization.

One of the most important chapters of the book for cyber-security management to read is how to build an intelligence program. Watching Scott and Rebekah go through this with many organizations has been impressive. Organizations that have benefited from their knowledge understand that "threat intelligence" is not a buzzword, and their approaches and requirements to step through is worth the read several times over.

For those who are security analysts, the book's main content steps an analyst through the intricacies of proper incident-response approaches, utilizing a threat intelligence mindset. Once exposed to the information contained in this book, it will permanently change the way you approach cyber security in your organization. It will transition you from being an average analyst into one with advanced operational skills that will continue to pay off throughout your career.

I wish I had this book 20 years ago in my first intrusion cases while investigating Russian hackers during Moonlight Maze. Luckily, we have this book today, and I can now point to it as required reading for my students who want to move beyond tactical response and apply a framework and strategy to it all that works.

— Rob Lee
Founder, Harbingers Security/DFIR
Lead, SANS Institute

Preface

Welcome to the exciting world of intelligence-driven incident response! Intelligence —specifically, cyber threat intelligence—has a huge potential to help network defenders better understand and respond to attackers' actions against their networks.

The purpose of this book is to demonstrate how intelligence fits into the incident-response process, helping responders understand their adversaries in order to reduce the time it takes to detect, respond to, and remediate intrusions. Cyber threat intelligence and incident response have long been closely related, and in fact are inextricably linked. Not only does threat intelligence support and augment incident response, but incident response generates threat intelligence that can be utilized by incident responders. The goal of this book is to help readers understand, implement, and benefit from this relationship.

Why We Wrote This Book

In recent years, we have seen a transition from approaching incident response as a standalone activity to viewing it as an integral part of an overall network security program. At the same time, cyber threat intelligence is rapidly becoming more and more popular, and more companies and incident responders are trying to understand how to best incorporate threat intelligence into their operations. The struggle is real—both of us have been through these growing pains as we learned how to apply traditional intelligence principles into incident-response practices, and vice versa—but we know that it is worth the effort. We wrote this book to pull together the two worlds, threat intelligence and incident response, to show how they are stronger and more effective together, and to shorten the time it takes practicioners to incorporate them into operations.

Who This Book Is For

This book is written for people involved in incident response, whether their role is an incident manager, malware analyst, reverse engineer, digital forensics specialist, or intelligence analyst. It is also for those interested in learning more about incident response. Many people who are drawn to cyber threat intelligence want to know about attackers—what motivates them and how they operate—and the best way to learn that is through incident response. But it is only when incident response is approached with an intelligence mindset that we start to truly understand the value of the information we have available to us. You don't need to be an expert in incident response, or in intelligence, to get a lot out of this book. We step through the basics of both disciplines in order to show how they work together, and give practical advice and scenarios to illustrate the process.

How This Book Is Organized

This book is organized as follows:

- Part 1 includes chapters 1, 2, and 3, and provides an introduction to the concept of intelligence-driven incident response (IDIR) and an overview of the intelligence and incident-response disciplines. We introduce the concept of F3EAD, the primary model for IDIR that will be used in the rest of the book.
- Part 2 includes chapters 4, 5, and 6, which step through the incident-response-focused portion of F3EAD: Find, Fix, and Finish, as well as chapters 7, 8, and 9, which cover the intelligence-focused steps in the F3EAD process: Exploit, Analyze, and Disseminate.
- Part 3 includes Chapter 10, an overview of strategic-level intelligence and how it applies to incident response and network security programs, and Chapter 11, which discusses formalized intelligence programs and how to set up an intelligence-driven incident-response programs for success.
- The appendix includes examples of intelligence products that you may create during the dissemination phase (covered in Chapter 9).

Typically, people who are interested in integrating threat intelligence into incident response have a stronger background in one of those disciplines over the other, so it may be appealing to skim through the sections you are more familiar with and focus only on the parts that are new to you. While that is perfectly fine, you may find that we have discussed a new model or approaches to better integrate the two disciplines, so don't skip through too much, even if you think you know it already!

Conventions Used in This Book

The following typographical conventions are used in this book:

Italic
> Indicates new terms, URLs, email addresses, filenames, and file extensions.

`Constant width`
> Used for program listings, as well as within paragraphs to refer to program elements such as variable or function names, databases, data types, environment variables, statements, and keywords.

`Constant width bold`
> Shows commands or other text that should be typed literally by the user.

`Constant width italic`
> Shows text that should be replaced with user-supplied values or by values determined by context.

 This element signifies a tip or suggestion.

 This element signifies a general note.

 This element indicates a warning or caution.

O'Reilly Safari

 *Safari* (formerly Safari Books Online) is a membership-based training and reference platform for enterprise, government, educators, and individuals.

Members have access to thousands of books, training videos, Learning Paths, interactive tutorials, and curated playlists from over 250 publishers, including O'Reilly Media, Harvard Business Review, Prentice Hall Professional, Addison-Wesley Professional, Microsoft Press, Sams, Que, Peachpit Press, Adobe, Focal Press, Cisco Press, John Wiley & Sons, Syngress, Morgan Kaufmann, IBM Redbooks, Packt, Adobe Press, FT Press, Apress, Manning, New Riders, McGraw-Hill, Jones & Bartlett, and Course Technology, among others.

For more information, please visit *http://oreilly.com/safari*.

How to Contact Us

Please address comments and questions concerning this book to the publisher:

> O'Reilly Media, Inc.
> 1005 Gravenstein Highway North
> Sebastopol, CA 95472
> 800-998-9938 (in the United States or Canada)
> 707-829-0515 (international or local)
> 707-829-0104 (fax)

To comment or ask technical questions about this book, send email to *bookquestions@oreilly.com*.

For more information about our books, courses, conferences, and news, see our website at http://www.oreilly.com.

Find us on Facebook: http://facebook.com/oreilly

Follow us on Twitter: http://twitter.com/oreillymedia

Watch us on YouTube: http://www.youtube.com/oreillymedia

Acknowledgments

Rebekah would like to thank the following people (and places):

My wonderful kiddos: Emma, Caitlyn, and Colin, for encouraging me to write and for offering up helpful suggestions on how to catch hackers (the bad ones).

My parents, brothers, sisters, and extended family for supporting me throughout this undertaking.

My work family: Jen, Wade, Rachel, Jordan, Bob, Derek (and many more!) for always believing in me and not saying (out loud) how crazy I was to write a book.

My partner in crime and partner in life, for keeping me hydrated, caffeinated, and happy, and reassuring me that deadlines were made to be missed.

My coauthor, Scott, for being the best BFFFG a girl could ask for.

And finally, to the staff of 23 Hoyt in Portland, the Trademark in Alexandria, and countless flights in between, where the majority of my writing took place.

Scott would like to thank the following people (and places):

My amazing wife, Kessa: I wouldn't have gotten this done without your encouragement and insight, and I wouldn't have bothered to try without your inspiration. Thanks for supporting me during the early mornings, late nights, and all the times in between. I'm hopeful I can be half as supportive in all your endeavors. JTMC

My parents, Steve and Janet: from another epic writing project and my first computer to now, you've constantly supported my curiosity and have made getting to this place possible. I can't thank you enough and wouldn't be here without my basecamp.

The GitHub Security team: you have given me the freedom to learn, to write, to share, and to build in a way I didn't know I could.

Kyle: your fingerprints are still all over this thing. I appreciate you telling me when I am crazy and when I am just ambitious and telling me to go for it either way.

My many friends and mentors throughout the years: my guess is most of you don't know how much impact you've had or how much I appreciate the conversations, the experiences, and the willingness to listen to me sharing my passions.

To my excellent coauthor Rebekah, you're the gunny we need, not the gunny we deserve. I couldn't have done it alone, and it wouldn't be excellent without you.

The staff at O'Reilly for being the best in the business and for helping make our ideas a reality.

Lastly, the fine folks at Mission Coffee Company in Columbus for the espresso and bagels that fueled many of my words.

## PART I

The Fundamentals

When you begin implementing intelligence-driven incident response, it is important to have a solid understanding of both intelligence and incident-response processes. Part 1 provides an introduction to cyber-threat intelligence, the intelligence process, the incident-response process, and how they all work together.

## CHAPTER 1

Introduction

"But I think the real tension lies in the relationship between what you might call the pursuer and his quarry, whether it's the writer or the spy."

—John le Carre

Before diving into the application of intelligence-driven incident response, it is important to understand the reasons that cyber threat intelligence is so important to incident response. This chapter covers the basics of cyber threat intelligence, including its history and the way forward, and sets the stage for the concepts discussed in the rest of this book.

Intelligence as Part of Incident Response

As long as there has been conflict, there have been those who studied, analyzed, and strove to understand the enemy. Wars have been won and lost based on an ability to understand the way the enemy thinks and operates, to comprehend their motivations and identify their tactics, and to make decisions—large and small—based on this understanding. Regardless of the type of conflict, whether a war between nations or a stealthy intrusion against a sensitive network, threat intelligence guides both sides. The side that masters the art and science of threat intelligence, analyzing information about the intent, capability, and opportunities of adversaries, will almost always be the side that wins.

History of Cyber Threat Intelligence

In 1986, Cliff Stoll was a PhD student managing the computer lab at Lawrence Berkley National Laboratory in California when he noticed a billing discrepancy in the amount of 75 cents, indicating that someone was using the laboratory's computer systems without paying for it. Our modern-day, network-security-focused brains see this and scream, "Unauthorized access!" but in 1986 it was hardly cause for concern. Network intrusions were not something that made the news daily, with claims of millions or even billions of dollars stolen; the majority of computers connected to the "internet" belonged to government and research institutes, not casual users. The network defense staple tool tcpdump was a year from being started. Common network discovery tools such as Nmap would not be created for another decade, and exploitation frameworks such as Metasploit would not appear for another 15 years. The discrepancy was just as likely to have been a software bug or bookkeeping error as it was that someone had simply not paid for their time.

Except that it wasn't. As Stoll would discover, he was not dealing with a computer glitch or a cheap mooch of a user. He was stalking a "wily hacker" who was using Berkley's network as a jumping-off point to gain access to sensitive government computers, such as the White Sands Missile Range and the National Security Agency (NSA). Stoll used printers to monitor incoming network traffic and began to profile the intruder responsible for the first documented case of cyber espionage. He learned the typical hours the attacker was active, the commands he ran to move through the interconnected networks, and other patterns of activity. He learned how the attacker was able to gain access to Berkley's network in the first place by exploiting a vulnerability in the *movemail* function in GNU Emacs, a tactic that Stoll likened to a cuckoo bird leaving its egg in another bird's nest to hatch and which inspired the name of the book on the intrusion, *The Cuckoo's Egg*. Understanding the attacker meant that it was possible to protect the network from further exploitation, identify where he may target next, and allowed a response, both on the micro level (identifying the individual carrying out the attacks) and on the macro level (realizing that nations were employing new tactics in their traditional intelligence-gathering arsenal and changing policies to respond to this change).

Modern Cyber Threat Intelligence

Over the decades, the threat has grown and morphed. Adversaries use an ever-expanding set of tools and tactics to attack their victims, and their motivations range from intelligence collection to financial gain to destruction to attention. Understanding the attacker has gotten much more complicated, but no less important.

Understanding the attacker has been a critical component of incident response from the beginning, and knowing how to identify and understand the attacker as well as how to use that information to protect networks is the fundamental concept behind a more recent addition to the incident responder's toolkit: cyber threat intelligence. *Threat intelligence* is the analysis of adversaries—their capabilities, motivations, and goals; and *cyber threat intelligence* (CTI) is the analysis of how adversaries use the cyber domain to accomplish their goals. See Figure 1-1 on how these levels of attacks play into one another.

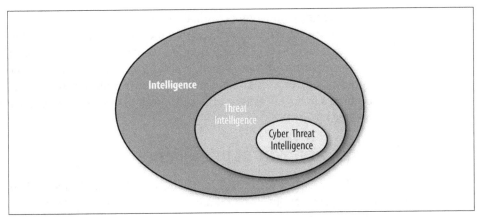

Figure 1-1. From intelligence to cyber threat intelligence

In information security, we traditionally focus on scientific concepts; we like things that are testable and reproducible. But there is both an art and a science behind cyber threat intelligence, and it is the art that most often eludes us. This art includes the analysis and interpretation of data about attackers, as well as how to convey that information to the audience in a way that makes sense and enables them to act. This is what will truly help us understand a thinking, reacting, and evolving adversary.

Security analysts love few things more than identifying malicious activity on their networks and tracing that maliciousness back to a known attacker, but in many cases early implementation of intelligence was ad hoc and largely intuitive. Over the years, new technologies were developed with the goal of better detecting and understanding malicious activity on networks: Network Access Control, Deep Packet Inspection firewalls, and network security intelligence appliances are all based on familiar concepts with new applications.

The Way Forward

These new technologies give us more information about the actions that attackers take as well as additional ways to act on that information. However, we have found that with each new technology or concept implemented, the enemy adapted; worms and viruses with an alphabet soup of names changed faster than our appliances could identify them, and sophisticated, well-funded attackers were more organized and motivated than many network defenders. Ad hoc and intuitive intelligence work would no longer suffice to keep defenders ahead of the threat. Analysis would need to evolve as well and become formal and structured. The scope would have to expand, and the goals would have to become more ambitious.

In addition to detecting threats against an organization's often nebulous and ephemeral perimeter, analysts would need to look deeper within their networks for the attacks that got through the lines, down to individual user systems and servers themselves, as well as look outward into third-party services and to better understand the attackers who may be targeting them. The information would need to be analyzed and its implications understood, and then action would have to be taken to better prevent, detect, and eradicate threats. The actions taken to better understand adversaries would need to become a formal process and a critical part of information security operations: threat intelligence.

Incident Response as a Part of Intelligence

Intelligence is often defined as information that has been refined and analyzed to make it actionable. Intelligence, therefore, requires information. In intelligence-driven incident response, there are multiple ways to gather information that will be analyzed and used to support incident response. However, it is important to note that incident response will also generate cyber threat intelligence. The traditional intelligence cycle—which we cover in depth in Chapter 2—involves direction, collection, processing, analysis, dissemination, and feedback. Intelligence-driven incident response involves all of these components and helps inform direction, collection, and analysis in other applications of threat intelligence as well, such as network defense and user awareness training. Intelligence-driven incident response doesn't end when the intrusion is understood and remediated; it actually generates information that will continue to feed the intelligence cycle.

Analysis of an intrusion, either successful or failed, can provide a variety of information that can be used to better understand the overall threat to an environment. The root cause of the intrusion and the initial access vector can be analyzed to inform an organization of weaknesses in network defenses or of policies that attackers may be abusing. The malware that is identified on a system can help identify the tactics that attackers are using to evade traditional security measures, such as antivirus or host-based intrusion-detection tools, and the capabilities they have available to them. The way an attacker moves laterally through a network can be analyzed and used to create new ways to monitor for attacker activity in the network. The final actions that an attacker performed (such as stealing information or changing how systems function), whether they were successful or not, can help analysts understand the enemy's motivations and goals, which can be used to guide overall security efforts. There is essentially no part of an incident-response engagement that cannot be used to better understand the threats facing an organization.

For this reason, the various processes and cycles outlined in this book are aimed at ensuring that intelligence-driven incident response supports overall intelligence operations. Although they provide specific guidance for utilizing cyber threat intelligence in incident response, keep in mind that wider applications can be used as intelligence capabilities expand.

What Is Intelligence-Driven Incident Response?

Cyber-threat intelligence isn't a new concept, simply a new name for an old approach: applying a structured analytical process to understand an attack and the adversary behind it. The application of threat intelligence to network security is more recent, but the basics haven't changed. Cyber threat intelligence involves applying intelligence processes and concepts—some of the oldest concepts that exist—and making them a part of the overall information security process. Threat intelligence has many applications, but one of the fundamental ways it can be utilized is as an integral part of the intrusion-detection and incident-response process. We call this *intelligence-driven incident response* and think it is something every security team can do, with or without a major capital investment. It's less about tools, although they certainly help sometimes, and more about a shift in the way we approach the incident-response process. Intelligence-driven incident response will help not only to identify, understand, and eradicate threats within a network, but also to strengthen the entire information security process to improve those responses in the future.

Why Intelligence-Driven Incident Response?

Over the past few decades, our world has become increasingly interconnected, both literally and figuratively, allowing attackers to carry out complex campaigns and intrusions against multiple organizations with the same effort that it used to take to target a single entity. We are long past the point where we can automatically assume that an intrusion is an isolated incident. When we better understand the adversary, we can more easily pick up on the patterns that show commonalities between intrusions. Intelligence-driven incident response ensures that we are gathering, analyzing, and sharing intelligence in a way that will help us identify and respond to these patterns more quickly.

Operation SMN

A good example of this is the analysis of the Axiom Group, which was identified and released as a part of a Coordinated Malware Eradication (CME) campaign in 2014 called Operation SMN. (*http://www.novetta.com/wp-content/uploads/2014/11/Executive_Summary-Final_1.pdf*)

What's in a Name?

The "SMN" in "Operation SMN" stands for "some marketing name," a not-so-subtle but amusing jab indicating how widespread the belief is that marketing often takes over intelligence products. For better or worse, threat intelligence has been eagerly embraced by marketing forces all touting the best threat-intelligence products, feeds, and tools. The first time many people are exposed to threat intelligence is through

---

marketing material, making it difficult for many to fully understand what threat intelligence actually is.

It is important that intelligence work is done with the end goal of better understanding and defending against adversaries. Sometimes marketing gets in the way of that, but ideally marketing can help with messaging and ensuring that the "story" behind threat intelligence reaches the right audience in the right way.

For more than six years, a group of attackers known as the Axiom Group stealthily targeted, infiltrated, and stole information from Fortune 500 companies, journalists, nongovernmental organizations, and a variety of other organizations. The group used sophisticated tools, and the attackers went to great lengths to maintain and expand access within the victims' networks. As malware was detected and the incident-response process began within various victim organizations, coordinated research on one of the malware families used by this group identified that the issue was far more complex than originally thought. As more industry partners became involved and exchanged information, patterns began to emerge that showed not just malware behavior, but the behaviors of a threat actor group working with clear guidance. Strategic intelligence was identified, including regions and industries targeted.

This was an excellent example of the intelligence cycle at work in an incident-response scenario. Not only was information collected, processed, and analyzed, but it was disseminated in such as way as to generate new requirements and feedback, starting the process over again until the analysts had reached a solid conclusion and could act with decisiveness, eradicating 43,000 malware installations at the time that the report was published. The published report, also part of the dissemination phase, allowed incident responders to better understand the tactics and motivations of this actor group.

Operation Aurora

Several years before the Axiom Group was identified, another (possibly related) group carried out a similarly complex operation named Operation Aurora (*http://bit.ly/2uF1MOJ*), which successfully targeted approximately 30 companies. This operation impacted companies in the high-tech sector as well as defense contractors, the chemical sector, and Chinese political dissidents. The patterns and motivations of the operation were similar to those in Operation SMN. Looking at these two examples of elaborate and widespread attacks, it becomes clear that these weren't random but rather were coordinated with strategic objectives by a determined adversary willing to expend a great deal of time and effort to ensure that the objectives were met. If we tackle the problem by jumping from incident to incident without stopping to capture lessons learned and to look at the big picture, then the attackers will always be several steps ahead of us.

Both the Axiom Group attacks and Operation Aurora were information-seeking, espionage-related attacks, but nation-state sponsored attackers aren't the only thing that incident responders have to worry about. Financially motivated criminal activity is also evolving, and those actors are also working hard to stay ahead of defenders and incident responders.

Conclusion

Despite the many advances in the computer security field, attackers continue to adapt. We are often surprised to hear about breaches where the attackers were loitering in a network for years before they were identified, or even worse, where the attackers are able to get back in undetected and reinfected a target after the incident-response process is complete. Intelligence-driven incident response allows us to learn from attackers; to identify their motivations, processes, and behaviors; to identify their activities even as they seek to outwit our defenses and detection methods. The more we know about attackers, the better we can detect and respond to their actions.

We have reached the point where a structured and repeatable process for implementing intelligence in the incident-response process is necessary, and this book aims to provide insight into that process. Throughout this book, we provide various models and methods that can be viewed as the tools of intelligence-driven incident response, as well as the background as to why these models are beneficial in incident response. There is no one-size-fits-all approach. In many cases, the incident or the organization will dictate which specific combination of models and approaches fits best. Understanding the foundational principles of intelligence and incident response as well as the specific methods for integrating them will allow you to build a process for intelligence-driven incident response that will work for you and to develop that process to meet the needs of your organization.

## CHAPTER 2

Basics of Intelligence

"Many intelligence reports in war are contradictory; even more are false, and most are uncertain."

—Carl von Clausewitz

Intelligence analysis is one of the oldest and most consistent concepts in human history. Every morning people turn on the news or scroll through feeds on their phones, looking for information that will help them plan their day. What is the weather report? What implications does that have for their activities for that day? How is the traffic? Do they need to plan for extra time to get to where they need to go? External information is compared to an internal set of experiences and priorities, and an assessment is made of the impact on the target subject—the individual in question.

This is the basic premise of intelligence: taking in external information from a variety of sources and analyzing it against existing requirements in order to provide an assessment that will affect decision making. This occurs at the individual level as well as at higher levels; this same process is implemented at the group, organization, and government level every single day.

Most individuals conduct some form of intelligence analysis on their own without formal training, and many security teams work through similar processes as they conduct investigations without realizing that they are, in fact, engaged in intelligence analysis. When businesses and governments conduct intelligence operations, it is based on a formalized process and doctrine that have been captured over the years. In addition, formalized processes are specialized for intelligence operations in information security and incident response. This chapter walks through key concepts, some from intelligence—some from security, and a few that combine both. We'll start with abstract concepts that are primarily pulled from intelligence doctrine and move toward the more concrete concepts that can be applied directly to your incident-response investigations.

Data Versus Intelligence

Before tackling anything else, it's important to clear up one of the most important distinctions of this discussion: the difference between data and intelligence. Both of these are significant terms in the security community. However, they are often used interchangeably, and many practitioners have a difficult time articulating the difference between the two.

"Joint Publication 2-0," the US military's primary joint intelligence doctrine, is one of the foundational intelligence documents used today. In its introduction, it states, "*Information* on its own may be of utility to the commander, but when related to other information about the operational environment and considered in the light of past experience, it gives rise to a new understanding of the information, which may be termed *intelligence.*"

Data is a piece of information, a fact, or a statistic. Data is something that describes something that *is*. In our previous example about the weather report, the temperature is a piece data. It is a fact, something that has been measured using a proven and repeatable process. Knowing the temperature is important, but in order to be useful for decision making, it must be analyzed in the context of what else is going on that day. In information security, an IP address or domain are data. Without any additional analysis to provide context, they are simply facts. When various data points are gathered and analyzed to provide insight around a particular requirement, it becomes intelligence.

Intelligence is derived from a process of collecting, processing, and analyzing data. Once it has been analyzed, it must be disseminated in order to be useful. Intelligence that does not get to the right audience is wasted intelligence. Wilhelm Agrell, a Swedish writer and historian who studied peace and conflict, once famously said, "Intelligence analysis combines the dynamics of journalism with the problem solving of science."

The difference between data and true intelligence is *analysis*. Intelligence requires analysis that is based on a series of requirements and is aimed at answering questions. Without analysis, most of the data generated by the security industry remains as data. That same data, however, once it has been properly analyzed in response to requirements, becomes intelligence, as it now contains the appropriate context needed to answer questions and support decision making.

Indicators of Compromise

There was a time when many people considered indicators of compromise, or IOCs, to be synonymous with threat intelligence. *IOCs*, which we will reference *a lot* and cover in depth later in the book, are things to look for on a system or in network logs that may indicate that a compromise has taken place. This includes IP addresses and domains associated with command-and-control servers or malware downloads, hashes of malicious files, and other network- or host-based artifacts that may indicate an intrusion. As we will discuss throughout this book, however, there is far more to threat intelligence than IOCs, although IOCs still remain one of the most common types of technical intelligence around intrusions.

Sources and Methods

Now that we have cleared up the distinction between data and intelligence, the natural next question is, "Where should I get this data from so that I can analyze it and generate intelligence?"

Traditional intelligence sources are most often centered around the *INTs*, which describe where the data is collected from:

HUMINT
> Human-source intelligence is derived from humans, either through covert or clandestine methods or from overt collection such as from diplomats. Human-source intelligence is the oldest form of intelligence collection. There is serious debate about whether cyber threat intelligence can be derived from HUMINT. One example is interviews or conversations with individuals who are involved with or have firsthand knowledge of intrusions. Another example that many describe as HUMINT is information gained from interactions with individuals via restricted or members-only online forums. This type of intelligence gathering could also be considered SIGINT, as it is derived from electronic communications.

SIGINT
> Signals intelligence includes intelligence derived from the interception of signals, including communications intelligence (COMINT), electronic intelligence (ELINT), and foreign instrumentation signals intelligence (FISINT). Most technical intelligence collection falls under SIGINT, because after all, computers function using electronic signals, so anything derived from a computer or other networking device could be considered SIGINT.

OSINT

Open source intelligence is gathered from publicly available sources, including news, social media, and commercial databases as well as a variety of other non-classified sources. Published reports on cyber-security threats is one type of OSINT. Another type is technical details about things like IP addresses or domain names that are publicly accessible; for example, a WHOIS query detailing who registered a malicious domain.

IMINT

Imagery intelligence is collected from visual representations, including photography and radar. IMINT is not typically a source of cyber threat intelligence.

MASINT

Measurement and signature intelligence is gathered from technical means, excluding signal and imagery. MASINT often includes signatures from nuclear, optical, radio frequency, acoustics, and seismic signatures. As MASINT specifically excludes signals intelligence, it is also not a typical source of cyber threat intelligence.

GEOINT

Geospatial intelligence is collected from geospatial data, including satellite and reconnaissance imagery, maps, GPS data, and other sources of data related to locations. Some organizations consider IMINT to be a part of GEOINT, and some believe it is a separate discipline. Similar to IMINT, GEOINT is not a typical source of cyber threat intelligence, but it can provide contextual information on threats to help you understand how attackers may use the cyber domain to achieve their goals.

At this point, many would bring up a variety of other INTs that have popped up over the years, including cyber intelligence (CYBINT), technical intelligence (TECHINT), and financial intelligence (FININT), but most of these new terms are already covered by other intelligence-collection methods. For example, cyber intelligence is primarily derived from ELINT and SIGINT. It is not important to get into an argument about the number of INTs in existence; the important thing is to understand the source of the data. At the end of the day, if it helps to refer to a specific collection type as its own INT, then go ahead; just be prepared to deal with the eventual terminology conflicts that tend to pop up in this field.

In addition to the traditional intelligence-collection disciplines listed here, some collection methods are often utilized specifically in cyber threat intelligence. It is useful to have a solid understanding of where this specific threat data comes from:

Incidents and investigations

This data is collected from the investigation of data breaches and incident-response activities. This is often one of the most rich data sets used in cyber threat intelligence because investigators are able to identify multiple aspects of the threat, including the tools and techniques that are used, and often can identify the intent and motivation behind the intrusion.

Honeypots

These devices are set up to emulate machines or entire networks and gather information about interactions with these devices. There are many types of honeypots: low interaction, high interaction, internal honeypots, and honeypots on the public internet. Honeypot information can be useful as long as you know the type of honeypots it comes from, what they were monitoring for, and the nature of the interactions. Traffic gathered from a honeypot that captures exploit attempts or attempts to install malware on a system are far more useful in analysis than scanning or web-scrapping traffic.

Forums and websites

A variety of companies claim to have deep web or dark web collection. In many cases, these companies are referring to forums and chatrooms with restricted access that are not easily accessible from the internet. In these forums and sites, individuals often exchange information that is valuable after it's analyzed. There are so many of these types of sites that it is nearly impossible for any one company to have complete coverage of *the dark net*, so be aware that the collection is often limited in scope and will differ from that of other companies that claim to have similar data.

Even these techniques are new iterations of common techniques of the past. What's old is new as technology evolves, and intelligence is no different. George Santayana's missive about forgetting the past is as true as ever.

Military Jargon

One common point of contention in information security is the use of military terminology. Although intelligence has existed for centuries, it was codified in doctrine by military entities in documents such as the US Army's "Joint Publication 2-0: Joint Intelligence (*http://www.dtic.mil/doctrine/new_pubs/jp2_0.pdf*)," and the UK's "Joint Doctrine Publication 2-00 - Understanding and Intelligence Support to Joint Operations (*http://bit.ly/2veFsZj*)." The majority of nonmilitary intelligence applications still pull heavily from the general principles captured in these documents, which results in a high volume of military terms in modern intelligence analysis. This means that related fields, such as cyber threat intelligence, often pull heavily from military doctrine. However, just as with marketing, military jargon is useful in some situations

---

and not useful in others. If the use of military terminology gets in the way of conveying your message, it may be a good time to use different terms.

Process Models

Models are often used to structure information so that it can be analyzed and acted on. A variety of models used in intelligence analysis are covered further in Chapters 3 and 8. In addition, several models are used to give structure to the process of generating intelligence. This section covers two models that are used to effectively generate and act on intelligence. The first is the OODA loop, which can be used in making quick, time-sensitive decisions, and the second is the intelligence cycle, which can be used to generate more-formal intelligence products that will be used in a variety of ways, from informing policy to setting future intelligence requirements.

Using Models Effectively

George E.P. Box said, "All models are wrong; some models are useful." Every model is an abstraction that's useful for understanding a problem. On the other hand, by it's very nature, every model is reductionist and throws out important details. It's not important to fit all data into a particular model, but it's always valuable to use models as a way to understand and improve your thought processes.

OODA

One of the most referenced military concepts in security is *OODA*, an acronym for "observe, orient, decide, act." The OODA loop, shown in Figure 2-1, was developed by fighter pilot, military researcher, and strategist John Boyd in the 1960s. He believed that a fighter pilot who was at a disadvantage against an adversary with more-advanced equipment or capabilities could be victorious by using OODA to respond more quickly to stimuli and effectively attack the opponent's mind through decisive actions.

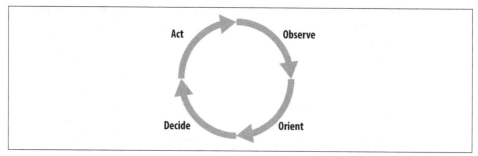

Figure 2-1. The OODA loop

Here's an introduction to each of the four stages.

Observe

The Observe phase centers around the collection of information. In this phase, an individual collects information from the outside world—anything and everything that could be useful. If the individual is planning to catch a baseball, this phase is about observing the baseball to determine its velocity and trajectory. If the individual is trying to catch a network attacker, the observation includes gathering logs, monitoring systems, and collecting any outside information that could help identify the attacker.

Orient

The Orient phase puts the information collected during the Observe phase into context with already known information. This takes into account past experience, preconceived notions, expectations, and models. For the baseball example, orientation uses what the observer knows about how a ball moves, taking into account its velocity and trajectory, to predict where it will go and how much force the impact will generate when it is caught. In the example of a network attacker, orientation takes the telemetry pulled from the logs and combines it with knowledge about the network, relevant attack groups, and previously identified artifacts such as specific IP addresses or process names.

Decide

At this point, information has been collected (observed) and contextualized (oriented); thus it's time to determine a course of action. The Decide phase is not about executing an action. It is about debating various courses of action until the final course of action is determined.

In the baseball example, this phase includes determining where to run and how fast, how the fielder should move and position her hand, and anything else needed to attempt to catch the ball. In the case of dealing with a network attacker, it means deciding whether to wait and continue to observe the attacker's actions, whether to start an incident-response action, or whether to ignore the activity. In either case, the defender *decides* on the next steps to achieve their goal.

Act

After all that, the Act phase is relatively straightforward: the individual follows through with the chosen course of action. This doesn't mean it's 100% guaranteed to be successful. That determination is made in the observation phase of the next OODA loop, as the cycle begins again back at the observation phase.

OODA is a generalization of the basic decision-making process that everyone goes through thousands of times a day. This explains how individuals make decisions, but also how teams and organizations do so. It explains the process a network defender or incident responder goes through when gathering information and figuring out how to use it.

The OODA loop is used by not only one side. While we, as defenders, go through the process of observing, orienting, deciding, and acting, in many cases the attacker is as well. The attacker is observing the network and the defender's actions in that network, and deciding how to act to changes in the environment and attempts to kick them out. As with many things, the side that can observe and adapt faster tends to win. Figure 2-2 shows the OODA loop for both an attacker and defender.

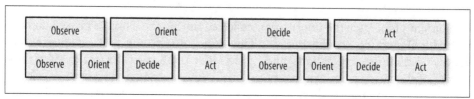

Figure 2-2. Competing OODA loop of the defender and the attacker

Multiple Defender OODA Loops

Beyond attacker-defender OODA loops, it's also useful to think about defender-defender OODA loops—that is, how the decisions we make as defenders can impact other defenders as well. Many decisions that defensive teams can make essentially set up race conditions for other defenders. For example, if a defender executes an incident response and then publicly shares information about the attack, then the first defender has started the clock on all other defenders to ingest that intelligence and use it. If an attacker can move through the OODA loop faster, find the public information about their activities, and change their tactics before the second defender can use the information, then they've *turned inside* (outmanuvered and achieved a more ideal position) the second defender and can avoid serious consequences.

For this reason, it's important to consider how your actions and sharing impact other organizations, both adversaries and allies. In all cases, computer network defense is about slowing down the OODA loops of the adversary and speeding up the OODA loops of defenders.

This generalized decision model provides a template for understanding the decisions of both defenders and attackers. We'll discuss the cycle more moving forward, but in the end, this model focuses on understanding the decision-making processes of all parties involved.

Intelligence Cycle

The intelligence cycle, pictured in Figure 2-3, is the formal process for generating and evaluating intelligence. The cycle begins where the last intelligence process ended and continues to build off itself. The intelligence cycle doesn't need to be followed to the letter. In fact, processes explored later in this book will build upon it. You do have to be careful not to omit critical steps, however. If you start skipping entire steps, you run the risk of ending up with more data and questions instead of intelligence.

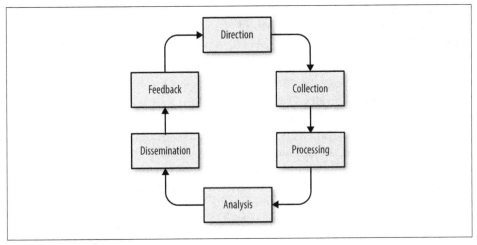

Figure 2-3. The intelligence cycle

To properly utilize the intelligence cycle, you need to know what is involved in the steps, which we will dive into next.

Direction

The first step in the intelligence cycle is direction. *Direction* is the process of establishing the question that the intelligence is meant to answer. This question can be delivered from an outside source, developed by the intelligence team itself, or developed by stakeholders and the intelligence team. (This is sometimes called the *RFI process*, which we'll discuss in Chapter 4). The ideal outcome of this process is a clear, concise question whose answer the stakeholders will find usable.

Collection

The next step is *collection of the data* necessary to answer the question. This is a wide-ranging exercise that should focus on gathering as much data as possible from many sources. Redundant information adds value here, because corroboration is often important.

This leads to a key idea of developing an effective intelligence program: *building a collection capability*. It's difficult to know exactly what data might eventually prove useful, so building a broad capability to collect a wide variety of information is important. This includes tactical information such as infrastructure, malware, and exploits, as well as operational strategic information such as attacker goals, social media monitoring, news monitoring, and high-level document exploitation (identifying reports, such as those that vendors release about groups, and gathering information from them). Be sure to document the sources and take care: news stories often republish or reference the same original material, making it difficult to know what's corroboration and what's just a rehash of the same material. If it is impossible to determine the source of a particular data set, you may want to avoid using it as a collection source.

Collection is a process, not a one-time action. Using information from the first round of collection (such as gathering IP addresses) leads to a second round (such as using reverse DNS to find domains related to those IP addresses), which leads to a third round (using WHOIS to gather information about those domains). This exploitation becomes exponential as it builds upon itself. The focus at this point is not understanding how the data relates but simply developing as much information as possible. Combining it comes later. Also, don't forget to consider internal sources, such as an incident-management system. It's common for organizations to discover actors or attacks they're already intimately familiar with.

Name Deconfliction

Naming presents a significant challenge in intelligence collection. While in the old days this focused on aliases and cover terms, today the field struggles with the fractured nature of intelligence collection and naming conventions. Every company, every intelligence sharing group, and every intelligence agency has its own names for various threat groups. The intrusion group APT1 is a great example: most commonly referred to as Comment Crew, this group was also known as ShadyRat, WebC2, and GIF89a by industry groups. Mandiant called them APT1. CrowdStrike called them Comment Panda. Ongoing intelligence determined their actual identity as Peoples Liberation Army Military Unit 61398. Collection against all of these names matters, as overlooking reporting that uses a particular name could lead to missing critical data.

Processing

Data is not always immediately usable in its raw format or in the format in which it was collected. In addition, data from different sources may come in different formats, and it is necessary to get it into the same format so it can be analyzed together. The *processing* neccesary to make data usable is often an overlooked task, but without it, generating intelligence would be nearly impossible. In the traditional intelligence cycle, processing is part of collection. However, when dealing with the types of data and organizations involved in incident response, it may be useful to consider processing separately. Here are some of the most common ways to process data related to cyber threats:

Normalization

Processing includes normalizing collected data into uniform formats for analysis. The collection process will generate nearly every conceivable kind of data result. Intelligence data comes in a variety of formats, from JSON to XML to CSV to plain text from email. Vendors share information on websites in blog posts or tables, but also in PDF-based reports or even YouTube videos. At the same time, organizations tend to store data in different formats. Some organizations use a purpose-built threat-intelligence platform, while other organizations build customized solutions from wikis or internal applications.

Indexing

Large volumes of data need to be made searchable. Whether dealing with observables such as network addresses and mutexes or operational data such as forum posts and social media, analysts need to be able to search quickly and efficiently.

Translation

In some cases, regional analysts may provide human translation of source documents, but this is generally not feasible for most organizations dealing with information from all over the world. Machine translation, while imperfect, usually provides sufficient value so that analysts can find items of interest. If necessary, they can then be escalated to specialists for a more accurate translation.

Enrichment

Providing additional metadata for a piece of information is important. For example, domain addresses need to be resolved to IP addresses, and WHOIS registration data fetched. Google Analytics tracking codes should be cross-referenced to find other sites using the same code. This enrichment process should be done automatically so that the relevant data is immediately available to analysts.

Filtering

Not all data provides equal value, and analysts can be overwhelmed when presented with endless streams of irrelevant data. Algorithms can filter out information known to be useless (though it may still be searchable) and bubble up the most useful and relevant data.

Prioritization

The data that has been collected may need to be ranked so that analysts can allocate resources to the most important items. Analyst time is valuable and should be focused correctly for maximum benefit to the intelligence product.

Visualization

Data visualization has advanced significantly. While many analysts fear vendor dashboards because of the clutter they typically contain, designing a visualization based on what analysts need (rather than what marketing and executives think looks good) can assist in reducing cognitive load.

Taking the time to process data effectively enables and improves future intelligence efforts.

Analysis

Analysis, as much an art as it is a science, seeks to answer the questions that were identified in the Direction phase. In intelligence analysis, data that has been collected is characterized and considered against other available data, and an assessment is made as to its meanings and implications. Predictions are often made as to future implications. There are various methods for conducting analysis, but the most common is to use analytic models to evaluate and structure the information. In addition to preexisting models, which we cover later in this chapter, it is also common for analysts to develop their own models that work with their particular data sets or way of interpreting information.

The goal of the Analysis phase is to answer the questions identified in the Direction phase of the intelligence cycle. The type of answer will be determined by the nature of the question. In some cases, the analysis may generate a new intelligence product in the form of a report or could be as simple as a yes/no answer, most often backed up with a confidence value. It is important to understand what the output will be before beginning the analysis.

Analysis is not a perfect science and must often be conducted with incomplete information. It is important that analysts identify and clearly state any information gaps in their analysis. This allows for decision makers to be aware of potential blind spots in the analysis, and can also drive the collection process to identify new sources in order to reduce those gaps. If the gaps are significant enough that an analyst does not think it is possible to complete the analysis with the current information, then it may be necessary to go back to the Collection phase and gather additional data. It is much better to delay the final analysis than to provide an assessment that the analyst knows is flawed.

It is important to note that *all intelligence analysis is generated by a human.* If it is automated, it is actually processing instead, which is a critical step in the intelligence cycle but is not by itself analysis.

Dissemination

At this point, the process has generated real intelligence: a contextualized answer to the question posed in the Direction phase. A report with an answer is useless until it's shared with the relevant stakeholders: those who can use this intelligence. In plenty of documented intelligence failures, analysis was spot-on but dissemination failed. *Intelligence must be shared with relevant stakeholders in the form they find the most useful.* This makes dissemination dependent on the audience. If the product is aimed at executives, it's important to consider length and phrasing. If it's aimed at implementation in technical systems (such as IDS or firewalls), this could require vendor-specific programmatic formats. In any case, intelligence must be usable by the relevant stakeholders.

Feedback

Often forgotten, the Feedback phase is key to continuing intelligence efforts. *The Feedback phase asks whether the intelligence that was generated answers the direction successfully.* This results in one of two outcomes:

Success
> If the intelligence process answered the question, the cycle may be over. In many cases, though, a successful intelligence process leads to a request for more intelligence based on either new questions or the actions taken based on the answer given.

Failure
> In some cases, the intelligence process failed. In this case, the Feedback phase should focus heavily on identifying the aspect of the original direction that was not properly answered. The following Direction phase should take special care to address the reasons for that failure. This usually comes down to a poorly structured Direction phase that didn't narrow the goal enough, or an incomplete Collection phase that was unable to gather enough data to answer the question, or improper analysis that did not extract correct (or at least useful) answers from the data available.

Using the Intelligence Cycle

Let's consider how the intelligence cycle can be used to start learning about a new adversary.

One of the most common questions a chief information security officer, often abbreviated as CISO, asks (hopefully before she gets asked it herself) is, "What do we know about this threat group I heard about?" A CISO will want a basic understanding of a group's capabilities and intention, as well as an assessment of relevance to a given organization. So what does the intelligence process look like in this situation? Here is an example of what is involved in each step of the intelligence cycle to meet the CISO's needs:

Direction

This came from a key stakeholder: the CISO. "What do we know about X threat group?" The real answer sought is a target package, which we'll explore in detail later.

Collection

Start with the original source, most likely a news article or report. That document will usually provide at least some context for beginning the collection. If indicators (IPs, URLs, etc.) exist, explore those as deeply as possible by pivoting and enriching. The source may itself point to additional reporting with IOCs, tactics, techniques, and procedures (TTPs), or other analyses.

Processing

This is very workflow/organization dependent. Getting all the collected information into a place where it can be used most effectively may be as simple as putting all the information into a single text document, or it may require importing it all into an analysis framework.

Analysis:

Using the collected information, the analyst will start by attempting to answer key questions:

- What are these attackers interested in?
- What tactics and tools do they typically use?
- How can defenders detect those tools or tactics?
- Who are these attackers? (Although this is always a question, it is not always one worth taking the time to answer.)

Dissemination

For a product like this that has a specific requester, the CISO, a simple email may suffice. Although in some cases limiting a response to this makes sense, a real product for proactive distribution to others will almost always create greater value.

Feedback

The key question: is the CISO pleased with the results? Does it lead to other questions? These pieces of feedback help close the loop and may begin a new series of collections.

The intelligence cycle is a generalized model that can be used to answer questions large and small. However, it is important to note that following the steps will not automatically result in good intelligence. We will discuss the quality of intelligence next.

Qualities of Good Intelligence

The quality of intelligence relies primarily on two things: collection sources and analysis. Many times in cyber threat intelligence we end up working with data that we did not collect ourselves, and therefore it is critical that we understand as much as possible about the information. When generating intelligence ourselves, we also need to ensure that we understand collection sources and are addressing biases in our analysis. Here are some things that should be considered to ensure that quality intelligence is produced:

Collection method

It is important to understand whether the information is collected primarily from incidents or investigations, or whether it is being collected from an automated collection system such as a honeypot or a network sensor. Although knowing the exact details of the collection is not imperative—some providers prefer to keep their sources confidential—it is possible to have a basic understanding of where the data comes from without compromising collection resources. The more details you have about the way information was collected, the better your analysis of this information will be. For example, it is good to know that data comes from a honeypot; it is better to know that it comes from a honeypot configured to identify brute-force attempts against remote web administration tools.

Date of collection

The majority of cyber-threat data that is collected is perishable. The lifespan of that data varies from minutes to potentially months or even years, but there is always a period of time when this information is relevant. Understanding when data was collected can help defenders understand how it can be acted upon. It is difficult to properly analyze or utilize any data when you do not know when it was collected.

Context

The collection method and date can both provide some level of context around the data, but the more context that is available, the easier it will be to analyze. Context can include additional details, such as specific activities related to the information and relationships between pieces of information.

Addressing biases in analysis

All analysts have biases, and identifying and countering those biases so that they do not influence analysis is a key component of quality intelligence. Some biases that analysts should seek to avoid include *confirmation bias*, which seeks to identify information that will support a previously formulated conclusion, and *anchoring bias*, which leads analysts to focus too heavily on a single piece of information while disregarding other, potentially more valuable information.

Levels of Intelligence

The intelligence models we have examined thus far focus on a logical flow of information through a sort of analysis pipeline. But just as with incident analysis, this approach is not the only way to model the information. We can think about intelligence at different levels of abstraction, ranging from the highly specific (tactical) to the logistical (operational) to the very general (strategic). As we examine these levels of intelligence, keep in mind that this model represents a continuous spectrum with gray areas between them, not discrete buckets.

Tactical Intelligence

Tactical intelligence is low-level, highly perishable information that supports security operations and incident response. The customers for tactical intelligence include security operations center (SOC) analysts and computer incident-response team (CIRT) investigators. In the military, this level of intelligence supports small-unit actions. In cyber threat intelligence (CTI), this usually includes IOCs and observables as well as highly granular TTPs describing precisely how an adversary deploys a particular capability. Tactical intelligence enables defenders to respond directly to threats.

An example of tactical intelligence is IOCs related to an exploitation of a newly discovered vulnerability. These tactical-level IOCs include IP addresses conducting scans searching for the vulnerability, domains hosting malware that will be downloaded to the host if exploitation is successful, and various host-based artifacts that are generated during exploitation and installation of malware.

Operational Intelligence

In the military, *operational intelligence* is a step up from tactical. This information supports logistics and analyzes effects of terrain and weather on larger operations. In CTI, this usually includes information on campaigns and higher-order TTPs. It may also include information on specific actor attribution as well as capabilities and intent. This is one of the harder levels for many analysts to understand, because it is sometimes defined as intel that is too general to be tactical but too specific to be strategic. Customers for operational intelligence include senior-level digit forensics and incident response (DFIR) analysts and other CTI teams.

Following the preceding example about tactical-level indicators of active exploitation of a vulnerability, operational-level intelligence would include information on how widespread the exploitation is, whether it is targeted or opportunistic, who else is being targeted, the purpose of the malware that is being installed, and any details on the actors who are carrying out the attacks. Understanding these details can support the generation of follow-up intelligence, including what other actions that may be seen, and should include information on the severity of the threat to help plan a response.

Strategic Intelligence

In the military, *strategic intelligence* deals with national and policy-level information. In CTI, we think of this as supporting C-level executives and boards of directors in making serious decisions about risk assessments, resource allocation, and organizational strategy. This information includes trends, actor motivations, and classifications.

In the preceding example, strategic intelligence would include information on the motivations of the attackers, especially if the activity indicates a new or previously unidentified threat, and any information that indicates new tactics or attacker targeting that may require higher-level responses, such as new policies or an architecture change.

Confidence Levels

As mentioned previously, intelligence typically has different confidence levels associated with it. These confidence levels reflect the analysts' trust that the information is correct and accurate. For some types of data, this confidence may be on a numeric scale (for example, 0 to 100) and calculated using traditional statistical methods, while in other cases the confidence assessment is provided on a qualitative, subjective basis by analysts directly. It is important to identify confidence in two important areas: confidence in the source of the information, and confidence in an analyst's conclusions.

One common way of describing source reliability is the Admiralty Code or NATO System found in FM 2-22.3 (*https://fas.org/irp/doddir/army/fm2-22-3.pdf*). This consists of two scales. The first evaluates the reliability of a source based on previous information, ranging from A (reliable) to E (unreliable). The second scale evaluates the degree of confidence in the information content itself, ranging from 1 (confirmed) to 5 (improbable). These two scores are combined for a particular piece of information based on the source and specific content, so that information known to be true from a source with a history of valid information might be evaluated as B1, but information that is improbable from a source with a history of invalid information would be evaluated as E5.

Sherman Kent, often referred to as the father of intelligence analysis, wrote an essay in 1964 called "Words of Estimative Probability," which describes various qualitative ways to describe confidence in an analyst's judgment. In that essay, Kent shares one of the charts that he and his team use to assign and describe confidence (shown in

Figure 2-4) but also writes that other terms may be used in their place as long as the meaning is understood and the terms are used consistently.

```
100% Certainty
The General Area of Possibility
93% give or take about  6% Almost certain
75% give or take about 12% Probably
50% give or take about 10% Chances about even
30% give or take about 10% Probably not
7%  give or take about  5% Almost certainly not
0%  Impossibility
```

Figure 2-4. Sherman Kent's chart on estimative probability

Conclusion

Intelligence is a critical component of incident response, and many processes can be used to integrate intelligence principles into incident-response (IR) investigations. It is important to understand the sources of intelligence that you will be relying on; there is a big difference in the way that you treat intelligence that came from a previous IR investigation in your network and the way you treat information that comes from a honeypot. Both types of information are valuable; they just have different applications. Popular models for structuring intelligence analysis and response are the OODA loop and the intelligence cycle. The next chapter dives into the specifics of incident response and the models that help analysts implement intelligence-driven incident response.

## CHAPTER 3

Basics of Incident Response

"We now see hacking taking place by foreign governments and by private individuals all around the world."

—Mike Pompeo

Intelligence is only one half of the intelligence-driven incident-response puzzle. While computer incident response isn't nearly as old as the art of espionage, in the last 40 years it has rapidly evolved into a major industry. *Incident response* encompasses the entire process of identifying intrusions (whether against a single system or an entire network), developing the information necessary to fully understand them, and then developing and executing the plans to remove the intruders.

Intrusion detection and incident response share many characteristics. Both are abstract. They are both complicated topics, and as a result people have sought to simplify them by abstracting them into cycles or models. These models make understanding the complex interplay between defender and adversary possible and form the basis for planning how to undertake responding to these incidents. Just like intelligence models, they are rarely perfect and can't always be followed explicitly, but they provide a framework for understanding the attackers' intrusion and the defenders' response processes.

Just like the exploration of intelligence, this chapter starts with the most overarching models and moves to more-specific models. Afterward we'll dig into common defensive techniques and finish with the integrated intelligence and operations models we'll use for the rest of the book.

Incident-Response Cycle

In the same way that we need a standard language for discussing intelligence concepts, we need a language to discuss incidents. This process can be viewed from the defender's perspective and the attacker's perspective. Let's start with the defenders.

The *incident-response cycle* is made up of the major steps taken in intrusion detection and incident response. The goal of this model is to be agnostic to the type of attack (phishing, strategic web compromise, SQL injection, etc.) and generalize the steps that are generic to all of those attacks (and many others). Figure 3-1 illustrates this cycle.

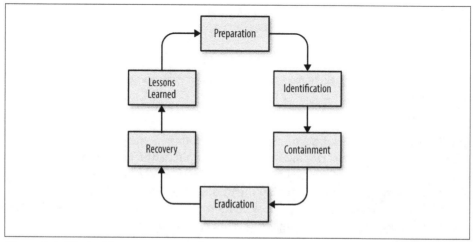

Figure 3-1. The incident-response cycle

There's some argument about where the concept of the incident-response cycle began. The first references seem to come from the National Institute of Standards and Technology's seminal document on incident response, "NIST 800-61 Computer Security Incident Handling Guide (*http://bit.ly/2tGfwUz*)." Now in its second revision, this document is the basis for government agencies handling incidents. Although this guide introduced a huge number of key concepts, one of the most important is the description of the incident-response cycle, which provides a defender's view of the incident-response process.

Preparation

For a defender, the first stage of an incident comes before the attack begins: the *Preparation phase*. Preparation is the defender's chance to get ahead of the attacker by deploying new detection systems, creating and updating signatures, and understanding baseline system and network activity. This is a combination of network security architecture and security operations. Many of these steps go beyond the security team, impacting and being impacted by general network operations, network architecture, system management, and even help desk and support.

Preparation should focus on four key elements, two technical and two nontechnical:

Telemetry

> You can't find what you can't see. Specialized systems are required for incident responders to identify and investigate intrusions. These systems range from network to host and should provide the ability to investigate a wide variety of activities at multiple levels.

Hardening

> The only thing better than identifying an intrusion quickly is it never happening in the first place. Preparation is the stage for ensuring that patches are deployed, configurations are locked down, and tools that limit attacks such as virtual private networks (VPNs) and firewalls are in place.

Process and documentation

> On the nontechnical side, process is the first line of defense that can be prepared ahead of time. Few things are worse during an incident than trying to figure out what you're doing as you're doing it. Along with processes (such as an incident-response plan, notification plan, and communications plan), having documentation for common questions such as network configurations, system configurations, and system owners will also speed up responses.

Practice

> The last thing preparation allows is the chance to practice your plans. This will speed up future incidents and identify issues that can be corrected (something we'll touch on more in "Lessons Learned" on page 33). The best incident-response teams are those that have been through incidents together, and the best way to do that is practice.

When discussing computer network defense, many (mostly pessimistic) people are quick to point out all the advantages an attacker has. Most of these advantages boil down to surprise: in computer network exploitation, the attacker gets to pick the location and time of the attack. What many don't take into account is the key advantage of the defender: namely, the ability to prepare for an attack. The adversary can do reconissance, but in many cases is attacking a black box, without full understanding of the target until the attack is underway. Defenders can leverage this by preparing adequately.

Identification

The *Identification phase* is the moment where the defender identifies the presence of an attacker impacting their environment. This can occur though a variety of methods:

- Identifying the attacker entering the network, such as a server attack or an incoming phishing email
- Noticing command-and-control traffic from a compromised host
- Seeing the massive traffic spike when the attacker begins exfiltrating data
- Getting a visit from a special agent at your local FBI field office
- And last, but all too often, showing up in an article by Brian Krebs

Whatever way it occurs, the Identification phase begins when you first gain awareness of the attack against your resources. In this model, the Identification phase is the entire intrusion-detection phase, glossing over many details in a complicated topic. This is obviously a simplification, but reasonable given that this cycle focuses on the end-to-end process of incident response. This phase typically leads to an investigation, identifying even more information about the attack and the attacker, before beginning to respond directly. One of the key goals of threat intelligence is to augment the Identification phase, increasing the accuracy and quantity of methods to identify attackers earlier.

 Identification, at least in the incident-response sense, is not simply hearing about an attack that took place or learning about a new attacker. Identification starts when there is direct impact to your users, systems, or resources. For it to be an incident, there has to be impact.

On the other hand, if an adversary has capability, intent, and opportunity, that adversary does represent a threat. This isn't the start of the incident cycle, but the intelligence cycle. Only after the adversary is identified in your environment should an incident begin.

Containment

The first two phases of the cycle can be considered primarily passive and are focused on information gathering. The first phase of actual response, meaning that specific actions are being taken in response to a specific attack, is containment. *Containment* is the initial attempts to mitigate the actions of an attacker, stopping them in the short term while preparing a longer-term response. These shorter-term responses may not make the attack impossible, but they dramatically reduce the ability of the attacker to continue to achieve the objectives. These actions should be taken in a rapid but controlled manner to limit the adversary's opportunity to respond.

Common containment options are as follows:

- Disabling the network switch port to which a particular system is connected
- Blocking access to malicious network resources such as IPs (at the firewall) and domains or specific URLs (via a network proxy)
- Temporarily locking a user account under the control of an intruder
- Disabling system services or software an adversary is exploiting

In many incident responses, defenders may choose to skip over the Containment phase entirely. Containment risks tipping off the adversary by changing the environment while that adversary still may have control.

Skipping Containment

Containment tends to be most effective against less-sophisticated adversaries that make limited changes to their approach, such as commodity malware threats. So what about sophisticated adversaries? In many cases, the Containment phase can tip them off. They may set up new tools, establish secondary backdoors, or even just start being destructive. For this reason, most of these incident responses may move straight into eradication. We discuss this more in Chapter 6.

Eradication

Eradication consists of the longer-term mitigation efforts meant to keep an attacker out for good (unlike the temporary measures in the Containment phase). These actions should be well thought out and may take a considerable amount of time and resources to deploy. They are focused on completely obviating as many parts of the adversary's plan from ever working in the future.

Common eradication actions are as follows:

- Removing all malware and tools installed by the adversary (see the sidebar "Wiping and Reloading Versus Removal" on page 32)
- Resetting and remediating all impacted user and service accounts
- Re-creating secrets that could have been accessed by the attacker, such as shared passwords, certificates, and tokens

Often responders will go for a *scorched-earth* approach to eradication. In these cases, responders will take remediations on resources with no indications of compromise; for example, regenerating all VPN certificates after an adversary accessed one VPN server. Scorched-earth approaches are effective at mitigating the *unknown unknown* situations, where it's impossible to know 100% what the adversary did, but comes with the compromise that it may require a significant effort to make these changes.

The effort necessary varies based on the sort of service or information involved. Forcing full password resets in an active directory–managed Windows environment is relatively easy. Regenerating and redeploying extended validations (EV) TLS certificates with domain pinning in major browsers is hard. The incident-response team needs to collaborate with the corporate risk management and system/service owner teams to determine how far to go in these situations.

Wiping and Reloading Versus Removal

One of the most common debates between information technology and security teams is the question of how to handle malware-infected systems. Antivirus systems claim they can remove malware, but most experienced incident responders have been burned by this in the past and prefer to insist on a full wipe of the system and a reload of its operating system. An evidence-based approach is key, so each organization needs to fight this battle for themselves.

In the spring of 2015, Pennsylvania State University took its entire engineering network offline for three days in response to a compromise (*http://bit.ly/2u7R5Bu*). Afterward it had to bring the network back online and return it to normal service. A recovery like this requires removing malware from systems, resetting credentials such as passwords and certificates, patching software, and many other changes set on completely removing the attacker's presence and limiting that attacker's ability to return. In this case, the mitigation action, taking the entire network offline (likely to limit the attacker's ability to make changes during the remediation phase), preceded the remedation actions. This is a common pattern when dealing with persistent adversaries.

Recovery

Containment and eradication often require drastic action. *Recovery* is the process of going back to a nonincident state. In some regards, recovery is less from the attack itself, but more from the actions taken by the incident responders.

For example, if a compromised system is taken from a user for forensic analysis, the Recovery phase involves returning or replacing the user's system so that user can return to previous tasks. If an entire network is compromised, the Recovery phase involves undoing any actions taken by the attacker across the entire network, and can be a lengthy and involved process.

This phase depends on the actions taken during the prior two phases, the attacker's methods, and the resources that were compromised. It generally requires coordination with other teams, such as desktop administrators and network engineering.

Incident response is always a team sport, requiring actions by a wide variety of security and nonsecurity teams, but none is quite as obvious as recovery. Security may set certain requirements for the way systems are recovered (most of these will take place during eradication), but recovery, after the incident-response team's all clear, is handled largely by IT and system owners. Figuring out how to work together and collaborate effectively is key. Few things can compromise a response faster than IT beginning recovery before the IR team has fully eradicated the threat.

Lessons Learned

The last phase of the incident cycle, akin to many other security and intelligence cycles, includes taking time to assess past decisions and learn how to improve in the future.

This Lessons Learned phase evaluates the team's performance through each step. Basically, this takes the incident report and answers some basic questions:

1. What happened?
2. What did we do well?
3. What could we have done better?
4. What will we do differently next time?

As an exercise, this can often be daunting. Many teams resist reviewing lessons learned or conducting after-action reviews. This occurs for a wide variety of reasons, from being concerned about mistakes being highlighted (and thus blamed on the IR team) to simply not having enough time. Whatever the reason, nothing will keep an incident-response team from advancing like skipping lessons learned. The goal of the Lessons Learned phase is to discover how to make the next incident response go faster, smoother, or ideally never happen at all. Without this crucial step, IR teams (and the teams they collaborate with) will make the same mistakes, suffer from the same blockers, and fail to identify improvements.

Although it's important, conducting a Lessons Learned phase doesn't have to be daunting; in fact, it should be the opposite. A good after-action doesn't need to take hours or require everyone involved in the incident response. Here are a few detailed starter questions you will want to ask when evaluating each phase during the Lessons Learned process:

Preparation
- How could we have avoided the incident altogether? This includes changes to your network architecture, system configuration, user training, or even policy.
- What policies or tools could have improved the entire process?

Identification
- What telemetry sources (IDS, net flow, DNS, etc.) could have made it easier or faster to identify this attack?
- What signatures or threat intelligence could have helped?

Containment
- Which containment measures were effective?
- Which were not?
- Could other containment measures have been useful if they'd been more easily deployable?

Eradication
- Which eradication steps went well?
- What could have gone better?

Recovery
- What slowed the recovery? (*Hint*: focus on communication, as that's one of the toughest parts of recovery to do well.)
- What did the response to recovery tell us about the adversary?

Lessons Learned:
> Not to be too meta, but even evaluating how the Lessons Learned process could be done more effectively; for example, would it help if responders took notes throughout the process? Did you wait too long and things were lost or forgotten?

Lessons Learned can also be practiced (the same as any other piece of the incident-response process). Don't just do Lessons Learned for actual incidents, but take the time to build and follow your Lessons Learned process for red team and tabletop exercises as well.

Ultimately, the key to Lessons Learned is having the understanding that although early lessons learned will be painful, they will improve—and that's the point. Early Lessons Learned exercises will call out flaws, missing technology, missing team members, bad processes, and bad assumptions. Growing pains with this process are common, but take the time and gut through them. Few things will improve an IR team and IR capability as quickly as some tough lessons learned. In addition, capture these lessons and share them with your leadership and related teams. Although it seems like calling out a team's flaws, in many cases these reports provide concrete justification for making changes that will improve your incident-response capability.

The incident-response cycle is one of the first models that incident responders learn for good reason: it succinctly describes the life cycle of an investigation. Where it becomes key is by taking the time to evaluate your team's ability to execute at each stage, from Preparation through to Lessons Learned.

Kill Chain

Another military concept that has made its way into cyber threat intelligence vernacular is the *kill chain*. In fact, it has become so popular that finding information on the original kill chains is difficult because of the extent of information security use cases and marketing. While this concept was on the fringes for years, a paper by Lockheed Martin researchers Eric M. Hutchins et al. titled "Intelligence-Driven Computer Network Defense Informed by Analysis of Adversary Campaigns and Intrusion Kill Chains (*http://lmt.co/2miXqrZ*)" brought the concept into the information security mainstream with a formalized mapping of the most common intrusion pattern as a formalized kill chain.

Since their report, the kill chain has become a go-to model for cyber threat intelligence, referenced by nearly every vendor, and a staple guiding process of defensive teams. The kill chain provides an ideal abstraction for the phases an attacker moves through when exploiting a target.

But what is a kill chain? In its simplest form, a *kill chain* is series of steps an attacker must conduct in order to achieve an objective (see Figure 3-2). In our case, we're discussing a computer network attacker, but it works for many adversarial activities. This means abstracting the incident process, but whereas the incident cycle is focused on the *defender's* actions, the kill chain focuses on the *attacker's* actions.

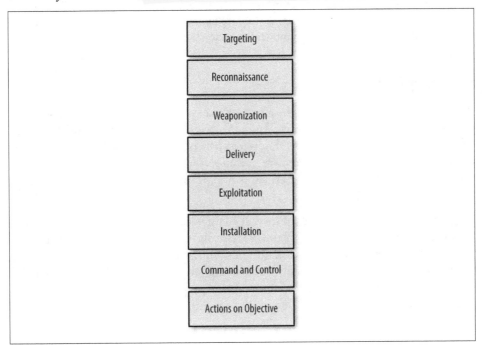

Figure 3-2. Cyber kill chain

The kill chain is a good way to abstract an attacker's tactics, techniques, and procedures (TTPs). It provides a structure to understand the abstract actions of an attack.

Though the earlier phases of the kill chain, especially Targeting and Reconnaissance, are sometimes opaque to the defender, usually difficult and circumstantial to detect, they're worth understanding. Defenders tend to think that attackers succeed every time with zero effort. This is far from the truth. In fact, our ability to disrupt these preintrusion phases later might be one of the strongest advantages defenders have.

Kill Chains in General

Kill chains existed long before the Lockheed Martin Cyber Kill Chain as a group of interrelated steps necessary to achieve a military objective, originally of lethal nature (going back to Vietnam era airstirkes (*http://bit.ly/2uDjZvj*)). The current US military version of the kill chain is described in "JP 3-60 Joint Targeting (*http://bit.ly/2uJdyI8*)." The kill chain paper by Lockheed Martin is just one cyber kill chain model for describing computer network operations; there is no "right" kill chain. Depending on the attack, certain aspects may be omitted or combined as necessary. Like all models, it's simply a method of thinking about intrusions.

As a result, we will make our own changes, including adding our own stages (targeting and breaking out persistence, for instance), as we describe the kill chain. This isn't meant to take away from the great work done by the Hutchins et al. but is meant to enhance it as you build your own model for understanding intrusions.

Targeting

Before the kill chain proper begins, the attacker must decide what to attack (for example, who is the potential target). In many cases, this occurs in consultation with some form of sponsor or stakeholder, often as part of their own intelligence or operational requirements. As defenders, we commonly think of the target as the victim organization, but in many cases that is less important than the information or capabilities being targeted.

Targeting is an interesting aspect of the kill chain because it speaks to motivation and thus the general category (though not necessarily specific identification or attribution) of an attacker. For example, an attacker who wants to steal money needs to go where the money is. Understanding what's being targeted gives insight into what the attacker is after (the attacker's ultimate goals) and may lead to better defensive techniques (discussed later in "Active Defense" on page 50).

Reconnaissance

After deciding *what* and *who* to target, the attacker begins conducting reconnaissance. In the *Reconnaissance* phase (or simply *recon*), the attacker develops as much information as possible about the planned victim. Reconnaissance can fall into multiple categories based on the type of data sought (hard data versus soft data) and collection methods (passive versus active).

Hard data versus soft data

The intelligence world has multiple ways of dividing information based on subject (SIGINT, TECHINT, etc.) as we discussed in Chapter 2, but for computer network operations, we can think of things a bit more simply.

Hard data includes information about technical aspects of a network and the systems attached to it. For an attacker (and defenders while investigating attackers), this usually includes open source intelligence:

- Footprinting or enumerating the target network
- DNS information such as reverse DNS
- Operating systems and application versions
- Information about system configurations
- Information about security systems

Soft data includes information about the organization behind the network and its systems:

- Organizational charts, public relationships, and other hierarchy documents
- Business plans and goals
- Hiring information, which can often leak information such as technologies in use
- Information on employees, both professional and personal, for use in social engineering attacks

Active versus passive collection methods

Attackers may use different methods of collecting information. We can categorize these methods as *active* or *passive*:

Active methods require interacting directly with the target. An active hard intelligence collection could be port scanning a system directly. An active soft collection could be a social engineering attack to gather information about internal hierarchy and contact information.

Passive methods are based on collecting information without interacting directly with the target, often by gathering information from a third-party information service such as DNS or WHOIS. A passive hard collection might exploit domain information from a public service. A soft passive collection gathers information about an organization from a site such as LinkedIn, where people often share considerable information (even information they shouldn't).

A defender's ability to detect this recon activity varies tremendously. Active methods are much easier to detect than passive methods, for example, and most network defenders have more control over hard information than soft information. Detecting active hard collection in the form of a port scan is easier than detecting soft passive collection in the form of reading job postings for positions that describe specific technologies in use at an organization.

Chasing Ghosts

While reconnissance gathering is useful to add to your kill chains, it's a dubious place to start most kill chains. Gauging the level of intent an actor has simply based on a port scan is virtually impossible. Anything on the internet is likely to be scanned aggressively and not necessarily by bad guys (such as Project Sonar (*https:// sonar.labs.rapid7.com/*), Censys (*https://censys.io/*), Shodan (*https://www.shodan.io/*), and others), so consider reconnissance low signal/high noise. On the other hand, taking indicators identified later in the kill chain correlated with reconissance activity may give surprising insight into targeting, methods, and even other compromised resources.

Weaponization

If all security controls, or all software in general, worked as intended (that is, as their designers imagined, not as they were built), then attackers would almost always fail. Thus, the goal for attackers is to find places where the intention and implementation don't match—a vulnerability. This vulnerability must then be exploited reliably and packed into a form that's ready to be delivered to a target (for example, a malicious document or exploit kit). The process of finding this vulnerability, crafting an exploit, and combining it with a payload is *Weaponization*.

Vulnerability hunting

The vulnerability subphase of weaponization is particularly interesting given its effect on what targets can be attacked. This forces the attacker to make a decision. Some widely deployed pieces of software are likely to be found in any environment, such as Adobe Acrobat and Reader or Microsoft Windows and Office. This means that any exploit targeting them is widely usable. However, these pieces of software have been attacked for years, and their respective companies have made considerable efforts to identify and mitigate vulnerabilities. The alternative is attacking a more esoteric piece of software that may be less defended but also less widely deployed. This limits where an attacker can use it. This process can be tied in with the cyber kill chain's *Reconnaissance* phase. The effort that attackers are willing to put in may also be influenced by their own direction and intelligence requirements.

As an example of this trade-off, consider the Stuxnet incident, in which unconfirmed attackers disabled centrifuges within the Iranian nuclear facility at Natanz. Part of this included deploying exploits against programmable logic controllers (PLCs) in Siemens equipment. While this equipment is not widely deployed in most organizations, it existed in the target environment. Vulnerabilities in those PLCs thus provided a vector for the attackers to carry out their mission.

We, as defenders, disrupt this process constantly by using development-centric security approaches. Good development practices such as Microsoft's Security Development Lifecycle (*https://www.microsoft.com/en-us/sdl/*) reduce the introduction of the mismatches that become vulnerabilities. Application security teams and related reviews constantly hunt for these vulnerabilities in source code. Strong patch management can help eliminate old vulnerabilities within an environment.

Every vulnerability that is patched constrains attackers a little bit and forces them to find new vulnerabilities to exploit. This is a time-consuming and expensive process. The longer a vulnerability is in the wild, the more value it has to an attacker because of its longer effective life span. In turn, then, disrupting the return on investment (ROI) of a vulnerability brings defensive value.

Imagine that an attacker has a privilege escalation in Windows 95. The attacker uses it for years, and it finally gets fixed in Windows 7. This means the attacker could use that exploit for multiple years across multiple versions. The longer it lasts, the more ROI the attacker receives from the vulnerability hunting and exploit creation effort.

That same attacker later finds an Internet Explorer 11 code execution vulnerability and uses it in a series of attacks. However, after three months, defenders find and patch the vulnerability. The attacker had less time to get ROI out of that vulnerability, requiring him to go back to the drawing board and find a new one. This requires additional resource allocation for a smaller window of effectiveness.

Exploitability

A vulnerability is just a crack in the armor. It takes an actual exploit to take advantage of that crack. The exploitability process is all about finding a method to trigger the vulnerability and turn that into actual control of program execution. Much like vulnerability hunting, this phase may have its own specialists or occur in conjunction with other exploit phases. This is a topic unto itself, addressed well in the book *Hacking, The Art of Exploitation* (*https://www.nostarch.com/hacking2.htm*) by Jon Erickson (No Starch Press, 2008).

After an exploit is crafted, the attacker must make it reliable. This can be complicated because exploits don't always work, given things like language packs and specific defenses such as Microsoft's Enhanced Mitigation Experience Toolkit (EMET) or Address Space Layout Randomization (ASLR) for Linux. Further, exploits that crash target code or systems will draw attention.

An exploit, though, simply opens the door and gives the attacker a method to access the target (or at least an intermediate target). For the next step, the attacker will need an implant.

Implant development

Generally, the goal of an exploit includes delivering some sort of payload for the attacker to then use to further their goals (such as data exfiltration). The implant will allow the attacker to maintain access to the exploited system without having to continually exploit the device, which can be noisy, and if the system is patched, it would remove the possibility of exploitation at all. As a result, implant development follows many of the same processes as traditional software development, with an emphasis on stealth (to avoid detection) and capabilities (to allow attackers to achieve their objectives). Thus, if an attacker wants to be able to listen to conversations within range of a compromised system, the implant needs the ability to activate the microphone, record what it hears, and transmit the resulting audio files, all without triggering suspicion from the user or any security software that's running.

There are two primary types of implants. The first is a beaconing implant that calls out to a command-and-control server and will receive commands to be carried out on the target system. The second is an implant that does not beacon, but waits to receive a command and then begins to communicate with a command-and-control server. Implant development is often determined by the network topology and device type. Sometimes a previously developed implant can be used, but in other situations an attacker will need to develop something specifically for the network that is being targeted.

 Although many computer network operations still lean heavily on the need for an attacker to keep persistence and install capabilities with implants, a growing number of actors seek to achieve their objectives without installing any implants. The compromise of Hillary Clinton campaign chairman John Podesta's email was conducted without ever deploying an implant at all, just by stealing his password. In many ways, this style of attack is more difficult for investigators because without an implant, there's one fewer artifact to analyze. Implantless attacks are another case where understanding the attackers' goals will help contextualize their techniques.

Testing

Both exploits and implants then go through extensive testing as a part of the Weaponization phase. Much like software development, testing could be little more than a spot check, or it could mean extensive testing conducted by a separate quality assurance teams. For malicious code, the testing phase focuses on two aspects: *function* and *detectability*.

The functionality aspect is much like any other software development project; the testing team needs to ensure that the software does what it's designed to do. If it's meant to steal files, the implant must be able to read from the filesystem on the target host; find the correct group of files; usually bundle, encrypt, and compress them; and then exfiltrate them to a system the attacker controls. This may seem easy, but there are a wide variety of variables that the development team may not always be able to control, and thus need to be tested for.

The detectability aspect is unlike anything seen in normal software development. Testing teams will attempt to verify that their software is undetectable by security tools they might see in their target environment, such as antivirus or other endpoint software. This ties directly into the functionality aspect as many heuristics-based security systems look for certain behaviors that the malicious code may need to achieve its objective, such as setting registry keys to maintain persistence. These detectability requirements may be based on assumptions, or for especially hard targets, based on information gathered during reconissance.

Infrastructure development

While not strictly a part of the Weaponization phase, infrastructure development is another key preparation task an attacker needs to complete before the attack. Most attacks rely on pieces of infrastructure to support the malicious code deployed onto a victim's machines. Command-and-control servers are needed to direct attack actions. Exfiltration points are needed to upload and then retrieve stolen data from. Hot points are needed for attackers to pivot through to obfuscate their real location if their other infrastructure gets compromised. Attackers need a wide variety of infrastructure to execute the various phases of their operation:

Certificates
> For code signing and TLS connections.

Servers
> For misattribution, command and control, serving tools (like second-stage tool kits), and exfiltration points. Sometimes these are purchased directly, such as from a hosting provider.

Domains

Few network connections go directly to IP addresses, so most attackers use domain names.

Attackers know that tracking or shutting down malicious infrastructure is not difficult, so they will often have backup servers and domains to use when one system has been compromised or shut down.

Nondigital Infrastructure Needs

Not all infrastructure needs are digital. Attackers often need two other big needs to set up malicious infrastructure: identities and money. Both are often necessary to buy the resources needed to set up infrastructure. These are both challenging for attackers because in most cases they tie back directly to real people, something an attacker would most likely want to avoid.

Over the years, attackers have taken a wide variety of approaches to avoiding these pitfalls. Pseudonyms and fake identities are common, but even these can be tracked as an attacker often uses the same false name, false address, or registration email on domain name and certificate purchases. As for purchasing, some attackers avoid purchases entirely by compromising other, less well-secured systems, and using those instead of purchasing their own. Others have taken to using semi-anonymous payment systems such as Bitcoin. Finally, other attackers have taken to using online services such as GitHub, Twitter, and others for free infrastructure, as was demonstrated in the HammerToss report (*http://bit.ly/2u8GyGb*).

Delivery

Once the attacker has gathered enough information to craft an attack, the next kill chain stage is Delivery. Common delivery scenarios include but are not limited to the following:

Spear phishing

The attacker sends a weaponized resource, either as an attachment or as a link, via direct communications (often email) to a specific target. The communication is usually crafted to appear legitimate and reduce suspicion in the mind of the targeted user.

SQL injection

The attacker sends a command to a web application that is passed to the database server and interpreted directly. The attacker then has the ability to execute any database commands, including modifying credentials, exfiltrating information, or (in many cases) executing commands on the host operating system.

Strategic web compromise (watering hole)

The attacker first compromises a secondary resource, usually a website, and places a browser exploit on it. The assumption is that the target, usually focused at an entire group rather than a specific individual, will visit the site, becoming compromised.

The key to delivery is how simple it is: it's just getting the payload to the victim. This simplicity belies the importance of this stage. Delivery is the first active stage on the part of the attacker to the victim. While the previous stages can (in the case of Targeting and Reconissance) be active, Delivery is the first case where an attacker *must* be active. This means delivery is the first case where a victim is guaranteed to have indicators of compromise to build from. In the case of spear phishing, this may be email artifacts such as headers and an email address, while for SQL injection it may be an IP address that initiated the web server/database connections.

Exploitation

Understanding the difference between delivery and exploitation can be challenging. Up through delivery, the attacker has not had direct interaction with the target and does not have any control of the targeted system. Even in the case of a spear phishing email, it is possible that security measures will prevent successful delivery, so even though there was delivery, there was no actual exploitation. Exploitation is the point where the attackers gain control of code execution and begin executing their own code.

In a watering hole attack, this takes place the second a victim hits an infected page. For the spear phishing attack, this is when the victim clicks on a malicious attachment or link. From this point forward, the attacker has control of at least one process on the target's system. This foothold is the start of the attacker's move into the network.

Installation

Once attackers have code execution, their first move is typically to solidify their foothold. The Lockheed Martin Kill Chain paper describes this in the following way: "Installation of a remote-access Trojan or backdoor on the victim system allows the adversary to maintain persistence inside the environment." While this is what the attacker usually does at this stage, we find it useful to look at these actions as establishing system or network persistence (in many cases, the adversary will do both, but it still helps to consider them separately).

System persistence

At this point, the attacker has code execution on a single system, and likely just a single process at that. This is a useful start, but it doesn't persist past a reboot. A shutdown of the compromised application may even remove their access.

Most attackers begin by solidifying their hold on a small number of hosts by deploying a root kit or remote-access Trojan (RAT) style of implant. A root kit establishes kernel-level access to a system and, once installed, permits an attacker to evade many detection methods of the underlying OS. A RAT is a piece of remote-control software meant to persist past reboots and without relying on a certain exploit. This allows the attacker to persist on an individual host.

Network persistence

Most attackers aren't content to establish a single-system foothold. Instead, they want to establish deeper persistence. To do so, they'll typically establish a wider footprint, using one (or both) of two techniques:

Establish system persistence on multiple systems
> This means using captured credentials and installing RATs or similar access methods on other systems. An attacker has a variety of options for this, from custom software to native tools such as PsExec in Windows or SSH in *nix environments.

Gathering credentials that allow access to broadly utilized network resources without accessing a system on the network
> This often means VPNs, cloud services, or other internet-exposed systems such as web mail. This lowers the risk of detection in many cases and doesn't require a form of malware, instead using native tools.

These techniques can be used individually or together.

Command and Control

Once an attacker has established persistence, especially if they've chosen the RAT route, they need a method to send commands. Communication can come in a variety of methods and using multiple types of channels. In the past, many pieces of malware, especially distributed denial-of-service (DDoS) tools, communicated by joining IRC channels or HTTP calls to a server under the attacker's control. The Comment Crew (*http://symc.ly/2tHeLKX*) got its moniker from doing command-and-control with HTML comments on otherwise innocuous-looking web pages. Some attackers use multiple methods, including DNS lookups, social media, or popular cloud applications.

Self-Guided Malware

A relatively small number of malware families operate without any communication at all. These *drones*, or self-guided malware families, are rare, and particularly suited to attacking air-gapped networks. The famous example is the Stuxnet malware family, aimed at a group of Iranian nuclear research facilities, where network communication was impossible. Given the success of this family and others like it, it's possible more may be coming. Responding to self-guided malware requires a different approach because defenders can't focus on identifying network traffic used for command and control or exfiltration. Instead, defenders need to identify malware in use on the system and eradicate it before it spreads.

Attackers focus on making sure that their communication channels avoid notice and provide enough bandwidth to meet the needs of the attacker. In some cases, malware may communicate using only a few lines of text a day, while others include full virtual desktop capability.

Actions on Objective

In most cases, all of this is not the ultimate goal, but rather the setup. Attackers go through the process of setting up access in order to give themselves the capability to affect the target in a way they didn't have before. We call this new capability the *actions on objective*. The most common actions on target were categorized by the US Air Force as follows:

Destroy
> The attacker destroys a physical or virtual item. This could mean destroying data, overwriting or deleting files, or otherwise making a system unavailable until it is completely rebuilt. This could also mean destroying a physical object, though this is a rare occurrence in computer attacks. The Stuxnet destruction of Iranian centrifuges is one such example.

Deny
> The attacker denies usage of a resource (such as a system or information) by the target, such as in the case of denial-of-service attacks that do not permit access to a site. Another example that has gained currency in recent years is *ransomware*, which encrypts a user's data and requires payment before the attacker will (in theory) decrypt the data for use again.

Degrade

> The attacker degrades the utility of the target's resources or capabilities. This most often refers to the target's ability to control and command resources.

Disrupt

> By interrupting the flow of information, an attacker can disrupt the target's ability to carry out normal operations.

Deceive

> The attacker seeks to cause the target to believe something that is not true. In this context, the attacker may be inserting false information into a workflow to redirect assets or information, or cause the target to take a course of action to the attacker's benefit.

Most of these are straightforward and basic on the surface. However, the manner in which an attacker puts these together is key and often speaks directly to the attacker's identity and goals. An attacker can often hide malware, obfuscate command and control, and so forth; but ultimately the actions on the objective cannot be obfuscated, encoded, or protected. To steal information, an attacker must steal the files. To execute a DoS, an attacker must use compromised hosts to send massive amounts of network traffic. In short, the Actions on Objective phase can't be faked.

It's also important to understand that an attacker may combine multiple actions and vectors, including physical/noncyber actions. This could include anything from recruiting an insider to leak strategic information to a *kinetic action* (for example, bombing a geographic site).

As you can see in Figure 3-3, the attacker's kill chain stays tightly defined while the incident cycle has to react to it, which starts in the Identification phase. Identification can occur anywhere between the Identification and the Actions on Target phases of the kill chain, and causes dramatically different incident responses to occur. An incident identified during the Delivery phase is ideal. The defenders can block the attack at an email or web proxy and keep the attack from ever executing. An attack detected during a later phase, such as Command and Control or Actions on Objective, is likely going to be painful, involving many compromised resources and an expensive and lengthy incident-response investigation.

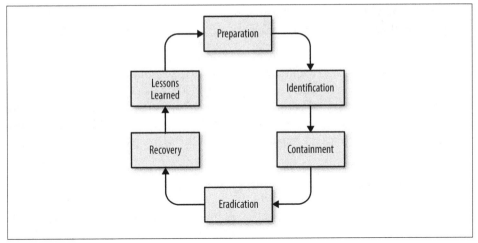

Figure 3-3. The kill chain and the incident cycle

Example Kill Chain

To illustrate the kill chain, imagine a series of attacks by a fictitious attack group code-named Grey Spike. This group conducts political intelligence collection against national campaigns in multiple countries. They seek to gain information about candidates' stances on economic, foreign policy, and military issues. Here's what their strategy would entail:

Targeting
> Grey Spike does not choose its own targets but receives *tasking* (intelligence jargon for what they're instructed to target) from national policy makers. This tasking describes specific target countries and candidates as well as key words of interest.

Reconnaissance
> Grey Spike begins operations by understanding the network footprint of its targets, including domain names, mail servers, key technologies, and web and mobile applications. The group also gathers information on key personnel, such as campaign management, social media managers, and the technology consulting firms retained by the campaigns.

Weaponization
> Grey Spike receives quarterly resource allocations including zero-day vulnerabilities, but in general prefers to use these when no other vector is available. In this case, Grey Spike has a suite of download macros that it implants as payloads in documents custom-written in the target languages by regional and cultural specialists on loan from other departments within their intelligence agency. Addi-

tionally, infrastructure in the form of private servers used for C2 and delivery is rented in the name of shell companies from providers around the globe.

Delivery

The operators send the weaponized documents to key managers in the campaign staff. Each document is written to appeal to that manager specifically, including offers to provide financial contributions and endorsements. Because of the rapid pace of the campaign trail, the targets open these documents with a high success rate, allowing the attacker's implants to run on their laptops.

Exploitation

The implant code runs in the form of a document macro that runs an older exploit for the PDF reader used by the campaign. Although a patch has been available for the vulnerability for some time, campaign staff have frozen all updates because of the belief by senior staff that this may cause outages at inopportune times.

Delivery

The exploit code is a downloader that then contacts a malware delivery server in a shared hosting environment at a popular ISP to install a remote access Trojan (RAT) on the target system. The RAT next contacts a C2 server at a bulletproof ISP in a third country.

Command and control

Grey Spike issues commands to the RAT via the C2 channel, in this case through encoded DNS lookups. Using their covert channel, they conduct searches for the target's email and relevant documents. In addition to some of the information they've been tasked with acquiring, they find emails documenting shared accounts, including passwords that they can then use to extend their access throughout the network.

Actions on Objective

In this scenario, Grey Spike is tasked specifically with information retrieval only. The policy makers do not wish to interfere directly with the campaign, largely because of concern about political consequences, despite having the technical ability to destroy most of the data and online infrastructure of the candidates.

Kill chains help to organize incident-response data in a way that allows you to visualize what the attack looked like as it took place, and can help identify patterns in activity. Another method to accomplish this is the diamond model, which we will discuss next.

Diamond Model

The diamond model (Figure 3-4) for intrusion analysis differs in many ways from the kill chain (though later in this section we'll discuss how they complement each other). Originally discussed in a paper by Christopher Betz et al., they summarize the model as follows: "An *adversary* deploys a *capability* over some *infrastructure* against a *victim*. These activities are called *events*...events are phase-ordered by adversary-victim pair into *activity threads* representing the flow of an adversary's operations." Ultimately, it is a paradigm for understanding the interaction between the various actors (the adversary and the victim) and the adversary's tools (infrastructure and capabiities).

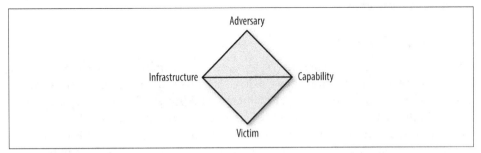

Figure 3-4. The diamond model

Basic Model

An *adversary* is an intelligent party (actor) with intent to gather information or do harm to an information system. We can further break this down into the *operator* carrying out the actions and the *customer* who will benefit from the actions. The same person might fulfill both roles (in a small mercenary or financially-motivated adversary group), but not always (as in the case of a nation-state SIGINT agency where the customer and operator could come from different agencies, let alone teams). Adversaries will have an intent, which could be as general as "make money through credit card fraud" or as specific as "acquire the communications of a specified person regarding a particular topic of interest."

An adversary has a set of exploits and techniques, called a *capability*, they can deploy to accomplish their goals. This includes the weaponized software and implants discussed in the kill chain, but it can also include the ability to carry out a social engineering attack or, in some cases, deploy some sort of physical ability, whether for gathering information or disrupting systems.

An adversary uses a set of communication systems and protocols, called *infrastructure*, to deliver or control a capability, or to cause some result on a victim. This includes systems owned directly by the adversary (e.g., desktops and network equipment in their physical possession) and systems compromised and re-purposed (e.g., end-user systems in a botnet).

Adversaries target a *victim* against which they deploy their capabilities in the attempt to accomplish a certain intent. The victim includes people and assets, and both may be targeted separately. And as noted, a victim system may then be used as infrastructure against another victim.

Each occurrence in which all four elements are present (an adversary using a capability across infrastructure against a victim) represents a single event. Events that feed into each other then are analyzed as *activity threads*, and we can further collect those threads into *activity groups* (related threads that may run in parallel or otherwise not necessarily flow linearly).

Extending the Model

One of the ways in which the model starts to demonstrate its power comes from looking at the axes across the diamond. The "north-south" axis connecting adversaries and victims represents a social-political relationship. The adversary has some interest in the victim, whether as a class (credit card numbers) or specifically (a CEO targeted for spear phishing to enable fraudulent wire transfers). Analysis of this axis can shed light on an adversary's motivation and possibly assist with attribution or operational and strategic planning for intrusion detection and incident response.

As mentioned at the beginning of this section, the diamond model complements the kill chain, and in fact the two integrate well. Each event in the diamond model can be categorized according to its phase in the kill chain. This allows the analyst to have a greater understanding of the relationship between events and consider investigating and documenting phases that you have previously neglected to investigate. (That said, not every phase of the kill chain will be present in every incident.)

Active Defense

One of the most talked about and least understood concepts about intelligence-driven incident-response cycles is the idea of active defense.

It is frequently equated with the idea of *hack back*, attempting to attack a malicious actor directly. Although this qualifies as one aspect of active defense, five other useful pieces of active defense are far more common. This mix-up is based on a fundamental misunderstanding of the purpose of active defense.

Most people who attempt or request some form of hack back have in mind a childish, schoolyard-style form of revenge. It's natural. You get hit; you want to hit someone back. There are reasons we've outgrown these juvenile tactics. First of all, in network intrusions, we often find it difficult to know the attacker's identity, leading to misattribution and thus a misdirected attack. Second, proportionate response is difficult for defensively oriented organizations. Third, it usually serves a limited purpose aside from a sense of revenge. Fourth, and perhaps most important, it is illegal in most countries to attempt to compromise an organization without its permission or appropriate legal authority such as granted to law enforcement and military organizations, which in theory submit to strict oversight.

Apart from hacking back, however, active defense includes several other valid and useful elements. Wendi Rafferty at the SANS DFIR Summit in 2015 described the goal of active defense as attempting to disrupt the tempo of an attacker. Like a detective, the goal of incident responders is to catch an attacker in a mistake, providing a chance to expose them. Active defense gives defenders a means to accelerate that by forcing the attacker into an error, generally while responding to a roadblock put into place by the incident-response team.

As previously discussed for attackers, defenders have the option to deny, disrupt, degrade, deceive, and destroy (Thus we call this model the D5 model of defense). Originally developed as a series of desired capabilities for computer network attack (CNA), it turns out the same D5 model provides a great list of capabilities for active defense.

Deny

The idea of denying an attacker is so straightforward and common that most organizations wouldn't even imagine it's a type of active defense. If we go by our traditional definition of disrupting the attacker's tempo, though, this is a perfect example. Denying can be simple, such as implementing a new firewall rule to block an attacker's command and control or shutting down access for a compromised email account. The key to denial is *preemptively excluding a resource from the malicious actor.*

Denial forces attackers to deviate from their plan and to find a different way to achieve their objectives. If the attackers don't change every single IOC before continuing, you can force them into revealing TTPs and pivot your investigation to their new activities. Additionally, many deny actions could be interpreted as mere coincidence, such as a user resetting a password because of a required window, not at the direction of the incident-response team.

Disrupt

If the Deny action preemptively excludes a resource from the malicious actor, then Disrupt *actively excludes a resource from the malicious actor.* In most cases, disruption requires active observation of an attacker in order to know when they're active so that they can be disrupted in real time. This could mean cutting off a command-and-control channel while it's being used or interrupting the exfiltration of a large archive file.

Degrade

Closely related to disrupting and denying an adversary, Degrade focuses on *marginal reduction of an attacker's resources while they're actively being used.* An easily understandable example is throttling an attacker's bandwidth during exfiltration, causing a large file to upload over an extremely slow time frame. This degradation of access attempts to frustrate attackers, hopefully driving them to attempt to access the data in a different way and expose additional infrastructure, tools, or TTPs.

Disruption and degradation present interesting but dangerous opportunities for a network defense team. While denial actions may be explained away as coincidence or normal passive defensive operations, disruption and degradation are clearly active. They begin to open up a dialogue with an attacker, giving the attacker an indication that the defender is deliberately responding. Attackers in situations like this can take a variety of actions. They may spool up attack tempo and severity by bringing advanced capabilities to bear, or they may go all the way in the other direction and cease operations entirely while they wait for the heat to go down. This is the risk of these types of active defense, and they need to be taken with a measure of caution and preparation.

Deceive

Easily the most advanced of available techniques, the Deceive active defense action is based on the counter intelligence concept of *deliberately feeding attackers false information* with the hopes they'll treat it as truth and make decisions based on it. This ranges from planting false documents with incorrect values to hosting honeypot systems or even networks.

Deception operations require a deep understanding of the attacker's goals, methods, and even psychology, as well as your own resources. Making deception material that an attacker is willing to accept as truth is incredibly difficult, as skilled attackers will attempt to corroborate any material they find with other sources.

Destroy

Destroy actions do actual harm, whether physical or virtual, to an attacker's tools, infrastructure, or operators. In most cases, this is the purview of law enforcement, intelligence, or military operators (so-called Title 10 and Title 50 organizations) that have the legal authority to commit such acts. For a commercial or private organization to do so is not only generally accepted to be illegal but also dangerous. It is unlikely that they have the tools, methodology, and operators to conduct a successful computer network attack, and there could be significant unintended consequences. Those resources are better allocated to improved defensive operations.

Is active defense for you? Active defense is a trendy topic, but should organizations make it a part of their security program? As with almost any simple question about complex topics, the answer is, "It depends." Active defense doesn't have to be implemented in its entirety. Denying an adversary is in the realm of any organization, and in fact most are probably already doing it. Disruption and degradation require maturity. Deception is an advanced tactic that carries high reward but also high risk and should be reserved for all but the most advanced security teams. As we just said, the Destroy active defense action requires special legal status that's not available to nongovernment organizations.

F3EAD

The last major cycle to cover combines the intelligence generation aspects of the intelligence cycle with the operations-centric aspect of the incident and kill chain cycles. Built as a targeting methodology for special operations teams, F3EAD addresses two key issues with both of the previous cycles:

- Intelligence cycles shouldn't just lead to more intelligence: they should lead to meaningful operations. In our case, this means threat intelligence shouldn't just lead us to more threat intelligence but instead to aggressive incident-response actions.
- Operations cycles shouldn't end after the objective is completed. The information gained during any operation should start feeding a new intelligence cycle. In our case, when an incident response is concluded, the information developed during it should be fed into the intelligence apparatus to start developing new intelligence, learn from previous incidents, and be better prepared for future intrusion attempts.

Thus these two cycles, operations and intelligence, *feed into each other* instead of just themselves (Figure 3-5. Each incident-response operation leads to intelligence operations, and each intelligence operation leads to an incident-response operation, continuing the cycle.

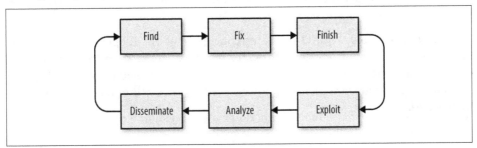

Figure 3-5. The F3EAD operations/intelligence cycle

To facilitate this process, F3EAD (*http://bit.ly/2uDMaKA*) uses a modified version of a combined intelligence and operations cycle: Find, Fix, Finish, Exploit, Analyze, Disseminate. As you'll see, this means going through the incident-response cycle and feeding the results into the intelligence cycle, and then connecting those results back into a new incident-response cycle.

Find

The *Find* phase includes the *targeting* phase of the operation, which is where you determine the threats that you will address. This can come from many sources, such as intelligence from a vendor or open source. Ideally, your own previous intelligence cycles should feed this process as well. Depending on the operation or investment, this phase may be determined by the IR team itself, in conjunction with the intelligence team, or even working with groups outside these teams, such as the SOC or management. This parallels the Preparation phase of the incident-response cycle.

Fix

Based on the information from the Find phase, the *Fix* phase establishes telemetry and determines where an adversary is on the network as well any external presence we can detect. Just to be clear, *fix* does not mean to repair (we were confused too!); it refers to the identification of operational presence of the attacker within the network. This involves taking available information and figuring out which systems, services, or resources an adversary may have compromised, what their channels of communications are, and how they're moving around your network. We can think of this as the Identification phase of the incident-response cycle.

Finish

The *Finish* phase includes the actual incident-response action (as opposed to the more kinetic and lethal actions intended for the original military version of this process—please do not do these). This is when you take decisive action against the adversary, carrying out the containment, mitigation, and eradication phases of the incident-response cycle.

The major transition in F3EAD is that the conclusion of the IR operation doesn't end the cycle. Whether the organization shifts resources and responsibilities between teams or the same team changes its own activity focus, the end of the Finish phase starts the beginning of the Exploit phase. The intelligence half of the F3EAD process then begins.

Exploit

The *Exploitation* phase maps directly to the Collection phase of the intelligence cycle. The goal is to gather as much information as possible that might be useful to the intelligence-focused phases of F3EAD:

- Any indicators of compromise, including IP addresses, URLs, hashes, and email addresses
- Automated enrichment for the IOCs (such as getting reverse DNS for given IP addresses or gathering WHOIS data)
- Exploit delivery examples
- Malware samples
- Common vulnerabilities and exposures (CVE) and exploits
- User and incident reports
- Communications from the attacker
- Previously identified TTPs
- Attacker objectives, goals, and motivations

It's impossible to list everything that might be useful, but analysts should collect as much information as they can about the various phases of the attack. Think through the kill chain and try to collect information about each stage where possible.

Analyze

The Analyze phase maps to (surprise) the Analyze phase of the intelligence cycle. During this phase, the idea is to develop the collected information through a few methods:

- Summarizing tactics, techniques, and procedures
- Developing timelines and kill chains
- Conducting in-depth malware analysis

Like the general intelligence phase, the Analyze phase itself is cyclical. Malware analysis may lead to more IOCs, which themselves can be enriched, and may lead to finding more malware. The overall goal is to develop a complete picture of the actor and his tactics, techniques, and procedures, with a focus on how to detect, mitigate, and remediate his actions.

Disseminate

Dissemination of this type of intelligence is focused primarily on the audience:

Tactical

The most immediate audience for the intelligence is the incident-response team, feeding back in to the beginning of the next F3EAD cycle. They'll want a focus on a IOCs and summarized TTPs.

Strategic

It generally takes only one significant incident for management to start having a strong investment and interest in the IR and threat intelligence team(s). Their interest will be in highly generalized TTPs (more focused on campaigns than individual incidents) and actions on target. This intelligence should be useful to decision makers in future resource allocation and larger business planning (for example, informing risk assessments).

Third party

Many organizations participate in some form of threat intelligence sharing group. Each organization has to determine its own rules of engagement for participating. Work with your leadership and legal teams to determine the best methods to do that. This may include intelligence from any level of abstraction, depending on your goals and appetite for collaboration.

Regardless of the level of intelligence or the audience you are addressing, you will want the information you disseminate to be clear, concise, accurate, and actionable.

Using F3EAD

F3EAD is one of the most powerful concepts that can be implemented to improve both the threat intelligence and incident-response side of security operations. It's also one of the most difficult. It's difficult to explain why an arcane Special Forces acronym that most people don't even know how to say should be a part of an IT department.

Rather than focus on the details, focus on the overall idea: security operations and incident response become an input to threat intelligence, and threat intelligence becomes an input to security operations and incident response. Whenever any part of the security operations team (whether that's a SOC, CIRT, or individual engineers) completes an incident response, all of their outputs and documentation, notes, forensic artifacts, malware, and research should be passed on to the intelligence team. From there, the intelligence team exploits and analyzes this information. Their output based on that incident should be provided back to the ops team, and then the cycle continues. This ends up forming a kind of security operations/threat intelligence OODA loop. The faster the security ops team can use this intelligence, the faster they can complete their operations tasks, which in turn drives more intelligence.

This ops + intelligence model doesn't need to be limited to the SOC and intelligence teams. This same process can be used with the vulnerability management and application security (AppSec) teams. For example, when the application security team finds a new vulnerability, that vulnerability can then be treated as a piece of intelligence. Nothing guarantees the application security engineer was the first person to find this vulnerability. Thus the AppSec team feeds as much information as possible to the SOC, which begins looking for any indications of previous attacks against that vulnerability.

Picking the Right Model

The purpose of models is to provide a framework that can be used to interpret information and generate intelligence. Hundreds of models are available for intelligence analysis. Some of these models are meant to be general purpose, and some have been developed for individual or specific use-cases. When deciding what model to use, there are several factors to keep in mind. The time available for analysis can help determine which model is appropriate. If there is time to conduct an in-depth analysis or an incident, the diamond model for intrusion analysis may work well. If you have time constraints, something like the OODA loop can be used to drive decisions. The type of information may also dictate which model is most appropriate, as some models are designed to be used with certain data sources such as netflow or endpoint data. Finally, it may all come down to analyst preference. If an analyst has found that a certain model works well within their processes, then by all means continue to use that model. There may even come a time when the best option is to develop a new model.

Scenario: GLASS WIZARD

Now that we've worked through many of the key models you'll need to understand intelligence-driven incident response, we're about to launch into the practical nuts and bolts of incident response, cyber threat intelligence, and how they can work together to help you defend your organization.

The rest of the book is laid out using the joint operations/intelligence model F3EAD. As we work through this process, we'll use our own investigation named GLASS WIZARD, digging into an actor. The F3EAD model breaks out like this:

Find
> The next chapter introduces how we target adversaries, both proactively and reactively.

Fix
> The first half of in-depth incident response is taking on the investigation phase, how to track an adversary in the victim environment.

Finish

The second half of incident response removes an adversary from the environment.

Exploit

Once the incident-response process is over, we'll start developing data that resulted from our incident response.

Analyze

Next we'll develop that data into intelligence that can be useful for protecting our organization going forward and helping others.

Disseminate

After developing the intelligence, we'll put it into a variety of useful formats for a variety of customers.

By the end, we'll have developed a full set of products, breaking down the actor we know as GLASS WIZARD.

Conclusion

Complex processes such as incident response often benefit from the use of models, which give the processes structure and can define necessary steps for task completion. Determining which models should be used depends on the situation, the data available, and in many cases the analyst's preference. The more familiar you become with these models and their applications, the easier it will be to determine which models to use in response to different incidents.

Now let's dive into Find!

## PART II

Practical Application

Once you understand the fundamentals, it is time to get down to business. Part 2 steps through the intelligence-driven incident-response process using the F3EAD process: Find, Fix Finish, Exploit, Analyze, Disseminate. These steps will ensure that you are gathering and acting on the right information in the right order to get as much as possible from the intelligence-driven incident-response processes.

## CHAPTER 4

Find

"Be very, very quiet; we are hunting wabbits."

—Elmer J. Fudd

The first half of the F3EAD cycle—Find, Fix, and Finish—are the primary operations components, which for us means incident-response operations. For these first three phases, the adversaries are targeted, identified, and eradicated. We use intelligence to inform these operation actions, but that's not the end of our use of intelligence. Later in the process, we will use the data from the operations phase in the second half of F3EAD the intelligence phase: Exploit, Analyze, Disseminate.

This chapter focuses on the Find phase, which identifies the starting point for both intelligence and operational activities. In the traditional F3EAD cycle, the Find phase often identifies high-value targets for special operations teams to target. In intelligence-driven incident response, the Find phase identifies relevant adversaries for incident response.

In the case of an ongoing incident, you may have identified or been given some initial indicators and need to dig for more; or in the case of threat hunting, you may be searching for anomalous activity in your networks. Regardless of the situation, before you can find anything, you need to have an idea of what it is you are looking for.

Various approaches can be taken in the Find phase. The method should be determined by the nature of the situation or incident as well as the goal of the investigation. Different methods may be combined as well to ensure that you have identified all possible pieces of information.

Actor-Centric Targeting

When there is credible information on the actor behind an attack, or you are being asked to provide information on a particular attack group, it is possible to conduct actor-centric targeting.

Actor-centric investigations are like unravelling a sweater: you find a few little pieces of information and begin to pull on each one. These threads can give you insight into the tactics and techniques that the actor used against you, which then give you a better idea of what else to look for. The result is powerful, but it can be frustrating. You never know which thread will be the key to unravelling the whole thing. You just have to keep trying. Then suddenly you may dig into one aspect that opens up the entire investigation. Persistence, and luck, are key aspects of actor-centric investigations.

Actors Versus People

Identity is a funny thing. In many cases, when we say *they* or *them* or refer to an adversary, it's easy to assume we're referring to the people behind an attack. In some, rare cases, we are talking about the actual individuals (this is called *attribution*, something we'll discuss more in the intelligence chapters). But in most cases when we're referring to actors, we refer to a persona based on the tactics, techniques, and processes (TTPS) used together to achieve a goal. We mentally group these together and personify them, since human beings understand stories told that way. This is an abstraction, because we usually don't know if it's one person or a large group. We call this abstraction of linked TTPs and a goal an *actor*, regardless of the number of people involved.

In some cases, incident responders will go into an investigation with an idea of who the actor behind the incident may be. This information can be gleaned from a variety of sources; for example, when stolen information is offered for sale on underground forums, or when a third party makes the initial notification and provides some information on the attacker. Identifying at least some details of an attacker makes it possible to carry out actor-centric targeting in the Find phase.

When conducting actor-centric targeting, the first step is to validate the information that has been provided on the attacker. It is important to understand if and why the attacker in question would target your organization. The development of a threat model, a process that identifies potential threats by taking an attacker's view of a target, can speed this process and can help identify the types of data or access that may have been targeted. This information can also feed into the Find phase, where incident responders search for signs of attacker activity.

A threat model can allow you to use actor-centric targeting even if you do not have concrete information on the actor by determining potential or likely attackers. Of the hundreds of tracked criminal, activist, and espionage groups, only a small handful will be generally interested in your organization. Assessing which of these groups are truly threats to you is not a perfect science, but you have to make your best guess and keep in mind that the list you come up with will not be an authoritative list but will still be a good place to start. After some time, experience will be the best guide to who you should be concerned about.

Once you validate the initial information, the next step is to identify as much information as possible on the actor. This information will help to build the *target package* on the attacker, which will enable operations to fix and finish the attack. Information on the actor can include details of previous attacks, both internal and external.

Starting with Known Information

In almost every situation, some information will be available on threat actors, whether that comes from previous incidents or attack attempts within your own environment (internal information) or intelligence reports produced by researchers, vendors, or other third parties (external information). Ideally, a combination of both types will be available in order to provide the best overall picture of the threat.

Strategic and tactical intelligence are both useful at the this stage. Strategic intelligence on actors can provide information on the actor's potential motivation or goals, where they ultimately want to get to, and what they ultimately want to do when they get there. Tactical intelligence can provide details on how an actor typically operates, including their typical tactics and methods, preferred tools, previous infrastructure used, and other pieces of information that can be searched for during the Fix stage and contextualize the information that is found.

It is also useful, though difficult, to understand whether the actors tend to operate alone, or whether they work with other actor groups. Some espionage groups have been known to divide tasks between several groups, with one group focusing on initial access, another focusing on accomplishing the goals of the attack, another for maintaining access for future activities, and so forth. If this is the case, there may be signs of multiple actors and multiple activities in a network, but further analysis should be conducted to see whether the activities fit the pattern of multiple actor groups working together or whether it is possible that several actors are operating independently.

Using Malware to Identify Threat Actors

Years ago, it was common to attribute attacks to a particular group based on malware or other tools used during attacks. PlugX is a perfect example, originally believed to be created and used exclusively by the NCPH Group (*http://bit.ly/2ff33Wv*). Since then, PlugX has been sold or shared and is in wide use by a variety of threat actors. The time for malware-based attribution has passed, as many attack tools and RATs have been published, sold, and repurposed by a variety of threat actor groups. Rather than base attribution solely on malware, it is important to take a variety of other factors into account, including goals and motivations as well as behaviors and other tactics. Identifying previously used malware is, however, useful in the Find phase and can lead to the identification of additional pieces of information useful to the investigation.

Useful Find Information

During the Find phase, our biggest goal is developing information that will be useful during the Fix portion of the F3EAD cycle. The most useful information is information that's hard for the actor to change. Incident responder David J. Bianco captured this concept, and its impact on the adversary, in his Pyramid of Pain (*http://bit.ly/ 2uKjNLN*), shown in Figure 4-1.

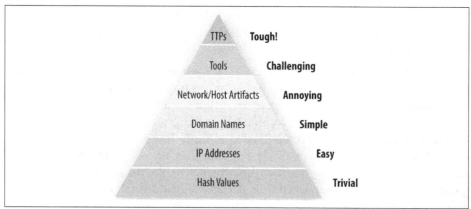

Figure 4-1. David J Bianco's Pyramid of Pain

The Pyramid of Pain is a model depicting how central various types of information are to an actor's tool chain and objectives, which corresponds to how hard they are to change. At the bottom, you have basic characteristics that attackers can change regularly by tweaking small details of malware or network configurations such as recompiling malware (to generate a new hash) or pointing a domain name at a new

IP address for command and control. At the top, you have core capabilities that are central to who an actor is, such as core techniques and methodologies.

Intelligence Versus Information

Keep in mind we are focused right now on threat *information* rather than threat *intelligence*. Intelligence is information that has been analyzed to answer a specific question, which we will get to later in the F3EAD process. At this initial stage, we are grabbing as much potentially useful information as we can find, which we will then analyze to determine whether it is something that we want to include in the remaining steps.

So how do we use this model? The Pyramid of Pain is all about understanding the relative value and temporal nature of different types of indicators of compromise (more on those in the next section!) and actor information. Are hashes useless? Not at all; they're incredibly useful in many contexts and provide a great starting place for an investigation, but they change often and easily (often just by recompiling a piece of malware). On the opposite end of the spectrum, an actor that specializes in compromising websites with SQL injection would have a relatively difficult time switching tactics to spear phishing with zero-day exploits. The result is when it comes to threat information, we prefer and get longer use out of information toward the top of the pyramid. Our goal in both incident response and intelligence analysis is trying to move higher up the pyramid, thus making it more difficult for the adversary to evade us.

Indicators of compromise

The simplest data (and thus lower on the Pyramid of Pain) to gather are commonly referred to as *indicators of compromise* (IOCs). The earliest definition of IOCs comes from Mandiant's OpenIOC website (OpenIOC is the Mandiant proprietary definition for IOCs compatible with its MIR products). While IOCs can come in a variety of formats (we'll discuss this more next chapter), they're all defined the same way: "a description of technical characteristics that identify a known threat, an attacker's methodology, or other evidence of compromise."

OpenIOC Versus Traditional IOCs

Most analysts would refer to a single piece of technical threat information as an IOC. However, OpenIOC wasn't based on individual atomic indicators but on compound indicators made up of multiple indicators grouped together around a particular threat. This is simply a difference between the original concept and the way the industry has embraced IOCs. Other organizations have created their own IOC formats, the most notable being MITRE's Structured Threat Information Expression (STIX).

IOC's typically focus on atomic pieces of information at the bottom of the Pyramid of Pain. These can be subdivided based on where the information is found:

Filesystem indicators
  File hashes, filenames, strings, paths, sizes, types, signing certificates

Memory indicators
  Strings and memory structures

Network indicators
  IP addresses, host names, domain names, HTML paths, ports, SSL certificates

Each type of indicator has unique uses, is visible in different positions (whether monitoring a single system or a network), and depending on the format it's in, may be useful with different tools.

Behavior

Far more complex for attackers to change are behaviors, captured in the top level of the Pyramid of Pain as TTPs. This is a loose group that goes beyond tools and instead focuses on how they're used to achieve an attacker's goals. Behavior is more abstract than TTPs and can't be easily described the way IOCs can.

Behaviors can often be best understood in terms of the kill chain from Chapter 3, as in how does an attacker achieve each piece? Here are a few hypothetical examples:

Reconnaissance
  (Usually based on inference.) The attacker generally profiles potential victims based on conference proceedings documents found online.

Weaponization
  The attacker uses a Visual Basic for Applications (VBA) macro sent inside a Microsoft Word document.

Delivery
  The attacker sends a phishing email from a fake industry group based on information from the proceedings of the conference identified during reconnaissance.

Exploitation
  The attacker's VBA macro executes when the victim opens the attached Word document and downloads the second-stage payload.

Installation

The attacker uses a privilege escalation exploit to install a second-stage payload, a remote-access Trojan, so it starts up at login and achieves persistence.

Command and control

The RAT uses connections to a micro blogging site to exchange encoded communication for command and control.

Actions on Objective

The attacker attempts to steal technical schematics and email by compressing them and uploading them through a file-sharing service.

Make sure that you document any information that you find in a way that will help you remember it for use in future steps of the intelligence-driven incident-response process.

Using the kill chain

Actor-centric targeting is often a good place to start, partially because it has the most straightforward model when combined with the kill chain. Any information that you are given or find at the start of your investigation will most likely come from one, or, if you are lucky, two phases of the kill chain. A good strategy is to use the surrounding phases of the kill chain to determine what other information to look for, so identifying where your existing information sits within the kill chain can determine where else you should look. In the previous example, if the only information you knew about the attack is that the attackers used macros in a Word document during the exploitation phase, you could research that behavior and identify that you should look for artifacts related to privilege escalation to determine whether the exploitation was successful. Another option would be to move in the other direction on the kill chain and to look for the delivery method, searching for email senders or subjects related to the original information that you received. Even if the attackers did not keep things 100% identical across attacks, similarities can be identified, especially when you know what you are looking for.

Scenario: building a kill chain. Building a kill chain for a new attacker is a great place to start building your understanding, even if there aren't a lot of things to fill in at the beginning. One of the great things about the kill chain, even one filled with question marks, is that it provides a structure for knowing what to look for next.

In our case, we're starting with a private report being passed around a variety of organizations similar to ours. (In reality, this report was released in 2014 as the Operations SNM report (*http://bit.ly/2u9wjkJ*).) Another security team thought the report could be useful. Using this report, we're going to start building a kill chain for the actor we're calling GLASS WIZARD, and will document what we know and what gaps we have.

GLASS WIZARD kill chain.

- **Goals**

  — Actor targets a wide variety of victims, including economic, environmental, and energy policy organizations as well as high-tech manufactures and service providers.

  — Actor targets a variety of domestic targets, indicating possible domestic security focus.

- **Reconnaissance**

  — Unknown.

- **Weaponization**

  — Use of stolen certificates to avoid OS-level code-signing protection.

- **Delivery**

  — Spear phishing.

  — Strategic website compromises.

  — Direct attacks against publicly facing services.

- **Exploitation**

  — Unknown.

- **Installation: Host**

  — Wide variety of malware varieities used: Poison Ivy, Gh0st Rat, PlugX, ZXShell, Hydraq, DeputyDog, Derusbi, Hikit, ZoxFamily (ZoxPNG, ZoxSMB).

  — Escalates privileges using local exploits, remote exploits (for example, the ZoxRPC tool), and compromised credentials from other systems.

- **Installation: Network**

  — Uses compromised credentials to move around the network using standard network administration tools such as RDP.

  — May install secondary malware on other hosts.

- **Communication**

  — Highly divided (minimally reused) infrastructure for each set of targets and campaigns.

  — Preference for DNSPOD and DtDNS DNS providers.

  — <target>.<holderdomain>.<tld> domain name pattern.

  — Use of compromised infrastructure to hide in legitimate traffic.

- **Actions on target**

  — Compromises large groups of machines and identifies useful material quickly, possibly indicating dynamic goals based on what's available.

  — Custom scripting for on-target actions.

  — Exfiltration?

Sometimes individual items could go in multiple categories. In our kill chain, the element *direct attacks against publicly facing services* is sort of Delivery, but could also be described as exploitation. In some cases, this is important, but the real important thing is capturing the information. It can always be edited, so when creating a kill chain, don't get too stuck arguing one phase versus another. Again, this is just a model, so it's not perfect; it just needs to be useful.

Though not a part of the kill chain, another thing this report tells us is related actors, campaigns, and operations including the following:

- APT1
- DeputyDog
- Elderwood
- Ephemeral Hydra
- Operation Aurora
- Operation Snowman
- PLA Third Department Unit 61486 and Unit 61398
- Shell Crew
- VOHO Campaign

How relevant these related actors are to our investigation depends on a lot of things, but for now we just want to keep them around. In addition, a wide variety of links make up the sources for the reports, and we'll want to keep those as well to reference and possibly analyze later.

Now we have an initial kill chain based on our first pieces of information about GLASS WIZARD. While it's obvious we have huge gaps in the structure of understanding, this actor is starting to come together. We know some of the techniques this actor might use to get into our organization, and we have considerable information about what they might do once they get in. Throughout the rest of the F3 operations phase, we're going to use the information we have to try to track and respond to the adversary and fill in some of these blanks as we go.

Goals

The attacker's goals are the most abstract of all of the information you will gather in the Find stage, because in many cases it has to be inferred from their actions rather than being clearly spelled out. However, an attacker's goal is one of the things that will rarely change, even if it is identified by a defender. An attacker focused on a particular goal cannot simply change goals to avoid detection, even if they may change TTPs, tools, or indicators. No matter what technologies the attacker chooses to use or how they choose to use them, they still have to go where their target is. As a result, goals are the least changeable aspect of an attacker's behavior and should be a core attacker attribute to track.

Attacker Moonlighting

From time to time, attackers will *moonlight*, conducting attacks with radically different goals but the same TTPs, by taking on other types of operations with different strategic goals. Espionage groups occasionally take on criminal operations, moving from stealing information to stealing money; or a criminal group shifts from using its botnet for spam to using it for DDoSing. In some cases, this may be in furtherance of another operation, such as developing secondary infrastructure for another attack, or even just for personal gain.

Seeing an attacker change goals is a key data point and should always be watched closely. It may signal a shift in interest or could be the setup for a new type of attack. Regardless, it gives considerable insight into attribution and strategic interests.

The goals for GLASS WIZARD are abstract:

- GLASS WIZARD targets a wide variety of victims, including economic, environmental, and energy policy organizations as well as high-tech manufacturers and service providers.
- GLASS WIZARD targets a variety of domestic targets, indicating possible domestic security focus.

It may even be worth referring back to the original report to understand these better, and possibly update the kill chain.

Asset-Centric Targeting

Asset-centric targeting is all about what you're protecting, and focuses on the specific technologies that enable operations. It can be incredibly useful for instances when you do not have specific information on an attack against your network and want to understand where and how you would look for indications of an attack or intrusion.

One of the most notable examples of this form of targeting is industrial control systems (ICS). Industrial control systems, which control things like dams, factories, and power grinds, are specialized systems that require specific domain knowledge to use and thus attack. A threat intelligence team can limit entire classes of attackers based on their ability to understand, have access to, and test attacks against ICS systems.

In a case involving specialized systems, we are talking about not only massively complex systems, but in many cases massively expensive ones as well. During an attacker's pre-kill chain phase, they have to invest incredible amounts of time and effort into

---

getting the right software to find vulnerabilities and then environments to test exploits.

Understanding who is capable of attacking the types of systems you're protecting is key to asset-centric targeting, because it allows you to focus on the kinds of indicators and tools that are useful for attacking your technology. Every extra system an attacker invests in being able to attack is an opportunity cost, meaning they can't spend the same time and resources working on another type of technology needing the same level of resources. For example a team putting effort into attacking ICS would not have the resources to also put effort into attacking automotive technology.

Third-party research can help and hurt technology-centric attacks, either by aiding the attackers with basic research (thus saving them time and resources) or by helping defenders understand how the attackers might approach it and thus how to defend it. Most defenders have a limited need to dig into these topic-specific issues, but they provide a focused view of the attacker/defender paradigm.

Using Asset-Centric Targeting

Because asset-centric targeting focuses on the assets that an attacker would target, in most cases the organizations that will get the most out of this method are those based around a unique class of technology such as industrial control, power generation, self-driving cars, flying drones, or even Internet of Things devices. Obviously, each has its own specific considerations, but should be approached with a similar but customized kill-chain-style approach. Robert Lee, a noted industrial control systems expert, demonstrated building a custom asset-centric kill chain in his paper "The Industrial Control System Cyber Kill Chain (*http://bit.ly/2uK7dMx*)."

What about the GLASS WIZARD team? So far, we have no information on them that would help in asset-centric targeting. The GW team, like the vast majority of actors, is targeting the widest range of systems, which means Microsoft Windows–based systems on a series of interconnected networks probably managed by Active Directory. This gives an adversary the widest attack opportunities. Asset-centric targeting is all about narrow specifics. In many cases, the actors themselves are known for focusing because of the complications of targeting hard-to-find systems.

News-Centric Targeting

This is a little bit tongue in cheek, but one of the most common targeting methodologies that occurs in less-disciplined organizations is what often gets called CNN-centric targeting or news-centric targeting. This usually starts with an executive seeing something on public news or hearing an offhanded comment from someone else that trickles down to the threat intelligence team, who are now tasked with analyzing the implications of the threat.

Let's set the record straight: these kinds of investigations are not an entirely bad thing. There is a reason even the largest traditional intelligence providers monitor news sources: journalism and intelligence are closely related. Current events can often have a dramatic impact on the intelligence needs of an organization. The key is often to distill what may seem an unfocused query into something more cogent and closely defined.

For example, if a stakeholder comes to you having seen the news clip "Chinese hackers infiltrated U.S. companies, attorney general says" (*http://cnn.it/2uK4NNV*) and wants to know whether this is relevant to your organization. There are a few key points to think about to answer this question:

- First take the time to read the article and watch the video and associated media. Who are the groups and people referenced? Don't just focus on attackers, but focus on victims and third parties as well.
- This article is discussing a specific group of attackers. Do you know who those attackers are?
- What is the question being asked? Start big and then get small. It's easy at first to look into the names mentioned in the article or video and say you're not any of those companies, or even related, but go deeper. The true question is likely, "Are we at risk of intellectual property theft from state-sponsored actors?"
- If possible, identify any information that will help you determine whether you have been compromised or will help you put defenses into place that would identify similar attack attempts. This is the beauty of the Find phase: you can identify any pieces of information that may be useful moving forward, regardless of what prompted the request, by making it part of the formal process.

It is useful to view this type of targeting as an informal request for information, rather than as offhanded (and sometimes annoying) requests. The request for information is the process of taking investigation cycle direction from the outside. We will discuss this concept more later in the chapter.

Targeting Based on Third-Party Notification

One of the worst experiences a team can have is when a third party, whether a peer company, law enforcement, or worst of all, Brian Krebs' blog, reports a breach at your organization. When a third party notifies you of a breach, in most cases the targeting is done for you. The notifier gives you an actor (or at least some pointers to an actor) and hopefully some indicators. From there, the incident-response phase begins: figuring out how to best use the information given (something we'll talk more about in the next chapter).

The active targeting portion of a third-party notification focuses primarily on what else you can get from the notifier. Getting as much information as possible is about establishing that you (the communicator) and your organization have a few key traits:

- Actionability
- Confidentiality
- Operational security

Sharing intelligence in a third-party notification is largely a risk to the sharing party. Protecting sources and methods is tough work, and harder when it's outside your control, such as giving the information to someone unknown. As a result, it is up to the receiver to demonstrate that information will be handled appropriately, both in protecting it (operational security and confidentiality) and in using it as well (actionability).

The result is that the first time a third-party shares information, they may be reluctant to share very much, perhaps nothing more than an IP address of attacker infrastructure and a time frame. As the receiver is vetted and shown to be a trustworthy and effective user of shared intelligence, more context might be shared. These types of interactions are the base idea behind information-sharing groups, be they formal groups like ISACs or informal groups like mailing lists or shared chats. Mature and immature organizations both gain from being members of these types of sharing groups. Just be sure your organization is in a position to both share what you can and act on what's shared with you. The more context that an organization can share around a particular piece of information, the more easily and effectively other organizations will be able to act on that piece of information.

 One thing that can be a struggle in many organizations is getting the authority to share information. Although most organizations are happy to get information from other security teams or researchers, many are reluctant to share information back, either to individuals or groups. This is a natural concern, but to be effective, teams must surmount it. This goes back to the childhood adage that if you don't share, no one will share with you. In many cases, this means engaging your legal team and developing a set of rules around sharing information.

Prioritizing Targeting

At this point in the Find phase, it is likely that you have gathered and analyzed a lot of information. To move onto the next phase, Fix, you need to prioritize this information so that it can be acted on.

Immediate Needs

One of the simplest ways to prioritize targeting a request from stakeholders is based on immediate needs. Did an organization just release a threat report about a particular group, and now your CISO is asking questions? Is the company about to make a decision that may impact a country with aggressive threat groups and they have asked for an assessment of the situation? If there are immediate needs, those should be prioritized.

Judging the immediacy of a Find action is a tough thing. It's easy to get caught up in new, shiny leads. Experience will lead to a slower, often more skeptical approach. It's easy to chase a hunch or random piece of information, and it's important to develop a sensitivity to how immediately a lead needs to be addressed. The key is often to slow down and not get caught up in the emergency nature of *potentially* malicious activity. Many an experienced incident responder has a story of getting too caught up in a target that *looked* important, only to realize later it was something minor.

Past Incidents

In the absence of an immediate need, it's worth taking time to establish your collection priorities. It's easy to get caught up in the newest threat or the latest vendor report, but in most cases the first place to start is with your own past incidents.

Many attackers are opportunistic, attacking once due to a one-time occurrence such as a vulnerable system or misconfiguration. This is particularly common with hactivist or low-sophistication attackers. Other actors will attack continously, often reusing the same tools against different targets. Tracking these groups is one of the most useful implementations of threat-intelligence processes. In many cases, analyzing these past incidents can lead to insights for detecting future attacks.

Another advantage of starting your targeting with past incidents is you'll already have considerable amounts of data in the form of incident reports, firsthand observations, and raw data (such as malware and drives) to continue to pull information from. Details or missed pieces of past incidents may be re-explored in the Find phase.

Criticality

Some information that you may have identified in this phase will have a much more significant impact on operations than other pieces of information that you have gathered. For example, if, during the Find phase you uncover indications of lateral movement in a sensitive network, that information is of a much higher priority than information indicating that someone is conducting scans against an external web server. Both issues should be looked into, but one clearly has a higher potential impact than the other: the higher-priority issues should be addressed first. Criticality is something that will vary from organization to organization based on what is important to that particular organization.

Organizing Targeting Activities

It is important to understand how to organize and vet the major outputs of our Find phase. Taking time, whether it's 10 minutes or 10 hours, to really dig into what information is available and understand what you are potentially up against will put you in a good position to move forward. You have to organize all of the information you have just collected and analyzed into a manageable format.

Hard Leads

Hard leads include information you have identified that has a concrete link to the investigation. Intelligence that is in the hard lead category provides context to things that have been identified and that you know is relevant. These leads have been seen in some part of the network, and during the Find phase you will be searching for things such as related activity in other parts of the network. It is important to understand what pieces of intelligence are directly related to the incident and which pieces of intelligence are only potentially related. Similar to the data sources we discussed in Chapter 3, the different types of leads are all useful; they are just used in different ways.

Soft Leads

Much of the information that you have discovered in the Find phase will fall into the category of soft leads. *Soft leads* may be additional indicators or behaviors that you have identified that are related to some of the hard leads, but at this point you have not looked to see whether the indicators are present in your environment or what the implications of that are; that will be done in the Fix phase. Soft leads also include things such as information from the news on attacks that target similar organizations to yours, or things that have been shared by an information-sharing group that you know are legitimate threats but not whether they are impacting you. Soft leads can also include things such as behavioral heuristics, where you are looking for patterns of activity that stand out rather than a concrete piece of information. This types of searches, those often technically more difficult to carry out, can produce significant results and generate a great deal of intelligence.

Grouping Related Leads

In addition to identifying which leads are hard and which are soft, it is also a good idea to keep track of which leads are related to each other. The presence of hard leads, either from an active incident or a past incident, will often lead you to identify multiple soft leads that you will be looking for in the Fix phase. This is known as *pivoting*, where one piece of information leads you to the identification of multiple other pieces of information that may or may not be relevant to you. In many cases, your initial lead may have limited benefit, but a pivot could be extremely important. Keeping track of which soft leads are related to hard leads, or which soft leads are related to each other, will help you interpret and analyze the results of your investigation. In this Find phase, you are taking the time and effort to identify information related to the threats against your environment. You don't want to have to spend time reanalyzing the information because you do not remember where you got it from or why you cared about it in the first place.

All of these leads should also be stored and documented in a way that will allow you to easily move into the subsequent phases and add information. There are a variety of ways that this information can be documented. Many teams still use good old Excel spreadsheets. Others have transitioned to tools such as threat-intelligence platforms (there are open source and commercial versions of these), which allow you to store indicators, add notes and tags, and in some cases link indicators together. The most important thing about documenting this stage of the incident-response process is that you find something that is compatible with your workflow and something that allows the team visibility into what has been identified and what still needs to be vetted or investigated. We have seen many teams spend far more time than they need to in the Find phase because of duplication of effort or a lack of good coordination. Don't fall into this trap! Once you have identified information about the threat you are dealing with and documented properly, you are ready to move into the next phase.

Lead Storage

Although we won't start talking about tracking incident-response activity and incident management until Chapter 7, it's important to take a second to discuss lead tracking. Every incident responder has stumbled across a piece of information in a lead that they've seen before only to fail to contextualize it. Taking the time to note your leads, even just solo in a notebook, is essential for success. Here's a solid format for saving your leads:

Lead
    The core observation or idea.

Datetime
    When it was submitted (important for context or SLAs).

Context
    How was this lead found (often useful for investigation).

Analyst
    Who found it.

This approach is simple and easy, but effective. Having these leads available will give you a starting point for reactive and proactive security efforts and also contextualize ongoing incidents in many cases.

The Request for Information Process

Similar to leads, requests for information (sometimes called a request for intelligence) are the process of getting direction from external stakeholders into a team's incident response or intelligence cycle. This process is meant to make requests uniform, and to enable them to be prioritized, and easily directed to the right analyst.

Requests for information (we'll call them RFIs for short) may be simple (only a sentence and a link to a document), or complex (involving hypothetical scenarios and multiple caveats). All good RFIs should include the following information:

The request
    This should be a summary of the question being asked.

The requestor
    So you know who to send the information back to.

An output
    This can take many forms. Is the expected output IOCs? A briefing document? A presentation?

References
    If the question involves or was inspired by a document, this should be shared.

A priority or due date
    This is necessary for determining when something gets accomplished.

Beyond that, the RFI process needs to be relevant and workable inside your organization. Integration is key. Stakeholders need to have an easy time submitting requests and receiving information back from it, whether that be via a portal or email submission. If you or your team are frequently overrun by a high volume of informal RFIs, putting a formal system into place is one of the best ways to manage the workload. We'll discuss RFIs, specifically as intelligence products, more in Chapter 9.

Conclusion

The Find phase is a critical step in the F3EAD process that allows you to clearly identify what it is that you are looking for. Find often equates to targeting, and is closely related to the Requirements and Direction phase of the intelligence cycle. If you do not know what your task is or what threat you are addressing, it is hard to address it properly. Find sets the stage for the other operations-focused phases in the cycle.

You will not spend the same amount of time in the Find phase for each project. At times the Find phase is done for you; other times it involves only a small amount of digging; and at still other times the Find phase is a lengthy undertaking that involves multiple people within a team focusing on different aspects of the same threat. When faced with the latter, make sure to stay organized and document and prioritize leads so that you can move into the Find phase with a comprehensive targeting package that includes exactly what you will be looking for.

Now that we have some idea about who and what we're looking for, it's time to dig into the technical investigation phase of incident response. We call this the Fix.

CHAPTER 5

Fix

"Never interrupt your enemy when he is making a mistake."

—Napoléon Bonaparte

We do not gather intelligence just for the sake of saying that we have intelligence; at its core, intelligence is meant to enable actions, whether those actions involve strategic planning or provide support to the incident-response process. Intelligence supports incident response in a few key ways:

- Providing better starting points by creating improved alerting criteria
- Contextualizing information identified in the response process
- Understanding attackers, methodologies, and tactics

The process of using previously identified intelligence or threat data to identify where an adversary is, either in your environment or externally, is called a *Fix*. In the Fix phase of F3EAD, all the intelligence you gathered in the Find phase is put to work tracking down signs of adversary activity on your networks. This chapter covers three ways to *Fix* the location of adversary activity—using indicators of compromise, adversary behavioral indicators, also known as TTPs, and adversary goals.

This chapter was tough to write, as entire books have been written about many of the items we'll discuss. This discussion is not meant to be comprehensive. If you want to learn malware analysis, it's not sufficient to read just a single section of a single chapter, but likely multiple books, and to do months of work. Additionally, many of the approaches taken in Fix will be dramatically different based on the technologies in use in your organization (for example, memory analysis on Mac and Linux has similarities, but is dramatically different on Windows). In order to focus on the application of intelligence, we'll cover important core concepts of incident response (focused especially on the intersection of these techniques and good threat intelligence) and will call out resources for learning the techniques themselves.

Intrusion Detection

Intelligence supports intrusion detection in a variety of ways. Integrating intelligence into intrusion detection is not always a straightforward process because there are various ways that an intrusion can manifest itself and various points at which an attacker's movements may be detected. Likewise, your security posture and internal visibility will also dictate where you will be able to identify attacker activity.

The two primary ways to detect intrusions are through network alerting, which looks for signs of attacker intranetwork and extra-network communications, and system alerting, which looks for indications of attacker presence on the endpoint.

Network Alerting

Network alerting involves identifying network traffic that could indicate malicious activity. Several stages of the kill chain involve network communications between the attackers and the victim machine, and it is possible to identify this activity by using intelligence. The activities we can identify by using network traffic include the following:

- Reconnaissance
- Delivery
- Command and control, and lateral movement
- Actions on target

Not all of these alerting methods are equally as effective, however. Let's dig into each of these activities in depth, including discussing under which circumstances they are useful and when they should be avoided.

Alerting on reconnaissance

Alerting on reconnaissance *seems* like the best place to start. After all, if you are able to identify potential attackers who are interested in your network ahead of time, you can prevent attacks outright. Unfortunately, alerting on reconnaissance is possible but generally not worthwhile. Why? In most cases, it's a matter of the volume of potential reconnaissance events. If you've ever run a system directly on the internet without running a firewall, you know why. Aggressive scanning is going on constantly, some of it malicious, some of it legitimate research activity. When defenders use scanning as a metric, they can claim extremely high numbers of cyber attacks, often citing millions of attacks in short time frames, but mostly they're referring to automated reconnaissance tools that may not be related to actual threats.

In short, if you alert on every Nmap scan or DNS zone transfer attempt, you'll drown in high-volume/low-signal noise without any concrete actions to take.

This doesn't mean gathering reconnaissance information is useless. In advanced cases, reconnaissance information makes an ideal place to start deception campaigns, something we'll talk about in the next chapter.

Alerting on delivery

The first concrete place to focus alerting on is the Delivery phase. In most cases, delivery means an email (for phishing), a website (for a watering hole attack), or web service compromise (accessing a web application, database, or other service).

Your ability to alert on delivery depends greatly on the technologies you have available. Email is notoriously hard to alert on and often requires a purpose-built tool or heavy modifications to existing tools. The three big concerns are attachments, links, and metadata:

Attachments
> The most common form of delivery in the last few years has been attachments, typically documents for commonly installed software containing exploits (although nonexploit social-engineering applications named to entice users to run them are also common, such as screensavers). Adobe Acrobat and Microsoft Office files are common. Organizations can alert on attachments based on filenames, file types, file sizes, or inspecting content (however, this last technique can be tricky, given the various ways of embedding or compressing attachments).

Links
> In some cases, malicious links in emails will lead users to a web page that is serving malware and will exploit the browser. Social-engineering attacks may also use links, sending users to fake login pages to harvest usernames and passwords for credential reuse attacks (described in the following sidebar).

Metadata
> Emails themselves contain many types of rich metadata that organizations can alert on, but these pieces of data are often transitive. It's easy to alert on malicious email metadata, but it's also simple for attackers to change such metadata. That said, tracking information such as sender email address, sender IP address, intermediate transit servers (especially viewed as a pattern), and user agent data can all be useful for alerting.

Identifying novel or unique ways that attackers initiate their activities (aside from these common methods) means that we can come up with additional ways to detect the Delivery stage of an intrusion.

Credential Reuse

According to the Verizon Data Breach Investigations Report (*http://www.verizonenter prise.com/verizon-insights-lab/dbir/*), and everyone we've ever talked to, credential reuse continues to be one of the top ways that attackers get access to or move through your network. It makes sense, because usernames and passwords are not difficult for attackers to get their hands on. Weak passwords, password reuse, and numerous public password dumps make it easy for attackers to identify the credentials that will get them into a network. Once they are inside, getting additional credentials is even easier. In addition, many phishing attacks are aimed at obtaining user credentials, which are then used to access the network.

Monitoring for credential reuse can difficult; after all, legitimate users should be accessing the network so that behavior doesn't automatically stand out. If you have the proper systems in place, there are ways to detect this behavior. Methods include looking for logins from strange locations; if Alice lives and works in San Diego, a login from Italy may be a sign that something is wrong. In addition, logins at odd times or concurrent logins can also be a sign that something strange is going on. Even if you are unable to detect a suspicious login at the time of the activity, once you are in incident-response mode and you know that there is an attacker in your network, you can use logs to look for any suspicious activity and flag those accounts for further investigation and, during the Finish phase, password resets.

Alerting on command and control

Eventually, the attacker needs to communicate with their systems. A lot happens between delivery and command and control, but those are all things most easily detected on the system level. Command and control (a.k.a C2) refers to the attacker interacting with their malware to execute actions, which by necessity results in network communication.

You can look for a few common characteristics in C2 communication:

Destination
> The first and simplest of approaches. Hundreds of threat-intelligence products are dedicated to listing known bad locations, in terms of IPv4 addresses and domains. Many tools will let you blacklist and alert on known bad destinations. While you're at it, geolocation also has its uses in identifying unknown/unexpected geographic destinations (for example, why is our print server connecting to X country?).

Content
> Most malware communicates by using encrypted messages to prevent detection. Although that does make it more difficult to know what is being transmitted, it

also provides defenders with the ability to search for encrypted messages where they shouldn't be. In an attempt to blend in, many pieces of malware will misuse common protocols, such as sending encrypted HTTP traffic over port 80/TCP, which is usually not encrypted. These mismatches of content and protocol can be a big tip-off. Metadata is also a fairly common class of content that attackers don't consider; for example, suspicious metadata includes always using the same user agent string or common headers.

Frequency

Unless the attacker manages to take over a publicly facing server, they likely won't be able to initiate communication with their malware at will, since it is likely unroutable. As a result, most malware reaches from a host on an internal network out to a command-and-control server, which we call a *beacon*. These usually take place at regular intervals, as often as every few minutes (generally for operational, in-use malware) and as long as every couple of months (generally to enable reinfection if the initial malware was removed). It's often possible to identify patterns in the frequency of communication and search for that.

Duration

Most malware isn't that smart, and the messages it sends are often not that interesting. In some cases, even though the messages are encrypted, they may themselves not have a lot to say. If this happens with enough frequency, patterns may emerge, such as a no-operation message that always has the same byte length.

Combinations

Often one characteristic isn't enough, but a combination of them may be. This takes time, recognition, and sometimes a bit of luck to develop a pattern and find a way to detect it.

Many times it is possible to alert on indicators associated with command-and-control, such as a known malicious IP or domain, but by better understanding the nature of command and control behavior, we will be able to alert on suspicious traffic even when we do not know that the destination itself is malicious.

Command and control via misuse of shared resources. Command and control is often subject to trends. For example, in the late 2000s, most criminal malware used Internet Relay Chat (IRC) for command and control. Defenders caught on, alerting or blocking 6666–7000/TCP, the common IRC ports. Attackers then moved to running IRC on port 80/TCP, and so the cat-and-mouse game has continued, forming trends.

One of the current and likely ongoing trends in command and control is the use of social media and software-as-a-service (SaaS) sites. Given the ubiquity of SSL, it's often difficult to inspect this traffic, and given that the destinations themselves aren't malicious, it can be difficult to detect and respond to. This can be complicated, even more so with platform-as-a-service (PaaS) companies where shared resources can be used in many ways, making it difficult to build generalized profiles of nonmalicious traffic and usage.

No command-and-control malware.   In rare cases, malware will have no command and control at all. This is difficult to accomplish, as such malware needs to have 100% of its instructions before being delivered and must be able to accomplish its goals without any changes or updates. This is usually done only out of necessity, such as air-gapped networks. It usually requires considerable reconnaissance in order to understand the lay of the land before starting. In cases like this, detection needs to focus on delivery and actions over target.

Alerting on actions over target

Similar to detection of command and control, detecting actions over target on the network focuses on unusual traffic patterns that indicate data entering or leaving your network. Data entering the network isn't commonly seen (though may be seen more in the future as disinformation becomes more prevalent). What is highly common is data exfiltration.

Data exfiltration is often the goal of many attacks, especially those focused on the compromise and theft of intellectual property. Each attacker will have their own preferred method of exfiltration, but in the end they all have to accomplish the same thing: get a lot of information (anywhere from a few dozen lines up to hundreds of gigabytes) from victim systems to an attacker-controlled system. How this is accomplished varies, but the end goal doesn't.

Defenders can take a few approaches to detecting data exfiltration. One is to focus on content, which is what gave rise to data-loss prevention tools. For instance, this detection technique means that if you want to prevent the theft of credit card information, you'll search for examples of four groups of four numbers (the credit card number) followed by three numbers (the card verification value, or CVV) and then a month/year combo (the expiration date). On the surface this seems simple, but the devil is in the details. What if the credit card number is split into four sets of four numbers in one file, and the dates are in another file? What if the CVVs use a letter substitution for the numbers and instead of 123 the CVV is sent as ABC? It gets only more complicated from there, such as if the attacker uses secure socket layer (SSL) to block your packet-sniffing tools looking for card numbers.

The second approach that defenders can take is focus on metadata around the network connections itself. If the attacker stole 5 gigabytes of credit card data, they have to move 5 gigabytes of data no matter how it's encrypted (ignoring compression).

Fixing on malicious indicators from network activity is a good way to start to identify what is going on in your network and to better understand the attackers who are targeting you. It is not the only way, though. Next we will discuss how to Fix malicious activity from a system perspective.

System Alerting

The complement to network monitoring is system monitoring. In the same way that network alerting is focused on particular aspects of the kill chain, system alerting can be similarly be divided into the following areas:

- Exploitation
- Installation
- Actions over target

System alerting is always dependent on the operating system. With rare exceptions, most tools—open source and commercial—are focused on a particular operating system. This is necessary because most security alerting takes place at the lowest levels of the operating system, requiring deep integration into process management, memory management, filesystem access, and so forth.

The result is that you need to carefully consider the methods of integrating intelligence for system alerting, both in terms of the target operating system and tools you'll use. For example, some string-based indicators may be useful on multiple systems, but registry keys are useful indicators only on Windows. At the same time, tools such as commercial antivirus programs may allow no direct content integration, while open source tools such as osquery can't function without content development.

Alerting on exploitation

Companies—in fact, entire industries (like the antivirus space)—have been built on the idea of alerting on and blocking exploitation. Exploitation remains a natural place to alert because it is where the transfer of control shifts from the defender to the attacker. The second the attacker begins exploitation, they are affecting the operation of defender resources.

Exploitation usually manifests itself in one of two key ways:

- A new process begins running on a user's system, one that's created and controlled by the attacker.
- A previous, user-controlled process is modified and co-opted to do something new and different.

The ways these things may be accomplished varies, but result is the same: the compromised system is under the control of the attacker. The primary approach to alerting on exploitation is to track this activity in near real time, monitoring processes on a system at different points in time and identifying changes. Some will be natural, but indicators of unexpected activity can indicate an intrusion. This includes modification of underlying binaries, applications running from unexpected or incorrect directories, or even brand-new processes with names meant to blend in at first glance (using names such as *rundll32.exe* versus *rund1l32.exe* with a 1 instead of an l) to confuse analysts. Unknown or previously unseen processes make a good start for alerting on a system and can leverage a variety of tools.

Alerting on installation

Installation is the bread and butter of on-system alerting. Even if an attacker can get control of code execution (the attacker can run their own code) on a victim's system, it's usually not the end. An exploited process, whether modified from a normal user process or created after execution, will eventually end; and after it does, the attacker will lose their foothold.

As a result, after exploitation, the next step for most attackers is to make sure they can maintain access. In a single-system phishing-style compromise, this usually means installing a second stage that maintains persistence and adds capabilities the attackers can use to execute their objectives. These features are often bundled together into a modular tool, often called a remote-access Trojan (RAT), or a rootkit. During the Find phase, we should have identified information about the tools that are commonly used by actors, which can help us know what to look for in the Fix phase.

Alerting on actions over target

Depending on the desired outcome, an attacker may need to access specific resources in order to carry out their objectives. In most cases, the actions over target follow the CRUD acronym:

Create
    Writing new files to disk from original material

Read
    Reading files currently on a system

Update
    Changing the content of files already on the system

Delete
    Removing files on a system, generally with extra steps to keep it from being recovered later

In some cases, attackers may do more than one action at a time, tying them together for more complex results. Cryptolocker-style attacks do three of these in rapid succession:

Read

The cryptolocker malware reads all the personal files on the machine.

Create

It then creates a new file from all the read files, but encrypted with the attacker's key.

Delete

Finally, it deletes the user's original unencrypted files so the user must pay the ransom to get access to the original files.

Simple, easy, and often effective.

Cryptolocker attacks are one example, but actions over target very greatly from attack to attack. For instance, an attacker may read data in order to exfiltrate it across the network to steal intellectual property, one of the most common advanced persistent threat (APT) patterns. In another case, they may simply delete all files (or key files) to render the system's resources unusable. Finally, an attacker may create a new application to use the system for secondary attacks, such as pivoting within a network or launching denial-of-service (DoS) attacks.

Alerting on these actions is complicated because creating, reading, updating, and deleting files are common actions. Everything done on a computer does these. Much of it depends on understanding the actions an attacker may want to take. If you're concerned with stealing money in a bank, monitoring actions that can access ledgers is key. If it's intellectual property the attackers are after, you may want to identify large uploads of files across the network or creation of big archives on disk. This requires a combination of thinking like the enemy, creativity, and experience.

By combining the information that was found on a threat actor in the Find phase and the information about how we are able to detect malicious activity on our own network, we can now begin to plan how we will look for the signs of an attacker in our environment.

Fixing GLASS WIZARD

In Chapter 4 we developed a kill chain for the actor we named GLASS WIZARD, and now we can use that information to better understand what attacker tools and activities we should look for in this phase. We identified that GLASS WIZARD uses avenues such as spear-phishing and strategic web compromises to deliver their tools, and installs additional tools to maintain access and interact with the host machine, including Hikit, Derusbi, and the ZOX family of tools. We also know that they typically look for information related to economic, environmental, and energy policies, and that they often compromise large numbers of host machines in a network in order to find the information that they are looking for. Using this information, we can start to build a plan of the types of activities to look for. The following sections discuss types of activity to look for.

Network activity

Here are the types of network activity we want to look for while trying to detect the GLASS WIZARD actions:

Spear phishing emails
> Search mail logs for senders, subjects, or attachment names that are related to GLASS WIZARD. In addition, alerting users to the details of these spear-phishing campaigns can ensure that they can inform the security team if they remember seeing any similar emails in the past and will be on the lookout for any future such emails.

Web compromises
> Search web logs for any successful or attempted visits to websites that had been compromised by GLASS WIZARD. Scoping is important in this stage. If a website was compromised for only a short time before it was identified and remediated, search for activity to those sites only around the time that it was known to be compromised.

Command-and-control activity
> Identifying the tools that are commonly used by GLASS WIZARD for C2 activities can help know what activity to look for. Additional research will need to be done at this point to fully understand the actor's tools and how they function; for example, the ZOZ family has been known to use PNG images to communicate with a command-and-control server.

System activity. Now that we know more about what we are looking for in our network, we can begin the process of investigating suspicious activity, such as the following:

Exploitation
> Some actors are known to exploit certain vulnerabilities over others, so understanding which vulnerabilities are targeted, and if and where those vulnerabilities exist on your network, can give you a good starting point for where to look for attacker activity. GLASS WIZARD was seen exploiting CVE-2013-3893, which is a vulnerability in Internet Explorer, so it would be useful to understand which systems have this vulnerability present, and to look for additional signs of exploitation that were identified in the Fix phase.

Installation
> Knowing which tools are commonly used by the actor and how those tools work allows you to build a better picture of which tools would be effective in your net-

work. GLASS WIZARD uses both a 32-bit and a 64-bit variant of Hikit, depending on the victim's network topography, so understanding your network will help you know what to look for at this phase. Identify what files are generated during installation and which directories they are located in.

Actions on target

We know that GLASS WIZARD is looking for information on economic, environmental, and energy policies, so if we know which systems have that type of information, we can look for any signs of files being accessed, gathered, and moved off the system. However, we also know that the actor likes to expand their presence to many hosts to look for files and potentially move throughout the network, so we can look for signs of lateral movement in the network, even on systems we would not think of as a typical target.

Now that we have a good handle on what information from the Find phase is going to be applicable to our network and our environment, we can move on to identifying GLASS WIZARD's activity in our networks. Doing so involves activities such as traffic analysis, memory analysis, and malware analysis, which we will deep-dive into next.

Intrusion Investigation

Separating alerting and investigation workflows often requires walking a fine line because they often use the same tools, just in different ways. If alerting is about reduction (finding the smallest, most specific bit of data that will tip you off to malicious activity), then investigation is about gathering as much data as possible to get context and then reducing data again into a cogent analysis. This expansion (collection and processing) and then reduction (analysis and dissemination) workflow is common in both security analysis and intelligence analysis.

Next we are going to explore the key aspects of intrusion investigation techniques and tools. That said, this is a topic unto itself. If you're new to these topics, we recommend *Incident Response & Computer Forensics, Third Edition,* by Jason Luttgens et al. (McGraw-Hill Education, 2014).

Network Analysis

The first place most intrusion investigations begin is with hunting on the network. Unfortunately, most incidents aren't internally discovered. Many incidents begin with a third party reporting nothing but a command-and-control IP address.

Network traffic analysis can be broken into major techniques based on a combination of tools and volume of traffic:

Traffic analysis
  Using metadata to understand attacker activity

Signature analysis
  Looking for known bad patterns

Full content analysis
  Using every single packet to understand the attack

We'll dig into each of these in the upcoming sections. Let's start with traffic analysis.

Traffic analysis

Traffic analysis is not unique to computer networks. In fact, traffic analysis largely developed from analyzing radio transmissions, and many techniques can be traced to World War I (*http://bit.ly/2uNdTcF*). Traffic analysis involves identifying adversary activity based on metadata, the patterns of how the adversary communicates, rather than based on the content of the communication itself. As a result, this technique uses the sparsest data set (a record of megabytes of full content activity may create only 100 bytes worth of metadata), tracking information like this:

- Endpoints (either IP addresses or domains)
- Ports
- Bytes in/out
- Connection length and start/end times

We refer to these groups of metadata as *network flows*. Even with these small amounts of information, a huge amount of insight can be gained by a trained analyst. Analysts should look for the following activities:

- Connections to a known bad IP address can indicate command-and-control activity.
- Frequent, regular, short-duration, low-byte in/out connections can indicate malware beaconing, checking in for new instructions.
- A connection to a never-before-seen domain with a long duration and large bytes out/low bytes in could indicate data exfiltration.
- Port 445 connections from a known compromised host to other internal hosts could indicate data collection (445/TCP is Microsoft SMB file sharing).

All these and far more can be discovered based on just limited network traffic metadata.

A variety of methods are used to collect data for traffic analysis. Network flow data (Netflow being the Cisco-specific implementation, not the generic term) is often available from a variety of networking equipment. This data is often easy to collect because it's useful for both the security team and the network team, allowing for dual use and split infrastructure costs. Another security-specific method for getting network flow data is Bro, a network security monitoring tool that focuses on deeper metadata than basic netflow, including protocol information and signature-based detection (we'll get to that later). CERT/CC's SiLK (*https://tools.netsa.cert.org/silk/*) and QoSient's Argus (*https://qosient.com/argus/*) are other open source tools for capturing traditional flow information. Other systems that can generate flow information include network proxies and firewalls.

Tools for analyzing flow information can range from very general to very specialized. Logging and full-text search tools like Splunk are often used to great effect. Purpose-built tools like Flowbat (*http://www.flowbat.com/*) add flow-specific operators. It's also possible to build custom tools using graph databases like Neo4j (*https://neo4j.com/product/*), Titan (*http://titan.thinkaurelius.com/*), or NetworkX (*https://networkx.github.io/*).

Another advantage of flow-based data over signature-based or full content analysis is the density of information in flow. Since only the metadata is kept, storage per record for flow information is low, making it both less expensive to store and faster to process through. This means that while keeping and searching more than a few months of signature-based information can be cost-prohibitive, keeping significantly longer flow-based data may be possible. Although flow data cannot completely answer all network security questions the way full content can, this information density and long-term storage make it a valuable capability. Add to that the ease of collection and analysis, and it's clear why traffic analysis is such high-value data source.

Applying intelligence to traffic analysis.   The most common application of intelligence to traffic analysis is using traffic data to look for connections to known bad resources (IPs, domains, etc.) or to identify patterns of anomalous activity by trusted systems (such as scanning, lateral movement, or beaconing). While these are simple techniques, they are often effective and easily automated. The danger of using traffic analysis exclusively is that it may result in false positives based on a lack of content understanding, such as dual-use IPs and domains that are malicious for only short periods of time.

Another way to apply intelligence to traffic analysis is to look for traffic patterns that indicate malicious activity, such as short, repeated communications, communications during nonworking hours, or communications to newly observed domains, which are domains that have only recently become active. Most users do not visit domains mere hours after the domain has been created. This can be a sign of command-and-control activity. Combining PassiveDNS and network flow analysis makes it possible to automate hunting for those domains.

Gathering data from traffic analysis.   It may seem counterintuitive, but traffic analysis is often a great source to generate leads. By looking for top talkers (hosts generating or receiving the highest frequency or amount of traffic) or bottom talkers (hosts generating or receiving the smallest frequency or amount of traffic), you can often identify important leads. Detecting rare hosts (hosts with very little communication to or from your network) is especially important because attackers will generally use new infrastucture to avoid bad reputations, but don't underestimate looking at large traffic amounts (top talkers) as well. It's important to understand whether a system sending gigabytes of traffic on a Sunday morning is doing offsite backups or exfiltrating data.

Signature-based analysis

Between the sparseness of network traffic data and the comprehensive full content monitoring is signature-based analysis. While traffic analysis is purely focused on metadata around connections, signature-based analysis is monitoring for specific content. Unlike traffic analysis, which can be pulled from a variety of sources and tools, signature-based analysis is the realm of purpose-built systems called *intrusion detection systems*.

Intrusion detection systems (IDSs) combine network capture, a rules engine, and a logging method. The rules are applied to the network traffic, and when one matches, a log is generated. A wide variety of intrusion detection systems are available, in both commercial and open source options. At the same time, one ubiquitous standard exists for signatures: the Snort signatures. Here's an example of a Snort IDS signature (*https://github.com/mjruffin/snort_signatures*):

```
alert tcp any any -> any any (msg:"Sundown EK - Landing";
flow:established,to_server;
content:"GET";
http_method;
pcre:"\/[a-zA-Z0-9]{39}\/[a-zA-Z0-9]{6,7}\.(swf|php)$";
http_uri;
reference:http://malware.dontneedcoffee.com/2015/06/\
  fast-look-at-sundown-ek.html;
class-type: trojan-activity;
rev:1;)
```

Let's explore a subset of the keywords and actions for Snort signatures (Snort has a lot of options, check out snort.org (*https://snort.org/*) to find more!). This signature breaks down as follows:

```
alert
```

The first word specifies the action to take if the signature matches. Snort has a variety of actions (though other IDS that use Snort's signature format (*http://bit.ly/2tL59im*) may implement only a subset of these):

alert
Generate an alert using the selected alert method, and then log the packet.

log
    Log the packet.

pass
    Ignore the packet.

activate
    Alert and then turn on another dynamic rule.

dynamic
    Remain idle until activated by an activate rule, and then act as a log rule.

drop
    Block and log the packet.

reject
    Block the packet, log it, and then send a TCP reset if the protocol is TCP, or an ICMP port unreachable message if the protocol is UDP.

sdrop
    Block the packet but do not log it.

By far, the most common action is alert, but the others can be wildly powerful in the right situation:

```
tcp any any -> any any
```

The next clause specifies many of the same characteristics from traffic analysis and applies them as limiting factors. The first word specifies the protocol (most likely TCP or UDP). The second part of this clause is key and takes the following generic form:

```
SOURCE_LOCATION SOURCE_PORT -> DESTINATION_LOCATION DESTINATION_PORT
```

Locations can be a few different things. It's perfectly valid to use an IP address or domain name for a location, but Snort allows for lists of multiple locations as well.

Inside the parentheses (starting in our example with msg) is the bulk of the rule. There are a wide variety of options, far more than we can cover, but here are some core options to know:

```
msg:"Sundown EK - Landing";
```

The msg is the alert name. This is what comes through in logging (along with a bunch of other content):

```
content:"GET";
```

The content field finds regular ASCII strings in packet content:

```
pcre:"\/[a-zA-Z0-9]{39}\/[a-zA-Z0-9]{6,7}\.(swf|php)$";
```

Snort signatures can also contain Perl Compatable Regular Expressions, or `pcre`, a way of specifing patterns instead of explicit content:

```
reference:http://malware.dontneedcoffee.com/2015/06/fast-\
    look-at-sundown-ek.html;
```

Finally, the `reference` field includes links to information that gives details on the threat that a signature looks for.

Being able to understand and work with signatures is the key to implementing and using signature-based detection successfully.

Applying intelligence to signature-based analysis.   Once an IDS is in place, the key to applying intelligence is twofold. The first is in signature creation. An obvious direct way to apply intelligence is creating new signatures based on intelligence you've received or developed. Applying intelligence well requires understanding your IDS capability and experience creating and tuning signatures.

Second, effectively applying intelligence to signature-based analysis requires not just creation of signatures, but also modification and removal. Having inaccurate or inactionable signatures slows incident response, forcing teams to waste time on fruitless investigations or analyses. It takes experience to develop an understanding for when a signature is losing usefulness, and when it should be modified versus removed.

Gathering data from signature-based analysis.   Signature-based analysis is a limited but important technique, given signatures must be based on known bad patterns. It's difficult to write signatures for purely hypothetical activity. What signature analysis can do is key you into the patterns and content of past attacks, including bad sources and destinations, so when a signature triggers against a certain endpoint, that endpoint may be a good starting point for investigating. You may need to go to another data source, either traffic or full content, but chances are you may find a plethora of information.

Full content analysis

On the opposite end of the spectrum from traffic analysis is full content—literally capturing every bit and byte sent across the network. From there, information can be searched, reassembled, and analyzed in a wide variety of ways. Unlike traffic or signature analysis, which cannot be reanalyzed after real time, the huge benefit of full content is that it can be reanalyzed or analyzed differently as long as the traffic is still stored. The downside of full content analysis is the storage requirement. Full content monitoring literally requires keeping a copy of every bit of network traffic, which for most enterprises means storing immense amounts of data.

At the most basic, full content analysis lets you look at every single element of a piece of network traffic in a way that no other technique allows. Using a tool such as Wireshark, you can dig into every element at every level of the open systems interconnection (OSI) model. This is often the basis for creating IDS signatures This also allows you to look for specific items that other tools might not detect.

Full content analysis allows analysts to rerun traffic and signature analysis after developing new information. For example, if you create a new signature for C2 traffic after an investigation, full content would allow you to rerun that new signature against earlier network traffic. In this way, full content essentially acts as a network time machine, allowing you to use new intelligence on old network traffic.

Finally, using full content is the only way to do full user activity re-creation. For instance, if a user triggered an alert for data exfiltration via FTP, it might be useful to look at everything else that endpoint was doing at that time. This could reveal secondary but important information, such as the C2 mechanism controlling that exfiltration. This type of full content analysis requires specialized tools such as NetWitness or aol/moloch to re-create the many levels of most network packets.

Applying intelligence to full content analysis.   As you might expect, application of intelligence is particularly flexible with full content analysis. All the techniques from traffic analysis and signature analysis apply to full content, as well as a few unique options:

- At the packet level, tools such as Wireshark allow filtering based on a variety of characteristics, including IP addresses and other characteristics you can get from intelligence or even other network-monitoring tools.
- Intelligence can also be applied by rerunning new intelligence against old network traffic.
- Using intelligence at the full content re-creation layer allows for hunting for secondary activity.

Gathering data from full content analysis.   Where full content really shines is in gathering data. Full content analysis is the the easiest and most comprehensive source for gathering data and developing further intelligence. Actual packet data allows you to pivot from information about bad endpoints to information about bad data instead.

Learning more

There are a number of great places to learn more information about network analysis. Check out Richard Bejtlich's *Practice of Network Security Monitoring* (No Starch, 2013) or Chris Sander's *Practical Packet Analysis: Using Wireshark to Solve Real-World Network Problems* (No Starch, 2017). Want something more hands-on? Consider "SANS SEC 503: Intrusion Detection In Depth (*https://www.sans.org/course/intrusion-detection-in-depth*)" or "FOR 572: Advanced Network Forensics and Analysis (*http://bit.ly/2uep7UE*)."

Live Response

One of the less appreciated but often effective analysis methods is live response. *Live response* is analysis of a potentially compromised system without taking it offline. Most forensics analysis requires turning the system offline, losing system state information such as active processes. It also risks tipping off the attacker and is widely disruptive to users as well.

Live response pulls the following information:

- Configuration information
- System state
- Important file and directory information
- Common persistence mechanisms
- Installed applications and versions

Although not always providing everything necessary to investigate a system, most live responses at least provide enough information to determine whether more thorough analysis is necessary.

Live response tools are most commonly built scripting technologies such as Perl, Python, or lately PowerShell, and as a result, many are open source. Yelp's OSXCollector (*https://yelp.github.io/osxcollector/*) is an open source, Python-based live response script built for collecting security artifacts on macOS. For Windows, many people focus on Dave Hull's Kansa, a PowerShell-based incident-response collection framework.

So how to integrate intelligence into live response? Live response tools are typically built to collect a set group of artifacts without any configuration, making their use repeatable and fast. Intelligence integration is generally focused on the backend.

For example, OSXCollector outputs a JSON blob with system information. This is meant to be analyzed using another Yelp project, osxcollector_output_filters, which can be integrated with multiple intelligence sources, including custom indicators and intelligence services like OpenDNS. This post-processing approach is common for complicated collections.

Memory Analysis

Similar to live response, memory analysis focuses on collecting volatile system state in memory. Given that every process on a system requires memory to run, this technique provides an excellent vantage point to gather information, especially from tools that attempt to run stealthily with limited system footprint.

Also similar to live response, memory analysis has a clear break between collection and analysis, grabbing everything first and then focusing on processing results and applying intelligence after the fact. FireEye's Redline memory analysis tool (created by Mandiant) always collects system memory first, but uses OpenIOC later at analysis time.

Redline is one tool for memory analysis and is great as an all-in-one solution that's able to do collection and analysis together; but one of the best aspects of the split between collection and analysis is the opportunity to mix and match collection and analysis utilities. A great example is the Volatility toolkit.

Volatility is a Python-based, open source memory-analysis framework. Volatility does not gather memory itself the way Redline does. Instead, it reads the memory formats from a wide variety of collection tools that run on a wide variety of operating systems. What Volatility provides is a framework and set of scripts for analyzing memory; detecting malware running in memory, extracting cryptographic keys—in fact anything you can find a plug-in to do.

Integrating intelligence into memory analysis is obviously very tool dependent. Volatility makes this especially easy. Volatility makes it easy to use Yara signatures to scan memory for specific artifacts. Additionally, Volatility is highly scriptable, making it possible to automate hunting for specific processes, memory artifacts, cryptographic primitives, and so forth. Volatility's ability to parse out everything from basic strings to very high-level information like certificates means you can apply indicators from other phases to memory analysis. Using Redline instead? Redline will accept indicators in the form of OpenIOC, which can then be applied directly to an individual memory capture.

To learn more about memory analysis, check out *The Art of Memory Forensics: Detecting Malware and Threats in Windows, Linux, and Mac Memory* by Michael Hale Ligh et al. (Wiley, 2014).

Disk Analysis

Traditional disk forensics typically involves using specialized tools to extract filesystem information from the raw bits and bytes on a hard drive. The information on a hard drive is unintelligible at first glance. It contains endlessly nested structures at the hardware, filesystem, operating system, and data-format level, similar to the OSI model. Peeling through these layers is a process called *file carving.*

Carving works from the very lowest levels, building up the various data structures until files, data streams, and other operating system artifacts become available. This isn't done by hand, but by using specialized tools such as EnCase, FTK, or Autopsy. Once the data is carved, analysis can begin. From there, these tools make it possible to browse the system much like being on the system itself. An analyst can export specific files or look through logs and operating system-specific constructs, like alternate data streams and registries on Windows. The forensics software may have extremely powerful search, even allowing for searches across specific types of files such as email.

The power of an experienced forensic analyst is an understanding of exactly where to go looking, based on what's being hunted for. For instance, if you have a compromised machine, a forensic analyst should be able to look at common persistence mechanisms, identify any malware running, and then acquire any artifacts the malware dropped. Additionally, the analyst may pull secondary pieces of data, such as logs that took place around the time frame of malware installation or activity. This is often an interim step, and the forensic analyst will usually pass much of what they collect to other analysts for analysis (such as passing malware to a reverse engineer, which we'll get into).

Applying intelligence to disk analysis

Applying intelligence to disk analysis isn't terribly common. While some tools may allow searching for certain strings or indicators, in most cases this is more easily done in logging tools or networkwide systems like intrusion-detection systems or endpoint-detection systems. Typically, the whole goal of disk analysis is to carve out useful artifacts to be analyzed by others.

Gathering data from disk analysis

System disks, especially of compromised machines, are a treasure trove for investigators and in many cases hold answers that are difficult to discover with other means. Along with the information itself, disk analysis also benefits from being less volatile than other methods and more stateful. In memory analysis or live response, by contrast, the analysis takes place at a single point in time, so it's possible that an important artifact might not be observable, or that analysts would ask a different question based on what they've learned in the course of the investigation.

With disk analysis, the analyst can collect what he thinks he needs to start, say, a piece of malware—then after further analysis, realize he missed an important configuration file. Because of the time-dependent nature of disk analysis, that file is likely still on disk, and the forensic engineer can go back and collect that after.

The most useful sources of disk information for investigation and intelligence are as follows:

- Persistance mechanisms
- Temporary files
- Hidden files and data streams
- Files located in unallocated space
- Malware and configurations
- Indications of actions over target

Malware Analysis

In most incidents, the most deeply technical analysis that takes place is analyzing the malware involved. Sometimes this analysis is as basic as a shell script, sometimes thousands of lines of code with extensive anti-analysis capabilities. Few areas of security require quite so much breadth and depth of understanding. In many cases, a team will have a dedicated reverse engineer focused on analyzing malware, but there's still plenty even a nonexpert can do.

Two basic sets of techniques are used for understanding malware: static and dynamic. Basic static and dynamic analysis are skills every incident responder and intelligence analyst should have.

Basic static analysis

The easiest form of malware analysis is *static analysis*, the process of gathering metadata about an unknown binary. This includes gathering information such as the following:

File hashes
- Common hashes such as SHA1 and SHA256, which are useful for comparing files, including looking them up in other malware resources such as VirusTotal.
- Soft hashes such as SSDeep that allow samples to be compared to each other later. This is especially useful for tracking campaigns, as small edits to files that change their SHA hashes often won't change the SSDeep significantly.

File type
Not just the extension.

File size
Useful along with other data for identifying similar files.

Strings
Some binaries have useful information including IP addresses and authentication tokens in plain text. Also useful for soft grouping, similar to soft hashes.

The ultimate goal is developing information that can be used in wide-ranging detection and response systems and to track the evolution of campaigns. Basic static analysis also helps develop intelligence from outside your organization, such as vendor reporting.

Basic dynamic analysis

Generally, the next step after basic static analysis is basic *dynamic analysis*. In dynamic analysis, the analyst runs the malware in a controlled monitored environment in order to observe what it does. The key to dynamic analysis is having a safe environment to execute the malware that's collecting good telemetry.

The most common technique for dynamic analysis is using a sandbox. A sandbox typically manages running a sample on a purpose-built system, often in a virtual machine, isolated from the internet. The sandbox imports the sample to the virtual machine, executes it, and then monitors the behavior of the system to see what the malware does. Typically, this focuses on changes to the system, such as new processes, new files, changes to persistence mechanisms, and network traffic. Just as in static analysis, the goal is to gather indicators useful for identifying the malware in your environment.

Dynamic analysis has a few downsides, especially with sandboxes. Building a safe environment that can collect proper telemetry is difficult and carries some risks; it also needs to mirror your environment, including common software. In addition, some malware samples may do things to detect they're in a sandbox, such as looking for evidence of a virtual machine or trying to reach network services. While there are ways to fool malware under dynamic analysis, it's an important added complication to consider and address. Tools such as INetSim (*http://www.inetsim.org/*) and Fake-Net (*https://practicalmalwareanalysis.com/fakenet/*) can help.

Advanced static analysis

Finally, when analysts need to fully understand a piece of malware, they resort to full-on reverse engineering. Another form of static analysis (the malware is analyzed without running it), *advanced static analysis* focuses on understanding malware at the code level by using multiple tools, most notably a *disassembler*.

A disassembler works by breaking down a compiled binary application into the machine-code instructions that a victim host would run. This is an incredibly low-level set of instructions that take experience to understand. What makes disassembly so effective is that to an analyst who can understand it, the entire binary and all its capabilities are laid bare. By tracking every code path, it's possible to understand all the functions a piece of malware has, even ones that wouldn't trigger during dynamic analysis.

The downside to full reverse engineering is the level of effort necessary. Understanding a sample, depending on its size, complexity, and antireversing measures, could take hours or even days. As a result, comprehensive reverse engineering is usually saved for new or especially prolific samples where indicators aren't enough, but there is also a need to understand all capabilities that a piece of malware has. This may illuminate important action-over-target capabilities such as remote-control capabilities or exfiltration methods.

Applying intelligence to malware analysis

Other intelligence and analysis can often key a reverse engineer into useful avenues of investigation. If prior analysis suggests C2 based on encrypted HTTP, reverse engineering might want to focus on looking for the encryption keys. If indications exist that information was stolen that was never stored on the computer but discussed near the computer, it might make sense to focus analysis on alternative information collection capabilities such as using the microphone or camera.

Gathering data from malware analysis

Malware analysis is one of the most data-rich types of analysis that a team can undertake, in addition to being one of the most difficult. Malware analysis reports result in a wide variety of exploitable types of data, including indicators, tactics, and capabilities that lead to the actions over target available to an attacker, even sometimes indications of who the attacker might be. Malware analysis leads to useful information for detection and alerting on both the network and on hosts.

Learning more about malware analysis

Malware analysis is one of the toughest skills in information security to learn. It requires a deep understanding of general computer programming concepts, operating system concepts, and common malware actions. *The Malware Analyst's Cookbook and DVD: Tools and Techniques for Fighting Malicious Code* by Michael Ligh et al. (Wiley, 2010) teaches most of the basic static and dynamic analysis techniques necessary for most incident responders

If you're interested in developing a comprehensive reverse-engineering skill set, including understanding assembly, you'll want to work through *Practical Malware Analysis: The Hands-On Guide to Dissecting Malicious Software* by Michael Sikorski and Andrew Honig (No Starch, 2012).

Scoping

Throughout the period of alerting and investigation, one of the most important pieces of information you're trying determine is the *scope* of the incident: which victim resources (systems, services, credentials, data, users, etc.) are affected. This leads directly into numerous workflows later, such as determining the impact and methods of response.

Say, for instance, a piece of malware is found on one computer. Your reaction would be different if after scoping you found that piece of malware on only one computer versus on dozens of systems in your network.

Another important part of scoping is determining patterns among affected resources. Are all the infected systems related to a specific type of user or department? This data could be important for understanding the attack at a deeper level (something we'll get to in the Analyze phase of F3EAD). This type of understanding requires good inventory management and collaboration with IT management teams. One of the most important, and often frustrating, aspects of incident response is having a given system and needing to ask, "What does this system do?"

Hunting

Until now, all our discussion of incident response has focused on reactive incident response: what to do after we know a security control has failed and trying to understand it. Hunting is different. *Hunting occurs when we search for indications of compromise without any alert or notification of a security control failure.* Detection is far from perfect, especially signature-based detection. Security controls can fail silently. For any number of reasons, attacks could be ongoing with no indications.

To people outside the security team, hunting looks like lucky guessing, but it's far from that. Hunting is based on a combination of instinct, experience, and good intelligence. Like traditional hunting, it's limited by your tools. If you have limited network telemetry, this will limit your ability to hunt on the network. It's best to focus hunting on the deepest and widest pools of network and host telemetry and then pivot into less strong sources. If you have considerable application logs, start there, but correlate odd activity against network or host traffic after you have a lead. Hunting is all about developing leads (basically theories) and then testing them (confirming or denying the theory).

Developing Leads

We discussed leads briefly in Chapter 4. For most teams, the toughest part of getting started with hunting is knowing where to start. The easiest way to think about starting points is as a series of leads, just like an old-school detective story. So where do these leads come from? A combination of intelligence, instinct, and imagination:

- Looking at past incidents to spot patterns or trends. Have past attackers commonly used a given ISP for C2? Did you read about a group of attackers using Compiled Help files?
- Build leads around activities that are out of profile for your organization. With the exception of huge organizations, it may be odd to see connections to certain countries or at certain times of day, especially at a high volume.
- Build leads off the results of vulnerability assessments or red team penetration testing. Did the simulated bad guys attack a specific host? Take the time to see if nonsimulated bad guys did the same.

The list goes on and on. The exercise of developing leads is one of those "there are no bad ideas" kind of brainstorming exercises: write it down, no matter how crazy.

Testing Leads

Just as with alerting, it is possible to generate a high volume of noise or false positives when conducting hunting activities to look for indications of an attacker. Because of this, it is a good idea to test any hunting leads before you deploy hunting detection methods across your environment. You can conduct this testing in several ways. One way is to run a query with the information from your leads against a single, known good host to ensure that you are not bringing back a high volume of data that is related to normal operations. Another option is to run the query against a sample data set, such as a day's worth of proxy logs, again to ensure that the query will not bring back an overwhelming number of results. A high number of results can either indicate that your system is massively compromised (which we hope is not the case) or simply that the lead needs to be refined or reevaluated. It can take some time to develop good leads for hunting, but once you have mastered the practice, you will be able to identify potential badness even without a specific signature.

Conclusion

Integrating intelligence into alerting, investigation, and hunting is a combination of improving processes, deploying or modifying tools, and most important, training people to understand how everything fits together. Alerting is all about boiling down what you're interested in knowing about to the most essential aspects. Once you've identified an important alert, the process moves into wider collection to gather context. Investigation is about gathering a wide variety of information and then distilling it into a cogent understanding. Once you master these aspects of reactive tasks, it is possible to move on to hunting, proactively applying the lessons and techniques of alerting and investigation to look for undetected malicious activity.

The goal of all of the analysis in this phase is to understand the scope of the incident and make a plan for response. Once you have that plan, it is time to act on it and remove the threat. We call this next step Finish, and we will discuss how to accomplish it in the next chapter.

## CHAPTER 6

Finish

"Change is the end result of all true learning."

—Leo Buscaglia

Once you have identified the threats that you are facing and investigated how those threats have accessed and moved through your network, it is time to remove the threats. This phase is known as Finish and involves not only eradicating the footholds that malicious actors have put in your network, but also working to remediate whatever enabled them to get access in the first place.

Finish involves more than removing malware from a system, which is why we spend so much time in the Find and Fix stages. To properly finish an attacker's activity, it is critical to understand how that threat actor operates and to remove not just malware or artifacts left behind by an attack, but also communications channels, footholds, redundant access, and any other aspects of an attack that we uncovered in the Fix phase. Properly finishing an adversary requires a deep understanding of the attacker, their motives, and their actions, which will allow you to act with confidence as you secure the systems and regain control of your network.

Finishing Is *Not* Hacking Back

Finish does not mean hack back. That is because, unless you are a government department or agency with the proper authority, hacking back is a very, very bad idea! Why, you ask? There are several reasons:

- Attribution is rarely perfect, and you don't always know what you will end up hacking. Attackers will rarely attack you directly from their infrastructure. They will pivot through other victim machines to get to you, which means that if you take action against the machine you think is attacking you, it might end up being a hospital or your grandmother, or a computer in another country, introducing all sorts of new complications because you just violated that country's laws as well as probably violating your own.

- You don't know what will happen when you take action. You may think you will just be ending a session or removing some files, but unless you know exactly how the system you are targeting is set up as well as the intricacies of network operations (which, let's face it, we often don't even know about our own systems), it is difficult to know exactly what will happen when you take action. In military operations, including the traditional F3EAD cycle, understanding the exact actions you are taking and any potential for collateral damage requires practicing the operations against a simulated environment by using information from the Find phase. In intelligence-driven incident response, all of the Find activity takes place inside your own network, so you don't develop a picture of the attacker's networks. Developing that picture needed to carry out a successful offensive operation is also most likely a violation of law.

- You don't know who you are messing with. Even if you have done extensive research on the attackers in your environment and think that you have a good idea of their motivations and intentions and know how to stop them, you may find yourself facing an adversary who does not take kindly to your operations. This may result in additional attacks against you, or in the most extreme cases, where you may find yourself hacking back against a nation-state adversary, your actions may have national security implications, causing problems not just for you but for other organizations or agencies that had nothing to do with the original attack.

- It is probably illegal. 18 U.S. Code § 1030 (*https://www.law.cornell.edu/uscode/text/18/1030*), "Fraud and related activity in connection with computers," and similar laws in many other countries, make it illegal to gain unauthorized access to protect systems. Even if the people using those systems are bad actors, they are still considered protected computers under US law, and even accessing them can be a violation of the law.

In short, please do not take anything we say as a call to offensive action. The Finish stage occurs entirely within your own network, not outside it!

Stages of Finish

Finishing an attacker in your network can take many shapes. The nature of the activity that is identified during the Find phase, your organization's sophistication and tolerance for risk, and the legal authority that you have will all dictate the best way to remove an attacker and to keep them from returning.

The Finish phase has three stages: mitigate, remediate, and rearchitect. These stages acknowledge that you can't do everything at once. Even after a comprehensive investigation, some tactical response actions can take place quickly, but many strategic response actions, such as rearchitecting, will take longer. We will discuss the three phases next.

Mitigate

During an incident, the defensive team will often have to mitigate the issue. *Mitigation* is the process of taking temporary steps to keep an intrusion from getting worse while longer-term corrections are taken.

Ideally, mitigation should take place quickly and in a coordinated fashion to avoid giving the adversary a chance to react before you have cut off their access. Mitigation takes place at several phases of the kill chain, including delivery, command and control, and actions on target.

Tipping Off the Adversary

When an incident-response team moves from the Fix phase to the Finish phase, it is important to consider the adversary's potential response to your finishing actions. Although the investigation process is largely passive (collecting and analyzing information), a response is, by necessity, active. This can result in tipping off the adversary, causing them to change tactics or take new actions. To avoid this adversary response, you need to plan your actions and then execute the plan as quickly as possible, taking care that the adversary can't leverage their access to stay in the environment.

Mitigating delivery

It is important to try to limit the ability for the adversary to reenter the environment. Blocking an adversary's way in involves using the information gathered during the Find phase, which can tell you how this adversary typically operates, as well as the Fix phase, which will tell you how the adversary got into your network. Mitigating delivery can involve blocking email addresses or attachments used for delivery or cutting off compromised credentials used to log in to the environment. Mitigating on delivery is usually the least likely type of mitigation to be detected because it doesn't impact active sessions but only future attempts to gain or regain access.

Mitigating command and control

If the adversary is using some form of command and control, cutting off this access is one of the most important actions before moving on to remediation. The overall key of mitigation is to keep the adversary from changing the environment as you are trying to regain control of it. The easiest way for an adversary to do this is to use the connection they have already established to set up an alternative means of accessing the system. One example is an attacker installing a secondary RAT with different signatures in addition to their primary RAT, but with a much longer communication interval that may not be detected as readily. In a situation like that, the attacker may allow their primary tools to be removed, knowing they they will be able to come back later.

Revoking Sessions

Unfortunately, many online systems such as email don't automatically revoke sessions when a compromised user password is changed. This can result in a situation where you think you have removed access, but the adversary remains logged in. This can be devastating to mitigation and remediation efforts, because the adversary may be able to reestablish complete control over a resource the IR team believes has been fixed, and can monitor additional responder actions and adapt to them. Few things feel worse as a defender than being recompromised by a vector you thought was fixed. Revoking sessions is important when changing account passwords.

In addition, don't forget application-specific passwords as well. Many services use one-time passwords for desktop clients or third-party services. These rarely change and may be used by an adversary for long-term access even when the victim regularly changes passwords.

Mitigating actions over target

Mitigating actions over target is something that stakeholders will often want done immediately. Knowing that there is an adversary in your environment who is potentially accessing or stealing sensitive information is not a thought that makes anyone feel comfortable or safe. Reducing the consequences or severity of an adversary's actions while going through the process of securing your network is a balancing act aimed at protecting information without allowing an adversary the opportunity to change tactics and find alternate ways to achieve their goals.

Most mitigation of actions over target focus on limiting access to sensitive information, reducing network transport options to prevent exfiltration, or shutting down impacted resources altogether. Remember that stealing information is not always the adversary's goal. They may be using your network as a hop point to reach another victim, or to conduct denial-of-service attacks against other targets. These actions can be remediated with network access controls or limiting outbound connections as necessary.

Mitigating GLASS WIZARD

In the past two chapters, we have focused on finding out how our adversary, GLASS WIZARD, operates—both in general by finding external information on their activities, and more specifically by understanding how they were able to successfully compromise our systems and what actions they took after the compromise occurred. Now that we understand our adversary, we can begin the Finish phase by mitigating their activities.

We identified that GLASS WIZARD was able to access our networks via spearphishing emails, and in the Fix phase we were able to identify email subjects, attachments (which were résumé themed and targeted HR), as well as the senders. To mitigate the risk of the attackers trying to reestablish access using the same or similar methods, we will reroute any similar emails to a sandbox for analysis, which will also allow us to look for any attempts to regain access. We will also talk with the HR department to let them know of the threat to raise their awareness.

To mitigate command-and-control activity, we will block traffic to the identified command-and-control servers, and will either block or monitor for other command-and-control-methods that we identified have been used by GLASS WIZARD. We know that the adversary may switch tactics after they realize that their activity has been detected, so we want to be prepared for any changes they may make to retain or regain their foothold.

Finally, we will force a password reset across the environment, including service accounts, and will revoke all sessions to online systems and applications that are used in the environment, knowing that the attackers almost certainly have captured both user and system credentials. We know the types of information GLASS WIZARD is likely look for on our network, but we have assessed that this information is widely distributed through the network, including on users' systems and email. We will increase monitoring on databases and other places where large amounts of information is stored, and we have made a note to focus on how to better track and protect sensitive information in the rearchitecture stage of Finish.

Once mitigation steps have been taken to stop or limit the damage being done by an adversary, it is time to move into remediation, which will have a more permanent impact on the attacker.

Remediate

Remediation is the process of removing all adversary capabilities and invalidating any compromised resources so that they can no longer be used by the adversary to conduct operations. Remediation generally focuses on a different set of kill-chain phases than mitigation does, most notably exploitation, installation, and actions over target, which we will break down in this section.

Remediating exploitation

In the vast majority of cases, remediation of exploitation means patching. Every exploit relies on a vulnerability, and so the number one way to keep an exploit from being used to compromise a system in the future is either make the exploit target unreachable (by putting a system behind a firewall or other using access-control processes) or by correcting the flaw. If a patch is already available, it is a matter of prioritizing patching of vulnerable systems and identifying why this wasn't done before, but in some cases a patch may not be available. In those situations, remediation involves working with the software creator, who may or may not be aware of the problem. During the sometimes lengthy process of creating a permanent fix, it is possible to put other mitigations in place, such as isolating a vulnerable system or enforcing and monitoring strict access controls.

Many organizations have plenty of custom code around, and in some cases you don't need to reach out to a vendor but instead to the responsible team. If your organization relies on custom tools or code, it is a good idea to develop a process for working with internal application development teams when security issues arise.

Patching Social Engineering

As the saying goes, "There is no patch for a human." Amusing quip aside, users often do not understand or identify the warning signs of an attack. Many successful attacks rely on this fact and avoid technical exploits entirely, using attacks such as fake applications or document macros coupled with clever social-engineering lures. Although technical options help in combatting these attacks, the key vulnerability isn't technical. The only root-cause solution is in training users to recognize and avoid these sorts of attacks, and to establish a process that allows users to report suspicious activity without fear of reprisal or public shaming.

Remediating installation

On the surface, remediating installation seems simple: you need to delete anything created during exploitation and installed at that point. Even though the concept is simple, remediating installed malware can be difficult and time-consuming, and often requires a great deal of time and effort.

What is malware, exactly? Typically, it's one or more executable files, possibly some libraries, and a persistence mechanism that makes sure the first executable file runs on a system in the case of a reboot or an error. At exploitation time, the attacker has control of the system and may take a large variety of actions. Understanding this fully takes a deep understanding of the system and considerable investigation.

Given that complexity, how do you successfully and completely remove malware after installation? It's not always as simple as just deleting the files. This leads to a fundamental argument between responders over whether the best approach is to remove malware or reformat the system and rebuild it completely. Antivirus works under the expectation that malware can be removed successfully, but many incident responders have found that that is not always the case. The decision on how to handle things is up to each incident-response team.

Our Opinion: Remove Malware or Reformat the System

This is normally the place we'd give a charming anecdote or humorously suggest you need to make the decision on your own (which you do), but instead we'll just give you our standard advice: *just reformat it!* Although you might have different factors in place and may need to make a different decision, we always recommend reformatting. It's the only way you can be 100% certain that any malware is gone and attacker system actions have been fully mitigated. On some specialized systems, such as control systems, this may not be possible; but when it is possible, it is the best way to know that you have not missed anything.

Remediating actions over target

Not every Action over Target phase can be remediated, but it's always worth considering. The ability to do so may be limited by your telemetry as well as the actions the attacker takes.

For data theft, it's usually difficult to do much more than determine what information may have been taken and develop an assessment on the damage done, though it highly depends on which data. For example, in 2013 Bit9, a security firm, was compromised specifically so attackers could steal the company's code-signing certificates. Software signed with these certificates was inherently trusted by the Windows operating system. As a result, the best way to remediate the attack was to issue a certificate-revocation request, which invalidated the certificate and thus any software signed with it.

Other examples of remediating actions over target could be blocking outbound network activity for a distributed denial-of-service bot, invalidating stolen credit card numbers by reporting them to the credit card providers, changing passwords or other stolen credentials, or even initiating full source-code reviews for stolen software. It's almost impossible to predict everything that could be done until the situation presents itself, but no matter what, good remediation of actions over target often requires a deep investigation getting back to a root cause of the problem and attacker goals, collaboration with those who work with the compromised resource, and a little bit of creativity.

Remediating GLASS WIZARD

We know that GLASS WIZARD is a sophisticated actor and uses a variety of malware, including Hikit and the ZOX family, both of which were present on our systems. Remediating compromised systems involves rebuilding those machines when at all possible. Doing so is not always possible, however; and although our plan is to rebuild all the compromised hosts, some of the compromised servers must be handled differently.

In the case of our domain controllers, the downtime associated with rebuilding the servers is not acceptable because of the many systems that rely on them, and therefore we must take a different approach. In this situation, we have decided that, after we take appropriate steps to mitigate the adversary's ability to access the systems using stolen credentials or command-and-control communications, we are going to build a new system, this time with specific whitelists for known good activity and alerting on anything that is not known good. We have high confidence based on reporting that GLASS WIZARD will attempt to get back into the network; and while we do not know exactly how they will accomplish that, we know to remain vigilant for any activity that is outside the normal. Once the new systems are properly configured and additional security measures are in place, we will replace the compromised systems all at once.

We have also identified that GLASS WIZARD used CVE-2013-3893 against some of our hosts, so we will need to partner with the information security team to identify and patch any systems using an outdated version of Internet Explorer. We have already enforced credential changes as part of the mitigation process, but we have decided that we will monitor attempts against several previous accounts to identify any adversary attempts to regain access using credentials.

Rearchitect

One of the most effective uses of intelligence-driven incident-response data is an advanced form of remediation: the incident-response team looks at past incident trends, identifies common patterns, and works to mitigate these at a strategic level. These mitigations are generally not small changes, and may range from small things like tweaks to system configurations or additional user training, to massive shifts in tooling such as the development of a new security tools or even complete network rearchitecture.

Often these massive changes occur after a single large breach, but don't underestimate the ability to identify trends with smaller intrusions or even failed intrusions and use the information on what vulnerabilities or weaknesses are being targeted as a driver for change.

Rearchitecting GLASS WIZARD

We have identified several architectural and process-related issues that contributed to the opportunity GLASS WIZARD had to compromise us. One is the fact that a vulnerability from 2013 was unremediated on several hosts. Because patches are usually installed as part of a larger package that addresses several vulnerabilities, we know that other vulnerabilities existed on those systems as well. We need to better understand why the process did not work in this case and make any changes that are needed.

We have also identified several issues with the way that authentication and access are controlled in our environment. GLASS WIZARD was able to use legitimate accounts to move through our environment, and nothing was in place to identify suspicious activity on these accounts.

Addressing this problem requires additional investments that we will not be able to make immediately. The mitigation and remediation steps we take will secure and protect the network while more lasting architecture changes can be planned and implemented.

Taking Action

The act of finishing adversary activity requires strategic and operational planning as well as tactical action. When a cohesive plan is in place and all responsible parties know what actions need to be taken and when, it is time to act.

In Chapter 2 we discussed the 5 Ds as they related to attacker activities: attackers take actions that deny, degrade, disrupt, deceive, or destroy the systems or networks that they target. In the Finish phase, we can use those same Ds to determine the actions to take to remove the attackers from the network. Once again, it is important to note that with all of these options, the actions that are being taken all occur inside your network and should never be directed outside the systems that you control.

Deny

Deny is one of the most basic response actions to take, and in almost all cases it will be the initial response to attacker activity. Attackers want access to your network. They want access to your information. They want to be able to move freely from system to system in order to find what they want and take it. The goal of Deny is to remove their ability to do any of these things.

The attackers got into your network somehow, and after they were able to get in, they likely installed backdoors or dumped user credentials in order to make sure that they could retain their access. Ideally, you have identified these activities during the Find phase, and in this phase you can focus on removing that access in a way that will completely deny the attacker access to your network. Here are some ways to deny attackers access or movements:

Credential-based access

If the attackers used stolen or default credentials to get access to the network, the best approach is to change those credentials or remove old accounts to deny the attackers that avenue of access. It's also key to look for accounts that the attackers created for themselves using stolen access.

Backdoors and implants

We discussed backdoors and implants in Chapter 2 so that you would have an understanding of how they operate and how attackers use them and be able to efficiently and completely remove their ability to leverage those tools to access your network. The process of denying access requires that you understand how the backdoor was installed in the first place. Often you will have to make sure you not only remove the attacker's tools, but also change credentials because the two often go hand in hand. Either an attacker used credentials to gain access and then installed the backdoor, or they dumped credentials after they had access.

Lateral movement

Denying access is not just about keeping an attacker from getting into your network from the outside; it also means making sure that they do not have the ability to move laterally through your network. As we mentioned, Finish is not just about kicking one attacker out of your network. This phase is about making sure that you deal with the things that allowed them access in the first place, and that means denying their ability to move throughout the network. During the Find and Fix phases, you likely identified methods that attackers used to move through networks—both common methods as well as methods specific to your incident and your environment—and it is important to address the issues that allowed those methods to work.

All of the information you gathered in the Fix stage will help develop the plan to ensure that you can completely deny access. However, sometimes denying access is not enough, as access is something determined attackers will try to immediately regain. It is important to also take steps to disrupt attempts to regain access to the network or gain access to information and to disrupt their ability to get that information out of your network.

Disrupt

In traditional operations, it is often impossible to deny an adversary's ability to take action. The goal then becomes to force an attacker to take ineffective actions and to diminish their ability to conduct operations. *Disrupt and degrade* are approaches to take when facing an advanced attacker with whom simply attempting to deny access is not likely to be successful.

Many organizations experience repeated breaches, often by the same attackers, because permanently denying access is a difficult thing to do. An attacker who is determined to get into a network will likely find a way, especially if that network has users who can be targeted to circumvent technical security measures.

Just because an attacker is able to get back into a network does not mean, however, that they will be able to get the information that they are after. To deny attackers access to the information that they are looking for, it is important to identify what it was they they were targeting (which should have been determined in the Find and Fix stages) and then take additional measures to restrict access to that information. This may mean setting up additional access-control measures around critical information, and additionally setting up alerting to detect when someone is attempting to discover or access that information, or it may mean requiring additional authentication when accessing shared resources. These steps can be taken only if you understand the information attackers are after and also know where this information is located in your network.

Degrade

The Degrade course of action is aimed at forcing an attacker to show their hand so that they can be more effectively countered. However, the goal is not to gather more information about an attacker's tactics, but to cause their previously identified activities to be less effective.

Deceive

Deception is the practice of trying to throw off an attacker by providing false or misleading information. In many cases, this focuses on actions over target; for example, trying to get an attacker who is focused on intellectual property to take a version of widget plans with the wrong type of metal that could cause failure. The idea is to devalue attackers' collection efforts, and hopefully force them to focus elsewhere.

Another common type of deception technique is *honeypots*, systems set up to look like a common system in the environment but secretly set up to provide enhanced telemetry. A good example is a system set up to look like a database server with all the right listening services on the right ports—maybe even deliberately set up with an inviting hostname like *ma-contracts-db* (*ma* in this case suggesting Mergers and Acquisitions). An attacker in the environment might look for hosts, see a tempting target where there might be useful data, and then attempt to access it. Given that those who should be in the environment know that there's nothing useful on this system, the only attempts to access it can be attributed to attackers. By identifying attempts to access this system, the defenders can be tipped off. Honeypots don't just have to be systems; the technique can be used in other contexts such as social networks or user personas.

Hypothetically, this sounds great. In practice, deception techniques can be useful, but they're hard to execute effectively. Most deception relies on a *dangle*, a lure that entices the attacker. The dangle has to walk a fine line. Not enticing enough, and the attackers won't bother attempting to access it. Too enticing, and the attackers may smell deception and avoid it. Even if you pick the perfect level of enticement, deception can still be a challenge, and authenticity is important. Say you want to identify phishing by using a fake persona on a social network. Even if the profile setup is perfect, it will quickly fall apart if the picture is pulled from a source that the attacker could find or if a user has too few connections.

Deception is hard. It's a challenge to get everything right and still be useful. It can often result in high rates of false positives as well. It can be useful but should be reserved for already sophisticated shops that can put in the time and effort to make it effective.

Destroy

Destroy means to cause some sort of physical damage to a system, and is not usually a good response, because we are talking about actions you take against your own network. You may discover an antiquated system that was compromised, and removing it from your network may be a good option, but even then you would not neccesarily destroy that system.

To be absolutely clear, we are not talking about the destruction of any systems owned or operated by the attacker in this section. As we mentioned, all of these actions take place within your network.

Organizing Incident Data

During—but most important, after—an incident, it is critically important to record details of the investigation and the actions taken. These details should focus on the following:

- Initial leads, sources, and outcomes.
- Details of the attacker kill chain, including both indicators and descriptions of tactics, techniques, and procedures.
- Information about compromised hosts, including their vulnerabilities, configuration, owners, and purpose.
- Details on actions over target, how the compromise impacted users, and what was stolen. (This can be especially important when/if you engage law enforcement.)
- Response actions taken on which hosts by which responder (important if you have to track down what went wrong).

- Follow-up leads or ideas for long-term actions.

You also may have additional information based on individual organizational needs. The ultimately goal is a single source of truth, a place where all responders can share what they've found and keep everyone coordinated. There are many ways to approach this, and in the end the key is not exactly how the information is stored, but that everyone works together, follows the process, and gets the job done.

Tools for Tracking Actions

A variety of tools are available to track your incident data as well as the actions that have been taken. This section covers ways to organize data, using both publicly available and purpose-built tools. When you are just getting started with incident response and do not have existing systems in place to track information and actions that have been taken, it is often best to start small and grow into increased capability and functionality. It's easy to get overwhelmed by adding complex ticketing systems with aggressive required fields and end up doing very little. The worst possible outcome is an incident-tracking system that analysts don't want to use, making it more difficult to track information about an incident. Fortunately, there are several easy places to start tracking incident information.

Personal notes

In almost every case, incident management starts with analyst notes. Good analysts will realize (or have it drilled into them) that they need to take notes for both formal investigations and casual observations. As a result, many analysts get in the habit of writing down whatever they stumble across throughout a shift in the SOC or day of hunting.

These notes can be invaluable to analysts, and are freqently their dominant reference when writing up formal reports, but are often less useful to the rest of their security organization. This is largely due to formatting. Analysts writing personal notes typically develop a personal style and format for their own investigations. This starts with the medium: paper notebooks or text files. From there, analysts do a wide variety of things, including using different structures of dates (12-1-16 versus 20161201), and creating written narratives, bullet points, or drawn graphs.

The tough part about individual notes is the difficulty in exploitation (not hacking exploitation but intelligence exploitation) of these notes. If they're written, it's basically impossible (short of using some form of handwriting recognition). If typed, opportunities for exploitation may exist, but not without a lot of lost context.

The result in most cases is that personal notes stay personal, for the analyst who wrote them only, and the team works together with a shared format for tracking information.

The Spreadsheet of Doom

In most cases, when a team starts tracking information together, the first attempt starts as a spreadsheet, jokingly referred to by analysts as The *Spreadsheet of Doom* (SOD) because of its content, sprawl, and general unwieldiness in working with it.

The SOD benefits from being easily structured. Typically, it's made up of multiple spreadsheets or tabs on a single spreadsheet, capturing the following information:

- Indicators of compromise
- Compromised resources (systems, services, data, etc.)
- Response actions (planned, taken, etc.)

Figure 6-1 shows an example SOD.

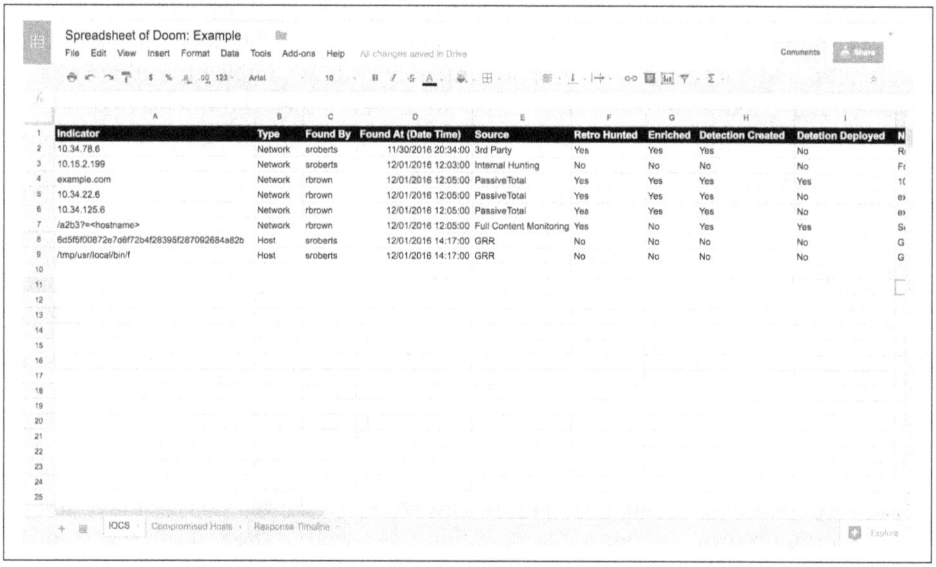
Spreadsheet of Doom: Example

Indicator	Type	Found By	Found At (Date Time)	Source	Retro Hunted	Enriched	Detection Created	Detetion Deployed	N
10.34.78.6	Network	sroberts	11/30/2016 20:34:00	3rd Party	Yes	Yes	Yes	No	R
10.15.2.199	Network	sroberts	12/01/2016 12:03:00	Internal Hunting	No	No	No	No	F
example.com	Network	rbrown	12/01/2016 12:05:00	PassiveTotal	Yes	Yes	Yes	Yes	1
10.34.22.6	Network	rbrown	12/01/2016 12:05:00	PassiveTotal	Yes	Yes	Yes	No	e
10.34.125.6	Network	rbrown	12/01/2016 12:05:00	PassiveTotal	Yes	Yes	Yes	No	e
/a2b3?=<hostname>	Network	rbrown	12/01/2016 12:05:00	Full Content Monitoring	Yes	No	Yes	Yes	S
6d5f5f00872e7d6f72b4f28395f287092684a82b	Host	sroberts	12/01/2016 14:17:00	GRR	No	No	No	No	G
/tmp/usr/local/bin/f	Host	sroberts	12/01/2016 14:17:00	GRR	No	No	No	No	G

IOCS | Compromised Hosts | Response Timeline

Figure 6-1. Using Google Sheets for a Spreadsheet of Doom

How the SOD is set up, what fields it has, where it's stored, and how people collaborate on it is up to each organization and will evolve over time. What is important is constancy and an agreed-upon format and conventions around names, dates, and categories. The need for consistency is important because the big advantage of the SOD versus personal notes is the ability to exploit spreadsheets easily.

Spreadsheets can be exported as comma-separated values (CSV) documents. These are easily read and written to by many tools and with a wide variety of scripting languages, making it easy to do more with a CSV than you could with other text-based documents, such as automatically resolving the reverse DNS of all IPs or checking hashes against VirusTotal. This type of automation can be invaluable.

The downsides of the SOD should be apparent at this point. It relies on discipline to use effectively and follow convention. There's no validation of any kind and nothing to keep bad data from polluting otherwise valid information. As soon as this falls apart, the SOD itself fails.

Third-party, non-purpose-built solutions

There are, of course, alternatives to using what is publicly or commercially available, and many teams have adapted their own tools to use for managing incident response and collecting incident information. This is a team decision and may be a stopgap or long-term solution. When evaluating using a third-party, non-purpose-built tool like a kanban board, semistructured flat file format like Markdown, a wiki, or a generalized IT ticketing system, consider the following needs:

Ability to automate
> The big advantage of having a data structure is the ability to build tools to automate common tasks.

Integration with typical team workflows
> Teaching new technologies is tough, especially when expecting those tools to be used in high-stress situations.

Once a tool is decided upon, the best approach is use it, given that relying on a new tool in an incident-response situation is dubious at best. It is highly recommended to put new workflow tools through their paces with multiple tabletop and sample exercises. Running into problems is common, but it is better to sort them out in practice than during an incident.

Purpose-Built Tools

Personal notes and apocalyptic spreadsheets are great, but eventually even the most seat-of-their-pants incident-response and intelligence teams want a purpose-built solution. This turning point will often arrive after they have spent too much time chasing down a mistyped or mistaken IP address or discover that confusion exists about whether a new detection was applied. The result is that most teams end up deploying or creating an incident-response platform.

Purpose-built incident-response systems provide important characteristics out of the box that we've discussed before. They're often easy to integrate with. Most provide a variety of integration points, often including email (for sending and receiving information sent as email) and an application programming interface (API) used for connecting directly to other tools.

One of our favorite purpose-built tools is FIR (*https://github.com/certsocietegenerale/FIR*) (Figure 6-2), short for *Fast Incident Response.* Built by the computer emergency response team at Société Générale, the third biggest bank in France, FIR is an open source ticketing system built from the ground up to support intelligence-driven incident response.

Figure 6-2. A screenshot of FIR

FIR is an ideal starting tool for teams looking for a dedicated platform to support their incident-response and threat-intelligence operations. One challenge of dedicated systems is striking a balance of customizability. Too few options, and the system ends up being so generic it may as well be a Spreadsheet of Doom downloaded off the internet. Too much customizability, and the analysts suffer from analysis paralysis, unsure which of a wide set of options to choose. FIR strikes a balance by having an opinionated workflow and set of defaults, but allows considerable customization.

Assessing the Damage

One important discussion that comes up at the end of every incident is assessing the damage. In some cases, this can be tied directly to dollars lost (such as events that impact retail operations or destruction of tangible resources such as physical hardware, or even the cost of incident-response services or internal IR time). In many cases, determining damage requires working with impacted business units, IT, and sales. Take special care to work with your insurance team, as they may have special insight into impact and costs.

Being able to put a dollar figure on incidents is often key for engaging law enforcement. In many cases, law enforcement will get involved only when an incident costs that affect organizations reach a certain minimum. The exact figure depends on your jurisdiction.

Monitoring Life Cycle

The last big piece of the Finish cycle is managing the monitoring life cycle. In the heat of an incident, it's easy to generate a wide range of signatures. These signatures need to work through a life cycle, and the end of the Finish phases is an ideal time to review them. The monitoring life cycle usually involves the following steps:

Creation

> The first stage is creation of the signature, which occurs when an analyst takes an observable and uses it to create a way to monitor for signs of that observable on internal systems.

Testing

> This is the most often skipped step, and if you skip it, you will pay for it in the refinement phase. The obvious form of testing takes place during the preceding step, creation, where a detection is applied against known bad, or a variety of known bad obseravables. Testing, however, should focus on known good, hoping to identify false positives. One way to achieve this is to put the detection into production, set to generate statistics but not alerts (such as using Snort's log action instead of the usual alert). This method is often effective and very real world, but time-consuming.

> Another method is having a corpus of known good data to test against. This technique is especially useful in an incident where deployment of alerts is often more important than false positives. The upside is that the results are much quicker, but not usually as thorough. In many cases, the ideal solution is combining both techniques, depending on the situation.

Deployment

> Once a detection is ready (hopefully after testing), it gets deployed. While some teams treat this step as the end of their responsibilities, that is a quick way to anger any SOC analysts or intrusion-detection team members. Working with the detection team and getting feedback is critical at this stage, because you will use that feedback during the next step: refinement.

Refinement

> Based on the feedback, the detection goes back to the drawing board to perform this step. This can take on a variety of improvements:
> - Overly specific detections can be broadened. This is especially useful when new, related samples are identified.
> - Overly broad detections are tightened up. Everyone who has spent time building detections has had an unexpected string that triggers on a common network service. Often this is discovered only after being in place.

- Refinement is often based on performance as well. Depending on the telemetry source, a given signature (especially in the case of intrusion detection systems) can not only run slowly, but also have significant impact on the entire system. Often signatures need to be reviewed and optimized for performance, either speed or memory.

Retirement

Eventually, a signature stops being useful, either because the threat has been mitigated (such as a signature that detects a vulnerability after the vulnerability is patched) or the attack falls out of favor. In some cases, it's useful, assuming the impact on performance is acceptable, to put a signature back into logging-only mode, allowing gathering continued statistics.

An interesting topic originally explored by Jeremy Johnson of Ford at the SANS CTI Summit 2017 was the idea of using seemingly less useful (high false-positive), indicators of compromise more effectively. In his talk "Using Intelligence to Heighten Defense" (*https://www.youtube.com/watch?v=NRY5fKZDGVU*), Johnson explained ways of taking noisy indicators and improving them not by refinement of the indicator itself but by judicious application to high-risk population. For example, if the detection team has a very general indicator for an adversary C2, one that causes too many false positives across the entire network, it may still be useful when used in an IDS on a network for research and development or executives.

Conclusion

As the active stage of incident response, the Finish section is one of the most important phases to focus on. If done effectively, an incident-response team can throw an adversary out, learn from the attacker's actions, and ensure a more secure network. If done poorly, it can tip off an adversary, allowing them to dig in, hide, and avoid being completely removed from a system. Taking the time to understand your mitigation and remediation options and how they fit in your response plans will make your team more effective in the long term. Finally, finding methods for managing all the output will set your team up to move into the next phase: Exploit, which is the first phase of the intelligence portion of F3EAD. The intelligence portion is where we will make sure that we learn from the attacker's actions and ensure a more secure network moving forward.

CHAPTER 7
Exploit

"If you focus solely on the enemy, you will ignore the threat."

—Colonel Walter Piatt

At this point in the incident-response process, it is common for the final incident-response report to be delivered and the responders to move on to the next matter requiring attention, but that is not where this book ends. Throughout the course of the investigation, we have gathered a lot of data on our attackers, looked for additional information from within our networks, and taken actions that have had an impact on the attacker's operations. Now we need to gather all of that data, analyze it for intelligence value, and integrate it into not only detection and prevention methods, but also more strategic-level initiatives such as risk assessments, prioritization of efforts, and future security investments. To get to the point where you can do all these things, you have to engage the intelligence portion of the F3EAD cycle: Exploit, Analyze, and Disseminate.

It is no secret why most people stop short of completing the F3EAD cycle: it's hard enough to generate intelligence, but managing it is a whole new series of headaches. Dealing with timing, aging, access control, and formats is enough to make anyone's head spin. And yet, as undeniably complex as these problems are, they have to be addressed head on. Having great intelligence that doesn't see the light of day is as disappointing as a star athlete sitting on the bench. Exploiting the intelligence that you have generated during the incident-response process ensures that all of the time and energy that went into identifying, understanding, and remediating the incident further supports network defense and response processes across the board. This chapter describes the various tasks you should do in the Exploit phase of F3EAD.

We've discussed the occasional difficulties between military jargon and common information security vernacular, and *Exploit* just happens to be one of the big ones. In information security, we tend to almost exclusively use the term *exploit* to refer to the exploitation of a technical vulnerability that will give you access or information. By contrast, in military terms, *exploit* more broadly means *to take advantage of* and is used not only when talking about vulnerabilities. In the context of F3EAD, it refers to using and benefiting from the intelligence that has been collected during the course of operations. When lined up with the traditional intelligence cycle, the Exploit phase can be considered a combination of collection (though usually more of an aggregation of internally gathered information) and processing to get that information into a usable format so that it can be analyzed.

What to Exploit?

When F3EAD is not properly implemented or is not carried out completely, you likely will find yourself dealing with the same intrusions or types of incidents not too far down the road. In the Find, Fix, and Finish stages of the cycle, we focused on a specific attack, a specific adversary, and the specific actions needed to deal with that particular incident. By the end of the Finish phase of the GLASS WIZARD intrusion, we had identified a large amount of information around the intrusion, the actors behind it, and how they operated. But even though that information is organized in a way that facilitated incident response, that doesn't necessarily mean it is in the right format for follow-up intelligence analysis.

In the Exploit phase, we begin the process that ensures that we learn from the incident. We focus on the threat, and not just the enemy. Because of this, it is important that we not only extract technical indicators related to the particular attack, such as malware samples and command-and-control IP addresses, but also the overarching aspects that led to the intrusion and allowed the attackers to be, at least to some degree, successful. This includes information about the vulnerabilities or weaknesses that were targeted in the attack and the information or systems that were targeted. We are not just trying to protect the network from a replay of the exact same attack, but to understand the various factors such as policies, technical vulnerabilities, or visibility gaps that led to the successful intrusion and to develop protections or detections for them as well. Because of this, we believe that there is very little information that should *not* be exploited and analyzed—but this, of course, makes managing that information complex.

After deciding what information will be exploited, it is necessary to extract that information from incident data, standardize it, and store it for future analysis and reference.

Gathering Information

Depending on how you manage your incident-response data, it is entirely possible that the most difficult part of the Exploit phase will be finding the important bits of intelligence from the investigation. When it comes to gathering incident-response data, we have seen it all—from elaborate systems, to Excel spreadsheets, to Post-It notes with IP addresses stuck to a whiteboard. There is no wrong way to gather that data, but if you want to be able to extract it so that it can be analyzed and used in the future, there are certainly some ways to make the process easier.

When you are dealing with exploiting information from a previous incident, you are often limited in the data that you have available. One of the goals of intelligence-driven incident response is to ensure that the incident-response process captures the information needed for intelligence analysis, but if you are just beginning the process of integrating operations and intelligence, you may not have been able to influence what information was gathered (yet). A good starting point for the Exploit phase is to understand exactly what you have available. We have found that the information that is currently available usually falls into one of two categories: high-level information, and technical details such as malware analysis.

If you have only high-level information in the form of a narrative about the incident, you will be looking at extracting strategic-level details, as opposed to if you have access to detailed malware analysis, from which you can extract tactical-level details about the malware's functionality. Initially, you may have access to only one level of information or the other, but ideally, as you implement this process in your organization, you will be able to gather both the technical details of an incident as well as the strategic information on the information targeted and what the impact was. Being able to combine information across all the levels is one of the things that makes intelligence most powerful.

Mining Previous Incidents

If you are reading this book with the intention of understanding how to start integrating operations and intelligence, it is important to note that you don't have to start with the next incident; you can go back through previous incidents and exploit that information. In fact, this type of activity is a great way to familiarize people in your organization with the F3EAD process and help them feel comfortable with it as you build your threat profile. Digging through and analyzing previous incident data can give you a great idea of the types of threats facing your network and identify the visibility or information gaps you may need to address as you move forward.

Storing Threat Information

At the end of an investigation—whether immediately following or six months after the fact—you will likely have a plethora of information. Your task in the Exploit phase is to take that information, whatever it may look like, and structure it into a format that can be analyzed and used moving forward.

Data Standards and Formats for Indicators

No discussion of threat intelligence would be complete without a discussion of the various data standards. We are about to dive into the details of the various data standards that may make you never want to talk about them again, but please stick with us. Data standards will make your life a lot easier once you find the one that works for you.

Several groupings of data standards are commonly used to store and share threat data. No one magical standard rules them all, so the best approach is to understand what standards are in existence and determine whether one of them will work for you. For example, if you are part of sharing organizations that utilize STIX/TAXII to share data, that may be a good choice for you. If your organization has already invested in security tools that use a specific format such as OpenIOC, that may work best. If there is more than one standard that you need to work with (which we see quite often), the next best approach is to make sure that you understand the fundamentals of the various standards and be prepared to do data-field mapping, because you likely will be dealing with information in one of these data formats at some point.

OASIS Suite—CybOX/STIX/TAXII

Oasis is an open standards organization that took over Mitre's role in supporting the CyBox, STIX, and TAXII data formats. These standards are some of the more well-known standards, in part because of US government adoption of this suite. The Oasis Suite components covered in this chapter are CyBOX, STIX, and TAXII.

Cyber Observable eXpression (CybOX) can be looked at as the building blocks for storing and sharing threat intelligence. CybOX is made up of observables, which are defined objects with stateful and measurable properties. There are multiple use cases for CybOX, ranging from event management to malware analysis and information sharing. There are a large number of CybOX objects for capturing observables, and not all of them are directly relevant to incident response, so you will not need to use them all.

Figure 7-1 shows an example of a CybOX object for a malicious executable we found in our environment related to the GLASS WIZARD intrusion. It includes several important pieces of information about the executable, including the name, size, and file type.

```
<cybox:Object id="example:Object-35e86e7h-d3e6-4138-891b-337376dc6f47">
  <cybox:Properties xsi:type="FileObj:FileObjectType">
    <FileObj:File_Name>setup_sx.exe</FileObj:File_Name>
    <FileObj:File_Extension>.exe</FileObj:File_Extension>
    <FileObj:Size_In_Bytes> 268832</FileObj:Size_In_Bytes>
    <FileObj:Hashes>
      <cyboxCommon:Hash>
        <cyboxCommon:Type xsi:type="cyboxVocabs:HashNameVocab-1.0">MD5</cyboxCommon:Type>
<cyboxCommon:Simple_Hash_Value>8fde69744886d6828165b1f12eb5a35c</cyboxCommon:Simple_Hash_Value>
      </cyboxCommon:Hash>
    </FileObj:Hashes>
  </cybox:Properties>
</cybox:Object>
```

Figure 7-1. CybOX file object

Structured Threat Information eXpression (STIX) is quite possibly the most commonly requested format for handling and receiving threat data. However, the sad fact is that many people like the *idea* of STIX without knowing the best ways to use it or implement it in their incident-response process. This is one of the reasons we end up finding so many people with their incident data in Excel spreadsheets!

STIX is built from the fundamental building blocks provided with CybOX. However, it allows for more contextual detail to be added to the CybOX objects, which enables further analysis and is a huge benefit when sharing threat data. These additional context fields include Threat Actors, Campaigns, Victim Targets, and TTPs. This allows you to take individual observables that are captured through CybOX and chain them together and add more context. This is when threat data can truly begin to become threat intelligence. Although it is good to know that a certain file is malicious, it is more useful from an analytic perspective to know that the file was used in a particular campaign targeting victims in a specific sector, and that after execution of the file, the actors attempted to exfiltrate intellectual property. When STIX, or any standard, is used fully, it can be a great tool for analysis, but just remember that work is required to get all of the information captured! That work is accomplished in the Exploit and Analyze phases of F3EAD, so for now, work on capturing all of the observables and surrounding context, and it can all be pieced together in the next phase.

Trusted Automated eXchanged of Indicator Information (TAXII) is not itself a data standard. It is paired with STIX so often that many people believe that the name of the data standard is STIX/TAXII, though they are separate things.

TAXII is a transportation and sharing framework and comprises four services: discovery, poll, inbox, and feed management. TAXII is the way that STIX is shared between entities or organizations. TAXII has three primary transport and sharing models:

Subscriber
> In this model, one central organization shares information with partner organizations, without the partner organizations sending any information back. This is the model that is most commonly seen with threat-intelligence providers, either commercial or open source, who send information to customers.

Hub and spoke
> One organization or source serves as the central authority for information sharing. It pushes information to other organizations, and when those organizations want to share back, they send information to the central organization, which redistributes the information to the group.

Peer to peer
> This model can be used by any two or more organizations that want to share information directly without going though a centralized organization. Several mesh networks utilize this model as well.

MILE Working Group

In addition to the Oasis Suite, another set of data standards is actively maintained and updated by the Managed Incident Lightweight Exchange (MILE) Working Group, which includes the following:

Incident Object Definition and Exchange Format (IODEF)
> RFC 5070 (*https://www.ietf.org/rfc/rfc5070.txt*), first published in 2007, defines IODEF as "a data representation that provides a framework for sharing information commonly exchanged by Computer Security Incident Response Teams (CSIRT) about computer security incidents." IODEF is an XML-based standard, and is used by groups such as the anti-phishing working group and ArcSite. It includes tags for sensitivity and confidence level. Figure 7-2 shows an example of the IODEF format capturing information on scanning from the original RFC.

```
        <Description>Source of numerous attacks</Description>
      </System>
    </Flow>
    <!-- Expectation class indicating that sender of list would like
         to be notified if activity from the host is seen -->
    <Expectation action="contact-sender" />
  </EventData>
  <EventData>
    <Flow>
      <System category="source">
        <Node>
          <Address category="ipv4-net">192.0.2.16/28</Address>
        </Node>
        <Description>
          Source of heavy scanning over past 1-month
        </Description>
      </System>
    </Flow>
    <Flow>
      <System category="source">
        <Node>
          <Address category="ipv4-addr">192.0.2.241</Address>
        </Node>
        <Description>C2 IRC server</Description>
      </System>
    </Flow>
    <!-- Expectation class recommends that these networks
         be filtered -->
    <Expectation action="block-host" />
  </EventData>
  </Incident>
</IODEF-Document>
```

Figure 7-2. IODEF scanning event

Real-time Inter-network Defense (RID)

Just as STIX has TAXII to facilitate the exchange of information in STIX format, IODEF and IODEF-SCI have RID. The goal of RID is to allow different organizations with incident data to share that information in a secure, easy-to-manage fashion. RID is defined in RFC 6545 (*https://tools.ietf.org/html/rfc6545*), and RID over HTTPS is defined in RFC 6546 (*https://tools.ietf.org/html/rfc6546*). Similar to TAXII, RID has several options for information-exchange models, including direct peer-to-peer and mesh peer-to-peer and client-to-subscriber.

IODEF—Structured Cybersecurity Information (IODEF-SCI)

This extension to IODEF provides a framework for capturing additional context around incident data. RFC 7203 (*https://tools.ietf.org/html/rfc7203*) defines the standards for IODEF-SCI and was first published in 2014. IODEF-SCI provides a structure for embedded additional contextual information into IODEF documents, including Mitre's Common Attack Pattern Enumeration and Classification (CAPEC), Common Vulnerabilities and Exposures (CVE), Common Vulnerabilities Scoring System (CVSS), and several other standards.

OpenIOC

As we discussed previously, the term *IOC*, or indicator of compromise, was popularized by Mandiant. In addition to coining the term, Mandiant developed a standard for capturing IOCs, which is called OpenIOC. *OpenIOC* is an XML-based schema (you may have picked up on a trend here) that is designed to capture and categorize forensic artifacts from compromised hosts as well network indicators related to malicious communications or other malicious activity. Mandiant identified over 500 possible artifacts that can be documented using OpenIOC. However, the framework also allows for customization and the creation of new fields as needed by organizations using OpenIOC. OpenIOC is interoperable with STIX (*https://github.com/STIXProject/openioc-to-stix*), and documentation has been published on how to transfer between the two standards.

 You will likely find yourself needing to convert data from one standard to another as you share and receive both threat data and intelligence. It is important to be aware of the various fields and components of the standards, because as you move between them (for example, from STIX to OpenIOC), you could lose or gain certain data fields. If you are unaware of the differences between the standards, you may find yourself searching for something that you *know* you had captured, but did not make it across in the conversion. When converting from one data standard to another, be sure to identify the important fields within the current standard, and then identify the equivalent field in the standard to which it will be converted.

Data Standards and Formats for Strategic Information

As we mentioned earlier, indicators that can be captured using the preceding formats are only half of the picture that you want to capture. Indicators are extremely useful for detection and response, but it is also important to gather other contextual information that will support strategic analysis. Although that information can be stored by using formats such as STIX, standards for capturing technical information are not often the best fit. Often such information ends up being stored in documents or PowerPoint slides, if it is captured at all. Not as many options exist for storing strategic information as for storing technical information, but frameworks can be utilized to avoid losing this critical component of incident information. We will explore two of the primary standards for storing strategic information: VERIS and CAPEC.

VERIS

The Vocabulary for Event Recording and Incident Sharing (VERIS) is a JSON-based standard that is well-known for supporting the Verizon Data Breach Incident Report (DBIR). The VERIS framework captures information that falls into four categories, known as the Four A's: Actor, Asset, Action, and Attribute, all of which answer a question about the incident:

Actor
> The Actor field answers the question, "Whose actions affected this asset?" This field captures high-level information about the actors responsible for an incident. The data schema enumerations for Actor include whether the actor is an internal, external, or partner actor, as well as the actor's motivation.

Action
> The Action field answers the question, "What actions affected the asset?" Action includes things such as how the attackers were able to get access, including the use of malware, hacking, or social engineering. It also includes the specific vector, such as exploiting a known vulnerability, or using phishing emails.

Asset
> This field answers the question, "Which assets were affected?"—an incredibly important question to answer from a strategic perspective. The enumerations include information about the type of asset affected, as well as information about its accessibility and management.

Attribute
> The Attribute field answers the question, "How was the asset affected?" It uses the traditional Confidentiality, Integrity, Availability triad.

VERIS also captures information about the timeline and impact of an incident. These fields provide places to capture how long it took to identify, contain, and remediate an incident and how severe the impact is for the organization affected.

The primary use case for VERIS is not generating rules or alerts, but for helping organizations understand the risks that they face. Therefore, the information is not as detailed nor as technical as the information that is captured in STIX or the formats that we mentioned previously. However, it can be used to tell a more complete story of what happened in a particular incident.

CAPEC

The Common Attack Pattern Enumeration and Classification (CAPEC) framework was originally designed to help with the development of secure software. The concept behind CAPEC is that if software developers were able to understand the common ways in which attackers targeted and exploited software, they would be able to design and build software that is not susceptible to those attacks. Rather than just capturing specific technical details, CAPEC attempts to capture the entirety of an attack as an attack pattern, which includes information on attack prerequisites, related weaknesses, related vulnerabilities, and attacker steps.

An organization can learn a great deal from an attack when a clear picture of what happened is available and is captured in CAPEC. An analysis of attack patterns over time can provide an understanding of the way attackers operate, the way they adapt to security measures, and any additional measures required to protect an organization.

Managing Information

Managing information does not simply involve capturing the individual indicators of compromise or artifacts from an investigation. A great deal of additional information needs to be captured as well so that you know how to manage and handle all the types of information moving forward.

Some key things are critical to capture in order to help manage information:

Date
> When was this piece of data or information seen? This will help with analysis as well as support expiration or retirement of data, essentially determining when data is still good to act on and include in analysis and when that data is no longer valid.

Source
> Few things are more frustrating than not knowing when and where a piece of information came from. Capturing the source of the information will help if you ever need to go back to get more information or if you want to assign the confidence of that piece of information, both of which will be useful during the analysis phase.

Data-handling information
> Often data will need to be handled differently based on the sensitivity and the source. We recommend using DHS's Traffic Light Protocol, which dictates how information can be shared:
>
> - TLP White: Publicly available information that can be shared with anyone using any method.
> - TLP Green: Information that can be shared with peers and partners, but not using publicly available channels, such as posting it on a blog or tweeting it to journalists. Seriously, don't do that.
> - TLP Amber: This information can be shared with people within your organization, but not outside it, and not using public channels. If there are ever questions about who TLP: Amber information can be shared with, such as whether it can be shared with customers of a managed security service provider (MSSP), it is always best to reach out to the original source of the information to request clarification. This is *not* a situation where it's better to ask

forgiveness than to ask permission; information-sharing relationships can be damaged that way.

- TLP Red: This is extremely sensitive information, usually related to an ongoing incident or investigation. It should not be shared outside the specific recipient, not even within the recipient's organization, without prior approval. Often TLP Red information will be reclassified as Amber or Green once the situation has been resolved.

Duplicate data

It is important to make sure that you are not duplicating data by accidentally capturing the same incident data or threat report more than one time. However, at times you will receive the same information from more than one source, and when that happens, it is important to capture that. Receiving the same indicators from multiple places, such as from an internal investigation *and* from a threat report from the FBI can have serious implications; but if you are not able to capture the details around both sources, you can seriously hinder the analytic process, which you will be moving into next.

Keeping these things in mind as you begin to store and manage your data will make using and maintaining your data much easier.

Threat-Intelligence Platforms

As you can probably tell from our coverage of standards and the numerous requirements for managing all the information that you have exploited during an investigation, capturing and analyzing all of this information is no trivial task. A threat intelligence platform is often used to simplify that process and make gathering, storing, and searching this information easier.

A *threat-intelligence platform* (TIP) is a database and user interface specifically designed to handle threat information. Various types of threat intelligence platforms exist—some that specialize in information sharing, and some that focus on the storage and management of large quantities of IOCs. Most TIPs can ingest information in the tactical formats described earlier in the chapter, and capture the additional information needed to manage the information as well. Using a TIP will significantly reduce the amount of work that needs to be done in the Exploit phase of F3EAD. Several popular open source platforms are available, and a variety of commercial solutions as well. We will discuss those options next.

MISP

The Malware Information Sharing Platform (MISP) is a free option for managing malware-based threat data. MISP was created by a group of developers in conjunction with NATO's Computer Incident Response Capability (NCIRC). MISP includes a database with a user interface that enables organizations to store both technical and nontechnical information related to attacks in order to facilitate correlation and sharing of information on threats. MISP can export information in OpenIOC, plain text, CSV, MISP XML, and JSON formats so that it can be used to support intrusion detection and prevention. MISP also has a robust sharing capability enabling users to share with other MISP users or groups. You can get more information on MISP on GitHub (*https://github.com/MISP/MISP*).

CRITs

Collaborative Research into Threats (CRITS) is another open source tool for managing and sharing threat data. CRITs was developed by MITRE, and therefore was designed to work with STIX and TAXII. CRITs stores threat information and includes the ability to add confidence and severity to the indicators that have been captured. It integrates with TAXII services to facilitate sharing, and is therefore a good choice for many organizations that receive or exchange information with the government or other organizations using STIX/TAXII. CRITs can export data into CSV, STIX, and JSON formats. Information and documentation for installing and using CRITs can be found on GitHub (*https://github.com/crits/crits*).

YETI

Your Everyday Threat Intelligence (YETI) platform is a newer threat intelligence management tool that was released for public use in March of 2017 (Figure 7-3). YETI was designed to enable analysts to organize and analyze the various components of threat intelligence in one place. It supports observables, indicators of compromise, and TTPs, as well as general knowledge on threats. One of the great aspects of YETI is that in addition to storing information that you have already found about threats, it can also do some indicator enrichment, including domain resolution and WHOIS lookups, as well as any additional integrations you want to configure. YETI can ingest data from MISP instances, JSON feeds, XML feeds, and various malware sandboxes. YETI was specifically designed to support many challenges that threat-intelligence analysts have identified in recent years, and to be flexible, as many analysts often need the same information, but have different processes or workflows. YETI has a GitHub repository (*https://github.com/yeti-platform/yeti*) where you can find more information on installation as well as documentation.

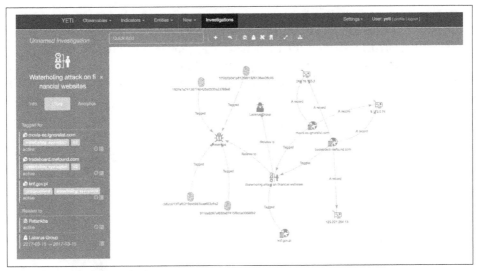

Figure 7-3. The YETI platform

Commercial solutions

A variety of commercial solutions are available for threat-intelligence management as well. Most of the commercial solutions include similar features to MISP, CRITs, and YETI, but also manage system configuration, take responsibility for setup and hardware management, and offer support for troubleshooting or feature requests. Commercial solutions can be ideal for organizations with limited development resources that want something easy to set up and maintain.

All of the threat-intelligence platforms, whether open source or commercial, have many of the same features and functionality, but may have been designed with a particular use case in mind, whether that is malware-based threat information, a specific information sharing, or supporting and enabling analytic processes. One of the best things about starting with open source threat-intelligence platforms is that you can find the best fit for your organization. If installation and support of the tools are a problem for your organization, you can explore several commercial solutions once you identify the best overall type of platform for your organization.

Conclusion

Information that is gained from an investigation should not be forgotten after the engagement is over—whether that investigation occurred at your own organization or happened somewhere else and you are fortunate enough to have access to the data. That information needs to be analyzed and disseminated so that organizations can learn and adapt to threats. Analysis and dissemination are not possible, however, without first going through the critical exploitation phase where information is gathered, processed into a usable format, and stored for analysis. As you learned in this chapter, you have many options for processing and storing this information, from the format it is stored in to the actual database it is kept in and the interface used to access it, so take time to explore your options and find a system or combinations of systems that will work well for you. Once the Exploit phase is completed, it will be much easier to move into the next phase of the F3EAD cycle: Analyze.

## CHAPTER 8

Analyze

"If you do not know how to ask the right question, you will discover nothing."

—W. Edward Deming

All of the information that you have gathered has been exploited and is now sitting—formatted and standardized—in a database or a threat-intelligence platform. So now what? The information sitting there does little good unless it is analyzed. The Analyze phase of F3EAD is one of the hardest to articulate but also one of the most important. The Analyze phase is where we take data and information and process it into intelligence. This chapter covers the basic principles of analysis, models such as target-centric and structured analysis, and processes to assign confidence levels and address cognitive biases.

The Fundamentals of Analysis

To properly analyze the information you have, you must go through another (thankfully, smaller) version of the intelligence cycle. You need to decide what your requirements are, or in other words, what questions you are going to answer. You need to collect the information that you will use to answer those questions. Most of that collection will come from the information you gathered throughout the investigation and collected and standardized in the Exploit phase, but other information will be needed to enrich or augment that information so it can be analyzed. Therefore, it may be necessary to continue to collect data as you move into the Analyze phase. The Analyze phase of F3EAD captures the entire intelligence cycle, pictured in Figure 8-1.

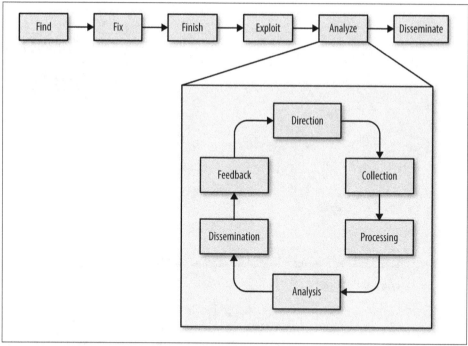

Figure 8-1. Analysis within F3EAD

During the response to the GLASS WIZARD intrusion, we identified domains and IP addresses that were used for command-and-control communications. That information helped us in the Fix and Finish stages, and will continue to help us as we analyze the intrusion, but in a different way. Rather than only identifying the technical details of the attack in order to respond and remediate, we can analyze those same domains and IPs to identify patterns that can be used to better understand the attacker's tactics. That involves gathering additional information about the domains and IPs, including who they were registered to and how the attacker used them, in order to determine whether patterns can be used to identify or predict future behaviors. This new information is then analyzed, intelligence gaps (critical pieces of information that are needed to conduct analysis) are identified, and more information is gathered as needed.

Case Study: The OPM Breach

One of the most significant breaches in recent history is the breach of the United State's Office of Personnel Management (OPM) (*http://bit.ly/2uI6oD1*), which resulted in the loss of personal, highly sensitive information about more than 20 million individuals who had undergone a background investigation for a security clearance. In addition to the size and sensitivity of the information that was stolen, the OPM breach is notable because of the multiple, missed opportunities for the attack to be identified and prevented. The intrusion was a complex campaign that spanned years and included the theft of IT manuals and network maps, the compromise of two contractors with access to OPM's networks, as well as OPM directly. Even when the individual intrusions were identified, no one connected the dots to identify that a larger threat needed to be addressed.

Even before the attackers began their campaign, opportunities existed to take what we know about attackers and how they operate and to identify that a government agency with access to highly sensitive, highly actionable personal information on every American with a security clearance was a high-value target for nation-state attackers.

The complete timeline of the breach is a lesson in how analysis, if done properly and in a timely fashion, can prevent or reduce the devastating impact of a successful campaign. It also shows just how bad it can be when incident responders, managers, and executives fail to connect the dots and see the bigger picture. The OPM breach was a classic and disheartening example of a failure to analyze, even when all of the information was available.

Unlike many traditional intelligence operations, in intelligence-driven incident response, many analysts are responsible for their own collection and processing, as well as analysis and dissemination. Using this model, the process of collection, analysis, and dissemination occurs as a subset of the overall intelligence cycle, with the process continuing until the questions that were posed during the requirements phase are properly addressed and the analysis is complete. The benefit of using the target-centric model in analysis is that it involves multiple check-ins between the various stakeholders involved in the process. It is especially beneficial to check in with the final recipients of the analysis, whether that is a CISO or a SOC analyst, to make sure that what is being analyzed and produced will meet their needs. There is nothing worse than conducting a lengthy analysis only to find that it is not what the target audience needed.

What to Analyze?

Conducting analysis is incredibly difficult if you do not know what you are trying to analyze. Often the thought of analysis conjures up images of someone standing in front of a wall with pictures and newspaper clippings haphazardly taped to it, waiting for that aha! moment when everything suddenly makes sense. Or maybe you think of the image of Newton sitting under a tree as an apple falls on his head, a simple (and over simplified) tale of an event that brings about sudden clarity, as everything you have been wondering about makes sense. Unfortunately, those are not methods that we can count on, although we do like to keep a wall of the house covered in newspaper clippings to scare the neighbors.

If your approach is to stare at all the data you have collected with the vague idea that you want to understand what it means, you will have a far more difficult time analyzing it than if you asked specific questions of the data, such as, "Why were we targeted?" or "How could this attack have been prevented?" You can certainly ask multiple questions of the information, and the questions can build on each other to increase your understanding of an attack and its implications—but without a starting point, most incident responders find it difficult to complete this phase of the process.

If you do not have specific requirements that are being analyzed for leadership or other internal teams, you can ask a standard set of questions that are helpful for analyzing each incident. However, some questions will always be unique to your organization or incident, so do not think of the following examples as the *only* things you should be analyzing. Here are some of the questions you can start with:

Why were we targeted?
> This question will provide a wealth of information on how to identify additional intrusions as well as how to protect your organization from future attacks. The nature of the attack, whether the attacker targeted integrity, confidentiality, or availability of your data, whether they used the attack to get access to third-party connected networks, and the actions they took after finding what they were looking for, can all provide insight into what you need to be looking for moving forward. Tactics and techniques may change, but an attacker's goals change far less frequently.

Who attacked us?
> This is often the first question that executives ask, but it is not the first question that we mention for a specific reason. Whatever it is that makes you a valid target for a specific criminal group may not be unique to that group; the same information may be targeted by another group with similar goals. Therefore, it's good not to focus exclusively on the group that you happened to catch this particular instance and lose sight of the overarching threats. Once you do understand their goals, however, it can be useful to understand more about the particular attackers. Analyzing information about attackers can include things such as the tactics they employ, what they target, how careful and cautious they were, what hours they operate, what infrastructure they use, whether it appears to be an individual or a group, and any other patterns that can be identified by analyzing the data.

How could this have been prevented?
> A significant goal of analysis is to understand what happened and why it happened so that it can be prevented in the future. When answering this question, you will focus on the things that went wrong within your own network. Were there unpatched vulnerabilities that the attacker exploited? Were there IDS alerts that were triggered but that no one looked into? Did a user reuse a password that had previously been leaked as part of an unrelated intrusion? This is not usually a

fun analysis to conduct, because no one likes to hear or see what they did wrong; but if your organization simply wipes a piece of malware from a system without understanding or addressing how it got there, then you will likely have to go through the whole incident-response process again, as the root cause was not identified or addressed.

How can this be detected?

This is where all of the delightful indicators you collected come into play. After the sometimes painful process of analyzing how you could have prevented the attack, it is nice to know that you can put things into place to prevent or detect future attacks. What you are able to do will depend greatly on the security systems that you have in place. While answering this question, it is important to focus on aspects that are unique to this particular attack, such as malware hashes and command-and-control IP addresses, as well as the aspects of the intrusion that are not as ephemeral, such as the systems that were targeted or the tactics utilized as the attackers moved through the network.

Are there any patterns or trends that can be identified?

This type of analysis is especially relevant when comparing internal incidents to incidents that have been reported either through information-sharing groups or through open source channels. When answering this question, you can attempt to identify patterns at various levels—from patterns related to targeting of organizations that may indicate a campaign, to patterns that identify reused or shared attack infrastructure, or patterns in social engineering avenues used by an attacker.

The output of the analysis that you conduct in this phase should enable action, whether that action is updating a threat profile, patching systems, or creating rules for detection. Focusing on the preceding questions and any other questions or requirements specific to your organization will help ensure that the work that you do in this phase will be able to cycle back into the operational phases of F3EAD.

Conducting the Analysis

As you go through the process of collecting information, you most likely subconsciously start to form a hypothesis about whatever question you are trying to answer, which is the beginning of analysis. Analysis involves taking all of the information you have and synthesizing and interpreting it in order to determine its meaning and ideally what should be done about it. In order for analytic judgements to be complete, accurate, and reproducible, it is best to follow a structured process to conduct your analysis.

Enriching Your Data

Throughout the incident-response and follow-up analysis process, we have focused primarily on indicators, whether they are host based or network based, that can be used to identify or detect attacks. We have mentioned an additional category of information that is required to conduct analysis: enrichment data.

Enrichment data contains additional details about an indicator that usually aren't used for detection, but for understanding more about a particular indicator and what it might mean if it is seen. Enrichment data can include things such as WHOIS, autonomous system number (ASN), website content, recent and historical domain resolutions, associated malware, and many other additional details. The point of enrichment data is to gather more context around an indicator you have already identified so that you can better interpret its meaning. In the Enrichment phase, you should focus on the patterns that emerge from the data rather than getting too caught up on one specific piece of information. One of the main reasons that many people end up with false positives and hundreds of thousands of indicators in block lists is that they take enrichment information and treat it as an indicator.

Enrichment sources

The types of enrichment data that will be used depends on the indicator you are investigating and your goals for the analysis. Most enrichment sources provide information that is beneficial for multiple use-cases, but some are specific, so make sure that you know what you are looking for before spending a significant amount of time digging into a particular enrichment source. With all enrichment sources, it is key to record the date that the data was identified, as it is likely to change in the future. There is nothing more frustrating than finding a piece of information that is key to your analysis, and not being able to identify when or how you found it after it changes again!

The following are some of the types and sources of enrichment information.

WHOIS information.   One of the most basic ways to get additional context and information about a domain or an IP address used in an attack is to get information about who registered or owns it. The WHOIS protocol, defined in RFC 3912 (*https:// tools.ietf.org/html/rfc3912*), was originally intended to pass additional information about the users of the original internet, ARPANET. You could originally get WHOIS information through a command-line query, and that functionality still works today, though additional resources are available now, including websites and tools to capture current and historical data.

WHOIS has gone through several updates, as the user base grew and the scope of the internet expanded greatly. Currently, WHOIS contains information on the registrant's name, email address, and additional contact information. WHOIS information can enrich analysis in several ways:

Tracking attacker infrastructure

Some (not all!) attackers reuse information when registering domains. By identifying a name or pseudonym used by a malicious actor, it may be possible to identify additional malicious domains related to the same attacker group.

Identifying compromised domains

In many cases, a legitimate domain may have been compromised and is being used by an attacker. Knowing the WHOIS information can help identify whether a domain is being run by an attacker or has just been compromised.

Identifying researcher-run infrastructure and sinkholes

Many researchers on the internet carry out activity that looks similar to attackers, but is used for research or identifying vulnerabilities before actual attackers do. In most cases, the IP addresses used for this research will be identified through the WHOIS record, which can prevent an analyst from spending too much time digging into a nonmalicious IP address.

Passive DNS information.   The original way that hosts on the internet were able to identify and communicate with each other was by using a single test file containing the names and IP addresses of all hosts. This file was aptly named *HOSTS.TXT* and was FTPed to all of the machines on the internet. This was a sustainable solution when a limited number of hosts were on the internet, as shown in Figure 8-2. However, it was difficult to maintain, and as the file grew, it took more and more bandwidth to transfer.

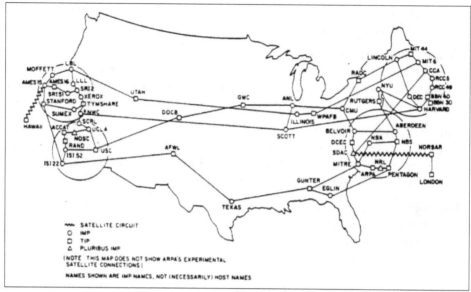

Figure 8-2. ARPANET

A more sustainable solution was developed, called the Domain Name System (DNS). It is essentially still a list of domains and hosts, but rather than a single file that is shared with everyone, the list exists on domain name servers that are queried when a host needs to look something up. The DNS is defined in RFC 1034 (*https://www.ietf.org/rfc/rfc1034.txt*) and 1035 (*https://www.ietf.org/rfc/rfc1035.txt*), and RFC 7719 (*https://tools.ietf.org/html/rfc7719*) released in 2015 defines modern DNS terminology. *Passive DNS*, originally called *Passive DNS Replication*, is a technique invented by Florian Weimer in 2004 as a way to gather and reconstruct information from the global DNS. The original use case identified in the paper "Passive DNS Replication (*http://bit.ly/2tNacPc*)" presented at the FIRST Conference in 2004 was the identification of domain names associated with botnet command-and-control IPs. Weimer noted that botnet C2 often uses multiple domain names rather than hardcoded IP addresses, and that these domains can resolve to multiple IP addresses, making filtering difficult. Identifying what IP address a domain resolved to at any given time, or vice versa, would require collecting the information ahead of time and storing it in a database so that it could be queried when needed.

Passive DNS provides an analyst with information on IP addresses and domains that were identified during an investigation. It can also provide information on the nature of the activity. Passive DNS information is especially useful when paired with WHOIS information to get a more complete picture of an indicator of compromise. Just remember that Passive DNS information, like WHOIS information, is not static, so make sure that you pay attention to the time frame.

Malware information. Information on malware can be extremely useful in analysis, and similar to Passive DNS information, many of the details around a piece of malware tend to change as time goes on and more information is discovered. Resources such as VirusTotal are living resources: the information changes as new entries are made, new detections are recorded, or users identify additional details around a sample. The following are examples of enrichment information on malware:

Detection ratio

> This number will change as time goes on and can be a useful indicator of the uniqueness of a sample that has been identified. When a sample first appears and is analyzed, the detection number, or the number of antivirus vendors who flag that sample as malicious, will be low. As time goes on, this number will increase.

File details

> This includes information that has been identified about a file, which is updated as more individuals or organizations analyze the sample. Even if you have conducted your own analysis of a particular malware sample, seeing what other analysis has been conducted can help to fill in any gaps you have and can also indicate how widespread the deployment is. It is helpful to know whether something has been used only against your network, or is being seen across many networks in several industries.

Malware behavior

> In addition to static information such as the hash of a malware sample, it is also possible to identify additional aspects of the malware's behavior, including where it installs, other files it calls or relies upon to execute, and any automated or scripted actions it takes upon execution. These details can help you understand other malicious activities you may find on your network and provide a glimpse into the sophistication of the attacker and whether the malware is unique or is a variant of a common malware family.

Internal enrichment information. Not all enrichment information comes from external sources. Internal enrichment information provides additional details on things such as compromised hosts, users, or accounts. Internal information to be aware of includes the following:

Business operations

> Knowing what is going on in your network and in your organization at the time of an incident can help answer questions about why you were targeted and why the attack was successful. Did you recently announce new partnerships? Were you involved in a new merger or acquisition? These are important details that can help you understand the nature of an attack and often can be obtained only by talking to people within your organization.

User information

Identifying which users were targeted or compromised can help you understand what information the attackers may have been after, if you have not already identified what was stolen. It can also provide information on the attacker's tactics; for example, if they initially target HR employees, and then attempt to move to a user with more access, such as a systems administrator.

Information sharing. Understanding when or if an indicator was previously identified can help put your particular incident into perspective. You should have identified some of this information during the Find phase, but it is useful to see what has changed or if any new information has been identified about any indicators that you are using in your analysis.

A good source of timely, nonpublic information of this nature is sharing relationships with other organizations. Public information is useful as well, and should be used in analysis; but information-sharing groups can provide details that often do not make it into the public domain, including specifics about when an indicator was seen, how it was identified, and what industry it was seen in. These are the types of details that many organizations do not want published but are often willing to share with partner organizations, especially when other organizations are sharing this sensitive information as well. There are formalized sharing groups, such as Information Sharing and Analysis Centers (ISACs), Information Sharing and Analysis Organizations (ISAOs), public/private partnerships, and informal groups. Many of the formal groups are arranged around industry or other shared interest groups. In some cases, information obtained from sharing groups can be used to detect malicious activity, but for the purpose of analyzing incidents, it can also be used as an enrichment source to help build out your understanding of the intrusion you are analyzing.

Once all information has been evaluated and enriched, it is time to move on to the next step: developing a hypothesis.

Developing Your Hypothesis

At this stage, we begin to get into the actual analysis, which begins with clearly stating your hypothesis. As mentioned, you usually begin to come up with some working answers to your question during the collection process. At the hypothesis development phase, you begin to document those working answers, no matter how speculative or far-fetched they are; the rest of the analytic process will weed out the obviously incorrect ideas. Make sure that when you document your ideas, you write them as fully as possible; and if specific information was found during collection, make sure to note what it was. This will help with evaluating the hypothesis further down the road. If you cannot clearly articulate an idea, or you discover that it is too vague or doesn't answer the question that you are asking, then it is not a good working idea, and you can move on to the next possible hypothesis.

In the case of our GLASS WIZARD intrusion, the first thing we want to understand is whether we were specifically targeted. Everything we have seen from this adversary indicates that they are a sophisticated threat group that is deliberate in their targeting, but we want to analyze the data we have to confirm that we were targeted. Our hypothesis, based on the information we gathered during the investigation and internal enrichment data about who at our company was targeted, is that this was in fact a targeted attack aimed at obtaining information on energy technologies. This hypothesis is specific and is based on our research, but it still needs to be verified by going through the rest of the structured analytic process.

Over the course of your career, developing a hypothesis will become easier for several reasons. First, many incidents have similarities, and it will become easier to identify indications of a particular behavior. While this can cut down on the time it takes to carry out the analytic process, it is important to not assume that this answer is correct; it is still just a hypothesis! Make sure that you go through the rest of the process even when the answer seems obvious, and make sure that you account for assumptions and biases, which we will discuss next.

The second reason that hypothesis development becomes easier is that after many iterations of this process as you step through numerous investigations, the mind often becomes more creative and less concerned when generating possible answers. After working through the analytic process and becoming comfortable with the fact that bad ideas *will* be identified and weeded out, an analyst can explore all possible ideas, often coming up with new ideas that they would not have identified before.

Regardless of how easy or difficult it is to generate your hypothesis, when you have a working hypothesis, the next step in the process is to evaluate the assumptions upon which that hypothesis is based so that you can move into the judgement and conclusion stage aware of and accounting for your biases.

Evaluating Key Assumptions

A *key assumption* is any part of a hypothesis that relies on a preexisting judgment or belief. Before continuing with the analysis, teams or individuals should take a few minutes or a few hours to identify these key assumptions and determine whether they are valid and should contribute to the analysis. For example, if an analyst has developed a hypothesis about how a particular attack could have been prevented, it is based on an assumption of how the attack was carried out, which would have been identified during the Find, Fix, and Finish phases. It should be relatively easy to evaluate whether that assumption is correct, but it should still be documented and discussed to make sure that all analysts have the same understanding of the information that contributed to the hypothesis.

The CIA's Tradecraft Primer (*http://bit.ly/2vrrGmm*) outlines how to conduct a key assumptions check and the multiple benefits of going through this process. These benefits include developing an understanding of the key issues that contribute to a hypothesis, identifying faulty logic, and stimulating discussions among analysts. The process for evaluating key assumptions is as follows:

1. Identify all key assumptions about a situation or hypothesis.
2. Identify why the assumption was made.
3. Assess the confidence in the assumption.
4. Identify how the confidence rating was determined.
5. Challenge each assumption and determine whether it is true and remains true for the current situation.
6. Remove any assumptions that are not true or that have a low confidence; these should not be used in the analysis.

Our hypothesis that the GLASS WIZARD intrusion targeted us specifically is based on several assumptions. First, we are assuming that the actor who targeted us is GLASS WIZARD. This is a key assumption, and it is made based on the fact that the information we obtained on the actor matched what we found in our network, including tactics, techniques, technical indicators, and targeting. We are confident in the accuracy of this assumption, based on the technical details and the timing. We are aware that additional information, especially information regarding deception activities on the part of the attacker, may change this assumption, and we will be prepared to change our analysis if any new information of that nature is identified.

Assumptions are not always easy to evaluate, and include things such as cognitive biases, which are logical fallacies or flaws in thinking that can easily cloud an analyst's judgment. It is not possible to completely remove biases from analysis.

Accounting for biases

Richard Heuer, one of the fathers of intelligence and the author of *The Psychology of Intelligence Analysis* (Military Bookshop, 2010) describes *cognitive biases* as "various simplifying strategies and rules of thumb to ease the burden of mentally processing information to make judgments and decisions." Cognitive biases are essentially shortcuts that our minds develop so that we do not have to go through the entire analytic process for every minute decision we make in our lives. A basic example is a child who complains of being cold, and whose parents immediately told him to put on a sweater. Years later, whenever that (now grown) child feels cold, he has the thought to put on a sweater. He probably also tells his children to put on a sweater. His mind does not have to run through the entire process of developing a hypothesis. (Maybe a hat would be best? Perhaps an extra pair of socks?) Testing and judging that hypothesis (clearly two pairs of socks are not enough) and coming up with a conclusion. He can simply shortcut to something that his mind tells them is an appropriate response to the situation.

Cognitive biases aren't always bad, and they do save a lot of time, but in intelligence analysis they can have a negative influence by causing an analyst to make assumptions and jump to faulty judgments. Another example of a cognitive bias at work is the use of previously identified malware, such as Poison Ivy, in the GLASS WIZARD intrusion. An analyst who has heard or experienced several instances where sophisticated attackers used sophisticated, previously unseen malware, may automatically generate the assumption that this actor is *not* sophisticated. In this instance, they would be using a cognitive bias called *anchoring* that lets one piece of evidence override any other piece of evidence without a sound analytic judgement.

Many types of biases exist. Here is an overview of some that are commonly seen in intelligence analysis and incident response.

Confirmation bias. With confirmation biases, we tend to seek out or focus on evidence that supports our preexisting judgment or conclusion. If, in the back of our minds, we think that we are going to find evidence of a specific type of activity, any evidence that seems to support that conclusion will be given more weight than something that disproves or questions that judgment. In the GLASS WIZARD scenario, we may have run into the issue of an analyst who thinks that the attacker was *not* a sophisticated actor because of the use of old malware. That same analyst may also identify the use of password-guessing techniques, also used by less-sophisticated actors, to prove this assumption. This judgment would require the analyst to ignore the historical cases where sophisticated actors also used password guessing, or give them less weight. Confirmation bias is one of the primary reasons that it is important to go through the exercise of evaluating key assumptions prior to coming to a final judgment.

Anchoring bias. In anchoring bias, analysts tend to become overreliant or give more weight to the first piece of information that they hear. Any subsequent information or evidence is compared to that initial piece of evidence, and the analyst often unconsciously debates whether the new evidence supports or refutes the first piece, making that first piece of information central to the investigation. If analysts were told going into the process of analyzing an intrusion that "we think it was Russia," then each piece of evidence will influence their interpretation of whether it was Russia, when that really is not the question that the analysts were meant to answer. Anchoring bias is one of the reasons that some experts such as Robert M. Lee (*http://www.robertm lee.org/tag/attribution/*) say that true attribution (attribution to a particular government or nation-state) makes it more difficult for analysts to do their job because that attribution becomes the anchor that they base their judgments off of. Again, going through the process of focusing on the requirements and what question is actually being asked, developing a hypothesis, and evaluating key assumptions should help an analyst account for and counteract anchoring bias.

Availability bias. In availability bias, there is an overemphasis on the information that is available, whether or not that information has itself been analyzed. Richard Heuer calls this bias the Vividness Criterion, which means that information that you personally experience or are most familiar with will become more important than information you are not as familiar with. It has also been referred to as the "I know a guy" bias, as in, "I know a guy who smoked a pack of cigarettes a day and lived to be 100; therefore, smoking can't be that bad for you." A newer version of the "I know a guy" bias is the "I saw it on the internet" bias.

Incident responders and intelligence analysts in particular need to be aware of this bias because this is what allows their previous experience to hurt rather than help them. If they focus on particular pieces of evidence that they are most familiar with because they have seen it before, then they may give that one thing too much weight or discount other pieces of evidence that they are not as familiar with.

Bandwagon effect. Bandwagoning occurs when an assumption seems more likely to be true as more people agree with it. Although there is something to be said for group consensus after a piece of evidence has been analyzed, the bias comes into play when this judgment occurs prior to analysis, or when the fact that others support the assumption becomes a basis for believing that assumption is true. There is some interesting psychological reasoning with bandwagoning, and it can therefore be hard to overcome, but it is important to note that "because everyone says so" is not a valid justification for an assumption to be labeled as accurate. If there is evidence to back up a group consensus, it is important to look at the evidence rather than the fact that everyone is in agreement.

Heuer also refers to an "oversensitivity to consistency" and writes that, "Information may be consistent only because it is highly correlated or redundant, in which case many related reports may be no more informative than a single report." To overcome this, Heuer recommends that analysts ensure that they are familiar with the body of evidence that previous analysis is based on, including the sample size and the information available, and question whether the same, consistent conclusion would likely continue with a larger sample size or the availability of more information. This is especially helpful with media reporting of an attacker. Multiple media reports may all be based on a single incident, so just because there are multiple reports does not mean that there were multiple incidents.

Mirroring. Mirroring, or mirror-image bias, occurs when an analyst makes the assumption that a target being studied thinks like the analyst and therefore would make the same decisions as the analyst would. This leads to an analyst making assumptions about what an adversary would or wouldn't do based on the analyst's own personal experiences, which are often completely different from those of the target. Instead of using the evidence to guide judgments, an analyst suffering from this bias uses her own opinions of what would have been a logical step, or "what I would have done" to determine whether an assumption is correct. Mirroring is often used during the generation of working ideas; but during the Evaluation phase, it is important to identify when mirroring, rather than evidence, is the basis of an assumption and remove that bias from the analysis.

Judgment and Conclusions

After the assumptions around evidence that supports a hypothesis have been evaluated and biases accounted for, the analyst can move toward making their judgment and conclusion about the hypothesis. Analysts can use several methods to interpret the evidence and identify whether a hypothesis is likely to be true or not, or whether they need to generate a new hypothesis either in part or in its entirety.

Analytic Processes and Methods

As we discovered with the use of models such as the kill chain and the diamond model, data is often better handled when we have a process or a method that we are applying to it. The processes and methods described in this section are common approaches to analysis and can be used on their own or combined.

Structured Analysis

Structured analysis is similar to the scientific method that forms the basis of many elementary-school science projects. You ask a question, do some basic background research, formulate a hypothesis, test or evaluate whether that hypothesis is accurate, and either report the findings or develop a new hypothesis if the original one did not prove to be accurate. The basic scientific method is pictured in Figure 8-3.

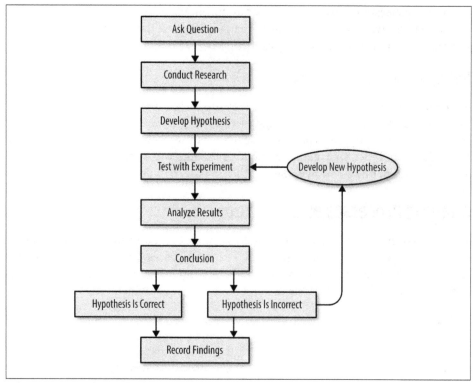

Figure 8-3. Scientific method diagram

Structured analysis takes this same general approach. However, the testing and evaluation of the hypothesis is not always as clear-cut as it is when conducting physical experiments. When performing intelligence analysis, it becomes critical to identify and evaluate key assumptions that have been made on the topic, which often involves identifying biases. After those key assumptions have been evaluated, several methods can be used to determine whether the hypothesis is accurate or likely, including conducting an analysis of competing hypotheses, which weighs various hypotheses against each other. Because analysis does not involve a definite yes or no answer and is instead based on of the analyst's interpretation of information, is it also important to add a step to assign a confidence to a likely hypothesis. Figure 8-4 shows the basic process for structured analysis.

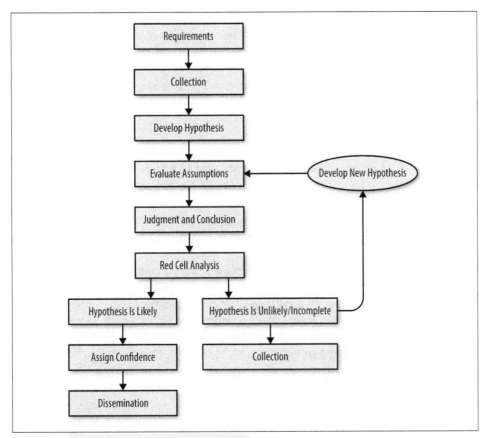

Figure 8-4. The structured analysis process.png

Here is an overview of each step of the structured analysis process:

1. Determine what question you are going to answer, ideally using specific requirements from your leadership. You can conduct multiple iterations of structured
   analysis in order to answer multiple questions present through requirements; but
   just as you do not try to test multiple variables within a single experiment, it is
   best not to try to answer several questions with the same analysis. Even if the
   processes are only slightly different, it is best to keep them separate to avoid
   clouding your judgment or contaminating your conclusions.
2. Collect data to ensure that you have all the information that you need to generate
   a hypotheses or multiple hypothesis to answer your question. This involves going
   through the information you gathered from the investigation as well as collecting
   additional enrichment information, and making sure that there is nothing else
   that you need.

3. Develop a hypothesis or a set of hypotheses that will be evaluated. In some cases, the hypothesis will seem clear, but in others it will seem like you are grasping at straws when trying to answer the questions of why you were targeted or what the long-term implications of a campaign are. Regardless of the situation, document your thoughts and work through the process of evaluating those hypotheses.

4. Evaluate key assumptions. This step deviates from the traditional scientific method. Because we are not dealing with factors that are readily measured or assessed, it is important to identify how our own thoughts or opinions about the various pieces of evidence may influence our analysis. It is easy to find qualitative evidence to support a hypothesis that you want to be true. To avoid this, we add this extra step to identify biases and ensure that the key assumptions around your analysis are sound.

5. You have enough evidence to make a judgment about your hypothesis. There are various methods to evaluate this, which we will go into in further detail later in the chapter.

6. Once a judgment has been made into hypothesis, you enter the next step of the structured analysis process: red cell analysis. In wargaming, the opponent or adversary was often depicted with the color red, and the friendly team with the color blue. The term *red team* means to think like an adversary or to challenge the position of the blue team. Red cell analysis provides an opportunity for the judgment to be evaluated and questioned, ideally by a third party.

7. If, after the red cell analysis, you determine that your hypothesis is not likely, you will need to go back and generate a new hypothesis, using the evidence you identified that negated the original hypothesis. You do not have to start over from scratch each time, and you will constantly learn more as you work through the process. Even if you determine that your hypothesis is likely correct, you will have to determine how confident you are in that assessment and document why you have assigned it that confidence. After that is done, you have completed your analysis and are ready to move onto the next question you need to answer.

Target-Centric Analysis

In the book *Intelligence Analysis, a Target-Centric Approach* (CQ Press, 2003), Robert Clark describes the traditional intelligence cycle as an attempt to give a linear structure to a decidedly nonlinear process, and introduces target-centric analysis as an alternative approach.

An example of the target-centric intelligence analysis process is shown in Figure 8-5.

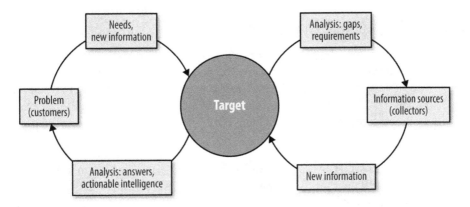

Figure 8-5. Target-centric intelligence analysis (http://bit.ly/2uPX9Sk)

At the center of target-centric analysis is the target model, also known as a conceptual model. A *conceptual model* is an abstraction of an analyst's thought process and describes what is being analyzed in as much detail as possible. A conceptual model can detail the hierarchy or structure of a criminal organization, or can describe the timeline of a network intrusion.

Once the conceptual model has been developed, we begin the process of understanding, based on the model that was developed, the answers we have, and the answers we still need. The answers we have take the form of *actionable intelligence*, intelligence that can be acted on or can answer questions. That intelligence is evaluated by the customer, or whoever will be using it; and if more or new information is needed, the model is updated, and we move back through the collection and analysis process again.

Target-centric analysis does not make the assumption that analysts step through the analytic process using a one-thing-at-a-time approach, but rather follow an iterative process, where information is gathered, analyzed to see whether it helps answer the questions presented, and occasionally ends up generating new requirements. If more or different information is needed, the collection and processing phases are reengaged, ensuring that all the necessary information is available to the analyst.

Analysis of Competing Hypotheses

Analysis of Competing Hypotheses, or ACH, is a method developed by Richard Heuer that is used to evaluate multiple, alternate hypotheses and identify the most likely hypothesis based on the evidence. ACH is an eight-step process that aims to force an analyst to look at all possibilities rather than to identify a hypothesis based on intuition and look for evidence that supports that hypothesis. The eight steps are as follows:

1. Identify the possible hypotheses to be considered. Heuer recommends using a group of analysts with different backgrounds and different perspectives to brainstorm the possibilities. It is also important to differentiate between an unproven hypothesis and a disproven hypothesis during this step. An *unproven* hypothesis is one where there is no evidence that it is correct, whereas a *disproven* hypotheses is one where there is evidence that the hypothesis is incorrect. Include an unproven hypothesis, no matter how improbable, in the ACH process, but do not include disproven hypotheses.

2. Make a list of significant evidence for and against each hypothesis. If you have already gone through the process of evaluating key assumptions, this step should be relatively simple; you already have the key pieces of evidence that contribute to the various hypotheses.

3. Create a matrix with hypotheses across the top and evidence down the side and evaluate whether each piece of evidence supports or refutes each hypothesis. See Figure 8-6 for an example of this matrix. There are several approaches to filling out the matrix. Richard Heuer suggests listing whether each piece of evidence is consistent with the hypothesis by putting a *C*, if it is inconsistent with the hypothesis by putting an *I* or if it is neutral or not applicable, in which case you would put *N/A*. Others suggest using a weighing scale such as a plus sign (+) if a piece of evidence moderately supports a hypothesis or two plus signs (++) if it strongly supports a piece of evidence, and so forth.

Figure 8-6. ACH matrix template

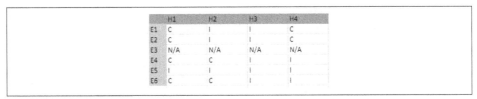

	H1	H2	H3	H4
E1	C	I	I	C
E2	C	I	I	C
E3	N/A	N/A	N/A	N/A
E4	C	C	I	I
E5	I	I	I	I
E6	C	C	I	I

Figure 8-7. Completed ACH matrix

In the matrix in Figure 8-7, we can see that H3 is not supported by any piece of evidence, and therefore would be removed from the matrix. Likewise, E3 is not applicable to any of the hypotheses, and E5 is inconsistent with every hypothesis, so the analyst would need to go back and reevaluate those pieces of evidence to make sure that they are both relevant to the analysis and are accurate. It is possible for a flawed or biased piece of evidence to make it through the evaluation stage, and this is another opportunity to identify whether something should be considered in the analysis.

4. Conduct initial analysis to refine the matrix. After step 3, the matrix should show a few things: some hypotheses may have Inconsistent (I or -) assessments for every piece of evidence. Although this doesn't disprove a hypothesis, if there is no evidence to support it, then it should be removed from the matrix (see Figure 8-7). Similarly, if a piece of evidence has an N/A assessment for each hypothesis, the analyst should either remove it from the matrix, or if it truly is a key piece of evidence, should reevaluate whether there is another hypothesis that needs to be considered.

One thing that incident responders may run into from time to time is evidence from a separate, unrelated intrusion ending up in the analysis, simply because it was identified around the same time as the other evidence. When something does not match up with any other evidence, it may be best to remove it from the current analysis and analyze it on its own.

5. Draw initial conclusions about the likelihood of each hypothesis. Focus on disproving the hypotheses rather than proving them to be correct. After the matrix has been initially refined, you can evaluate the likelihood of each hypothesis based on how much of the evidence supports it. In the example in Figure 8-7, H1 has the most supporting evidence, and if it is deemed by the analyst that E5 is not a valid piece of information, then there is no evidence that contradicts this hypothesis. H1 would therefore be considered the most likely hypothesis. H2 and H4 both have evidence that supports them and that is inconsistent with them; therefore, they are less likely. If any of the evidence that was marked as inconsis-

tent proves that those hypotheses are incorrect, they would be considered disproven hypotheses. It is easier to disprove a hypothesis than it is to prove that a
hypothesis is absolutely true.

6. Analyze how much of your conclusion is dependent on a single piece of evidence.
Re-analyze the information that led to your judgment of the most likely hypothesis or led to a hypothesis being disproven. Was there a single piece of evidence
that weighed most heavily? If so, how confident are you in that piece of evidence?
This will help determine the overall confidence in a judgment. If multiple pieces
of evidence from various sources strongly support a hypothesis, there will be
higher confidence in the assessment than if the judgment was based on one or
two key pieces of information from a single source.

7. Report your conclusions on the likelihood of all the hypotheses, not just the most
likely one. It is important to record and report all the hypotheses that were considered, as well as the evidence that led to the final judgement. This is especially
important if the analysis is going to go through a red cell analysis process, which
we will discuss later in this chapter. It can also help to identify whether the analysis needs to be reevaluated if new information is provided, which brings us to the
final step of the ACH process.

8. Identify situations in which the analysis would need to be reevaluated. Richard
Heuer writes that all analysis should be considered tentative, and that it is always
possible for new evidence to be presented that will require a new analysis. If any
intelligence gaps are identified or any information that you know is currently
missing but has the potential to change the judgment, these should be documented to assist in future analysis. An example in the GLASS WIZARD intrusion
would be the addition of information from another organization that experienced a similar intrusion, or information that the attacker's activity was detected
in the future due to additional security measures that were put in place. In those
situations, you would have access to new log information. If either of these things
happened, we would need to revisit the judgment.

Graph Analysis

In many cases, developing a hypothesis or evaluating evidence requires additional
analysis. In some situations, that analysis is best done visually, such as when you are
looking for patterns or relationships in a large amount of information. In situations
like this, graph analysis can be useful. Graphs are also especially useful when analyzing social networks or interactions between groups.

Graph analysis has several other names, often with only slight differences. Association matrices, social network analysis, and link analysis are all names to describe a
similar process. Social network analysis is used widely across the intelligence community as well as law enforcement agencies, because of the importance of understanding
the relationships between groups, whether they are carrying out terrorist attacks or

conducting criminal operations. This type of analysis can be useful for tracking cyber actors as well, as they often rely on others for logistics or support, or may work with different groups or teams as required. However, people and relationships are not the only thing can be analyzed with graphs.

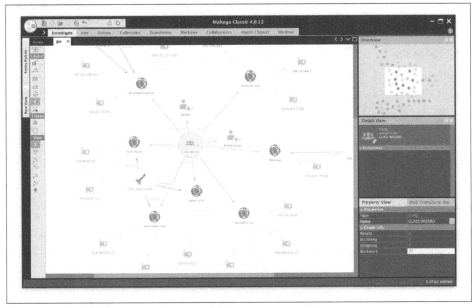

Figure 8-8. Graph Analysis of GLASS WIZARD using Maltego

In intelligence-driven incident response, an analyst is usually looking at activity related to machines or malware, rather than individuals. In the GLASS WIZARD intrusion, graph analysis can be used to look at the relationships between hosts that had been compromised by the attacker. A graph analysis would show that many hosts communicated with an attacker's command control node only once or twice, and a smaller subset of hosts had repeated contact with multiple command control nodes. Those hosts could then be analyzed by using internal enrichment information to understand why the attackers seemed to be more interested in those machines. Graph analysis could also be used to identify the domains related to a piece of malware found as part of the investigation to better understand the attacker's behaviors.

In many cases, graph analysis is used to better understand evidence or to develop evidence, and something like ACH or a red cell analysis should still be used to validate a hypothesis that is supported by graph or social network analysis.

Contrarian Techniques

The final type of intelligence analysis to cover includes several methods that are considered to be *contrarian*, meaning they seek to go against the existing standards or norms by providing a different view of the situation. In some cases, the initial analysis is conducted using contrarian methods, whereas in others contrarian techniques are used to question an existing judgment to ensure the analysis stands up in all possible situations. This type of analysis is not required in every case, but is strongly recommended for analysis for which a wrong judgment would have serious consequences, or where the judgment is expected to be contested.

Devil's advocate

Devil's advocate is used to challenge a widely accepted analysis of a situation by taking an opposing viewpoint and evaluating whether the available evidence truly disproves the alternative point of view. The devil's advocate approach does not truly intend to prove that the alternative viewpoint is correct and the accepted analysis is wrong. Instead, it looks to expose any weaknesses in the original analysis, uncover any biases that were not accounted for, and help the original analysis stand up to intense scrutiny.

"What if" analysis

This type of analysis attempts to introduce new variables into the situation to see how that would change the analysis. For example, "What if this key piece of evidence is part of a deception campaign by the adversary?" or "What if this log data has been tampered with?" Again, this type of analysis does not attempt to directly disprove a hypothesis, and in fact can help with assessing confidence in an overall judgment by determining whether the analysis is sound even when certain pieces of intelligence are called into question. This technique can be useful in step 6 of the ACH process, as the analyst determines how much of the analysis relies on one or two pieces of evidence.

Red team analysis

This technique seeks to analyze how an adversary would think or act in the given situation. The analyst tries to put themselves in the mindset of the attacker and asks questions such as, "What is important to me in this situation?" and "What actions would cause me to deviate from the plan?" When conducting red team analysis, it is critical that an analyst take on an adversary's persona. This technique can help counter mirror-imaging or mirroring bias by forcing an analyst to identify when an adversary's mind set would differ from their own. Red teaming helps to identify additional factors that an analyst may not have initially considered.

Red teaming is a well-known concept in the information security industry, and it is important to know that this type of analysis relies on an understanding of an adversary, including basing the decision on the adversary's social, political, and cultural tendencies, as opposed to some red team exercises that take a "just do whatever works" approach.

Conclusion

Analysis is often seen as an intuitive process: someone is either good at it or is not. This belief is not necessarily true. Sherlock Holmes certainly has natural talent when it comes to analyzing situations, but he still follows set processes, including accounting for biases, developing hypotheses, and using evidence to support or disprove those hypotheses. Analysts trying to answer specific questions about an incident or investigation follow a process as well. Although that process is not exactly the same in every instance—sometimes enrichment information is needed and ACH is conducted, and other times all the information is available and the analyst uses red teaming to evaluate a judgment—there *is* a process. Be flexible with your analysis, but be sure not to completely skip any of the steps; they are there to ensure that a sound analytic judgement is made based on the right information. After the analysis has been completed and a judgment made, it is time to decide how to best convey the finding to the appropriate audience.

## CHAPTER 9

Disseminate

"People tend to do one of two things with data: they hoard it, or they dump it on people."

—General Stanley McChrystal

"Tell me what you know. Tell me what you don't know. And then…tell me what you think…I will hold you accountable."

—Secretary of State Colin Powell, September 13, 2004, Intelligence Reform Hearing

At some point, the investigation needs to end, or at least pause, long enough to create outputs useful to other teams or organizations. We call the process of organizing, *publishing*, and sharing developed intelligence *dissemination*. This is a skill set unto itself and, just like any other skill, has processes and takes time to develop. Good intelligence can be ruined by poor dissemination. Although writing up something after hours of analysis may seem unimportant, it's worth the time for any intelligence team to focus and build their skills disseminating information.

Dissemination is such an important skill that in larger intelligence teams, resources may be dedicated just to the dissemination phase. These dissemination-focused analysts need the following:

- A strong understanding of the overall process and importance of the information they're sharing.
- A firm grasp of the types and needs of stakeholders that the intelligence will be going to.
- A disciplined and clear writing style. (Intelligence writing is a little different from typical narrative writing; we'll get into that later in this chapter.)

- An eye toward operational security to protect the valuable intelligence products and materials.

No matter how your team is set up, from a dual-hat CERT analyst and intelligence analyst up to large dedicated teams, it's important to develop processes for writing and editing and to practice them regularly. Dissemination, and the written output (known as *intelligence products*) that result from it, can only be as good as the analysis they're based on. In addition, bad intelligence product development can render good analysis useless.

This chapter covers building intelligence products for distribution within your organization. We'll focus on making these audience focused and actionable through building effective writing structure and process.

Intelligence Consumer Goals

Understanding intelligence consumer needs is all about understanding the consumer's goals. Usually, this is accomplished by contemplating the audience (we'll get to that next) and their needs. These two aspects define almost everything else about the product, from tone to structure to time frame. *Understanding the goals for an intelligence product is all about what the stakeholder can expect to get out of the product.* For example, here's a common goal: inform SOC on new actor TTP. This indicates the need for a shorter-form tactical product aimed at a highly technical audience (a.k.a. a target package).

The intelligence team needs to figure out what kind of product will help the consumer achieve their goal. That's why it can be helpful to start your planning by explicitly stating the consumer's goal for the product. This is especially useful when building a product with a team. A stated goal (a mission statement, if you will) can provide a common vision.

Audience

Also known as *consumers*, the *audience* is tied directly into the goal of any intelligence product. The execution of the goal is intrinsically tied to the stakeholders you're writing a product for. Every intelligence writer and team must develop an understanding of the audience they're writing for, as this understanding leads directly to creating useful and actionable products. This is never a one-time exercise, as teams you're writing for change, evolve, and learn.

For instance, an organization may have a highly technical CEO who can digest highly technical reports and revels in disassembly. That can drastically change the approach an intelligence team takes. Understanding your audience allows you to anticipate questions and needs more effectively. Executive teams will hear a topic and have a completely different set of questions than SOC analysts.

Although every situation and every consumer is a bit different, a few common threads exist. Common consumer types include executives or leadership, internal technical consumers, and external technical consumers. We will explore them in more detail next.

Executive/Leadership Consumer

For many analysts, the most intimidating audience to present to or provide an intelligence product for is executive leadership, either the C-suite or board of directors. In large part, this is due to the authority such leadership has and the fact that major leadership briefings often happen as a result of severe circumstances such as a major breach or threat. The stakes are almost always high.

Quantifying the Unquantifiable

Writing about intelligence, especially about strategic topics, for executive/leadership consumers, often means trying to quantify unquantifiable things. To do this, we need a language for describing abstract concepts in relative ways.

Thankfully, this is a problem that's been worked on before. The CIA Library has an excellent article with not just the answer, but also the process by which the intelligence community solved it, called Word of Estimative Probability (*http://bit.ly/2twTeth*). The CIA's result was a series of specific words, with precise meanings, to help describe certainty versus uncertainty.

Their words were as follows:

- Certainty: 100% chance
- Almost certain: 93% give or take about 6%
- Probable: 75% give or take about 12%
- Chances about even: 50% give or take about 10%
- Probably not: 30% give or take about 10%
- Almost certainly not: 7% give or take about 5%
- Impossibility: 0%

This provides a whole range that consumers can tie back to understandable, quantifiable percentages, while still being useful in prose and written intelligence. These words become key when they're used consistently and with understanding by your consumer. For instance, a group could decide to use the word *likely* instead of *probable* as long as the consumer understands how that term should be interpreted. If you don't stay consistent with your estimative words, you risk these estimates being confusing or even deceptive, instead of creating clarity.

As consumers, executive leadership is always a challenge. For one thing, every leadership team has a considerable range of skills and technical acumen. The same group can have former engineers and technicians turned leadership with deep technical skills alongside specialists from totally unrelated disciplines such as finance or human resources that while deeply skilled in their own areas are not always technical. These sorts of mixed audiences are often a challenge to target.

The following are common characteristics of C-suite executives:

- Deep knowledge in a specific area of expertise with above-average awareness of others (sometimes known as *T-shaped people* (*http://bit.ly/2tNwccZ*)). Although most C-level executives have one area of expertise, they have usually spent enough time around other fields (HR or finance, for example) to have more than a passing familiarity.
- They tend to be strategically focused above all else. If the executives are running a business, all decisions will focus on how to make or save money. If the organization is a non-profit, the focus above all else will be the mission.

 Although it's easy to write off a leadership team as nontechnical, many have done this at their peril. It's easy to forget that members of leadership may have gotten to their position as skilled engineers. It isn't unusual to stumble across a CEO or senior director who still knows their way around C code and understands key pieces malware disassembly code, or maybe just finished a masters in electrical engineering for fun (true story!). While assuming too much technical competency and drowning executives in jargon is bad, so is assuming no understanding.

The focus on your consumers goes deeper than just technical comprehension. Executive leadership, especially the C-suite, has specific focus areas of their own. A chief financial officer (CFO) is interested in threats to underlying finances of the company, expenses related to incidents (real or potential), and threats targeting the finance staff such as W-2 social engineering. Conversely, the chief technical officer (CTO) is probably not as concerned about W-2 theft attempts; after all, her staff probably doesn't have access to W-2s, but is likely to be concerned about distributed denial-of-service attacks, which would impact the technology department's function.

It is important to consider how a single intelligence product can speak to multiple aspects of the business. Above all, listen to your consumers. This is the feedback loop of the intelligence cycle we discussed in Chapter 2, when the final product is reviewed by the consumer and they share their insight. These insights can be about the intelligence itself, but it's important to also pay close attention to the consumer's response to formatting, process, and even wording. Taking these factors into account lets a team evolve their products and improve them with each new release.

When writing intelligence products for leadership, a few major characteristics make them most effective:

- Focus on intelligence necessary to make business decisions. Few executives, even the deeply technical ones, are highly interested in tactical intelligence. Their primary focus is on anything that will help them make better business-level decisions.
- Use intelligence to tell the story of the threat. There can be great value, if done correctly, in sharing relevant operational intelligence with leadership. The benefit of sharing operational intelligence, especially at the campaign level, comes in leveraging most humans' love of stories. Using operational intelligence makes it easier to share a narrative: good guys, bad guys, tools, and actions (think of the four corners of the diamond model, which we discussed in Chapter 3). The focus should still be on the strategic aspects, but the operational side can help support it with a powerful and relatable story.
- Keep it brief and to the point. In many cases, security is only one concern for this audience, and their time to focus on security is limited. Long reports may seem like they'll be impressive and thorough, but in most cases they'll end up sitting on a desk unread. This can be avoided with two techniques:
  - When in doubt, be brief. A well-written and dense one-page product is far more likely to be read in its entirety than 10% of a 50-page report.
  - Every product should start with an executive summary covering the most important points. It may be the only piece that gets fully read, so make it count.

Techniques like this are valuable to most consumers, not just leadership. Economy of language means the consumer can move more quickly to using the data instead of consuming it.

 It's easy to assume that your intel team is the single source of truth for your consumers. This is a dangerous assumption, especially with your board or executive team. In many organizations, these groups will engage outside resources and advisors. Be sure to keep this in mind when creating intelligence products. You should be prepared for a more in-depth critique than you might expect.

Internal Technical Consumers

For most analysts, the easiest consumer to write for is other analysts. This is largely because it's a persona we understand wholeheartedly: it's writing for ourselves. It's easy to make assumptions based on our personal ideas, preferences, and needs, but it's still important to treat analysts, even if you are one, as important intelligence product consumers with their own needs. It's valuable to study them, solicit feedback, and work to improve products to meet your consumers' needs rather than rest on assumptions.

Generally speaking, internal technical consumers (SOC analysts, incident responders, cyber threat intelligence analysts, etc.) want tactical and operational-level products to help them do their jobs—in most cases, intrusion detection and incident response. In some cases, these products will be aimed at developers or architecture-focused analysts or engineers trying to build more-defensible products or networks. As a result, these internal technical consumers ultimately have the most varied needs and uses of any group you're likely to build products for. Here are a few examples of the types of products you may need to create for internal technical consumers:

- An operational-level campaign analysis aimed at keeping SOC analysts familiar with a major ongoing spear-phishing campaign.
- A strategic discussion of major compromises of the last year for the systems architecture and vulnerability management teams, trying to identify improvements in system and network architecture.
- A tactical IOC list of domain names, after filtering out likely false positives, to be blocked at the web proxy.

All of these product examples are focused on improving detection and minimizing false positives. Analysts want to understand what bad looks like (generally) and how to verify that it's actually bad (specifically). These are two sides of the same coin, and the balance is key to consider when building products for other analysts.

As far as how to approach writing for analysts, the key is to keep the focus on the data.

- In most cases, you'll develop these products from analyst notes. This approach keeps the product close to the *ground truth* that analysts crave.
- These products can and should be highly technical and descriptive and also should be rich with references, including external research and internal telemetry references. Analysts often want to trace individual pieces of data to their original sources, and the best way to help them is by giving easy-to-follow references.
- The highest-quality products should be backed up by machine-consumable products, such as IOCs in STIX format or YARA signatures, to make it easier for other analysts in your organization to review the technical details.
- Always make sure you have a method for internal consumers to provide feedback and ask questions. This could be as simple as providing your email address, setting up a topic-specific chat room, or another method for readers to interact with the authors.

External Technical Consumers

Sharing intelligence can be wildly powerful, but creating products for external technical consumers presents its own unique challenges. Writing for external technical consumers is similar to writing for internal technical consumers, in terms of tone. The core differences are in *rules of engagement*, the process around how to interact with external technical consumers. There are four main rules of engagement:

Get permission
> Sharing internally with your own organization may have some sensitivity, but sharing outside your organization is often much more risky. In many cases, threat and incident data are considered highly sensitive and shouldn't be sent to third parties without sign-off.

Understand who you're sharing with
> Authorization may allow sharing with a certain type of organization (partners, law enforcement, ISACs, etc.) or specific individuals. Sharing outside these authorized individuals may risk exposure to unexpected third parties, including partner organizations or even the media.

Risks of Exposure

Even though organizations verify and trust those they share intelligence with (and do everything possible to protect information they receive), exposure happens. Intelligence consumers' mail accounts get hacked, and insider threats leak intelligence. As an intelligence producer, it's important to consider that intelligence you share may leak. This shouldn't discourage organizations from sharing, but does mean you need to consider the response of exposure, even if using strong cryptography.

Teams should avoid offensive or insensitive code names, unprofessional language, and unfounded speculation. Consider the embarrassment or negative ramifications that would result if your intelligence product were shared on Twitter. For an example of how this could happen, look at the exposure of Google's Looking into the Aquarium report (*http://bit.ly/2uhZ5RP*). Want to take this protection against exposure to the next level? Consider working with your organization's public relations team and get their feedback.

Create external intelligence products that focus on translatable intelligence
> Translatable intelligence is information that can be useful for both organizations. This is largely focused on indicators (for example, Snort signatures are useful to other organizations with intrusion-detection systems, but IP addresses are useful to almost all organizations), but should also be applied to timeline and narrative information. Taking the time to understand partner organizations will help with writing such intelligence products.

Have a method for feedback

Although sharing internally generally means a consumer will have a wide variety of feedback mechanisms, external consumers will have far fewer available channels. It's important when sharing intelligence to explicitly lay out methods of feedback, including channels, formats, and expectations.

Sometimes you will have more than one target audience for your intelligence; your SOC may be an internal technical consumer of incident-related data, but the C-suite wants a brief as well. At times like this, it is important to keep track of what information you need to get to each consumer, so we recommend that regardless of your audience, you have a consumer persona developed for them. We discuss developing these personas next.

Developing Consumer Personas

A highly useful exercise for understanding an intelligence program's audience is developing consumer personas, a technique pulled from common marketing practices. A *persona* describes a hypothetical prototypical consumer, and is focused on identifying the consumer's defining characteristics, challenges, and needs in order to help find the best way to address these needs. Keep the personas in a place where they can be accessed by members of the team during the Dissemination phase.

The approach starts with developing a template for the persona. Figure 9-1 provides an example template for a consumer persona.

Old Navy is famous for a whole family of consumer personas, but their main persona is Jenny (*http://bit.ly/2uHeeNL*), a 25–35 year old mother. For intelligence products, the size of the audience is important. Intelligence teams with lots of consumers may have a few generalized personas. Other teams may have a more limited number of consumers and may be able to make specific detailed personas for each consumer. A hybrid approach is likely best for most teams, meaning they build a few detailed personas for high-priority consumers and generalized personas for other groups.

The persona should help explicitly define many of the unknowns or generalizations about the consumers. Is the CEO highly technical and thus likes reading full-on reverse-engineering reports? That should be noted in their persona. Does your SOC lead prefer short, one-page products? That should be called out in their persona. Ultimately, the persona should be a recipe for providing a consumer with the most useful and stakeholder-relevant products. Take time to carefully consider (or even investigate and confirm) the persona's goals/challenges and values/fears. This will help ensure that you hit your target and provide the most useful products.

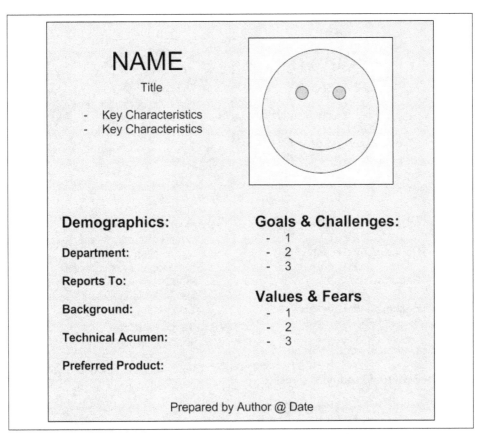

Figure 9-1. A simple consumer persona template

Figure 9-2 shows a real intelligence consumer profile. Shawn is a VP of security, which naturally leads to certain expectations about him in terms of interest and technicality (a form of bias). This is where the profile is important, because many of the assumptions we'd make about a vice president are wrong in this case. Shawn is highly technical and has high expectations about the accuracy and depth of any products sent to him. Whereas some VPs might be uncomfortable or intimidated at high levels of detail getting into packets and persistence mechanisms, Shawn expects them. At the same token, many of his interests are typical strategic needs. By combining the understanding of both interest and acumen, we can design custom products specifically aimed at Shawn.

Shawn

VP of Security

- Former engineer, highly
  technical
- Security program
  management focus

Demographics:

Department: Security

Reports To: CEO

Background: Unix Admin &
Security Engineer

Technical Acumen: High

Preferred Product: 1 Pager

Goals & Challenges:
- Identify strategic threats to
  organization
- Tying together security for
  varied business needs
- Sec Risk Management

Values & Fears
- Strong situational
  awareness
- Intel leading to strategic
  improvements

Prepared by Scott @ January 3, 2017

Figure 9-2. A real consumer profile

Although it's not crucial to build a detailed profile for every possible consumer of
your threat intelligence, creating personas can be a valuable exercise for key stakeholders. On the other hand, it can be valuable to build generic personas based on
common stakeholder roles, such as a SOC analyst. Such generalized profiles still provide key guidance when building intelligence products and function as an important
yardstick for determining whether products are meeting stakeholder needs.

 Many teams go through the persona process and treat those personas as gold. Personas should be only as static as the people or
roles they're attached to. Is there a new CFO? Take the time to create a new persona for that person; she may be dramatically different from the previous CFO.

Authors

Whereas the audience dictates what the consumers want, your authors dictate what you can talk about effectively. Any great product combines both the capabilities of the authors and the needs of the audience.

Authorship is about establishing and maintaining credibility. Your consumers (the audience) will get value only out of products they believe in, and much of this belief is based on the authors. In the same way that biases in analysis can discredit a team, so can trying to write about information outside your scope of knowledge. It's better to write strongly and authoritatively on topics that are well understood than to overrepresent speculation.

Authors should be knowledgeable enough about the topic to write with authority, and be familiar enough with the audience to convey information in the way the audience needs to receive it. Without the former, the product will be riddled with errors (which will damage credibility), and without the latter, good information will be wasted without any understanding.

As a report writer, you need to decide whether you're writing an intelligence product based on the analysts you have or the topic you want. If you're starting with a particular set of topics that you want to address in the product, you need to assemble a team capable of addressing the various needs that topic will cover. On the other hand, if you have a set team, the product topics should be limited based on the capabilities of that team.

Automated Report Information in Intelligence Products

One common technique used by intelligence product writers is including information that comes from automated tools. This approach is especially common in malware analysis, and many authors include output from sandboxes and online malware analysis services in their reports. This can be valuable, especially when the analysts and authors have limited experience, but in many cases, this is just data without context. Automated malware analysis may be useless because of anti-reverse-engineering techniques that cause the analysis to fail.

Anytime you include automatically generated information in a report, make sure of the following:

You completely understand the information
> Understanding the information is important not only for writing the report, but also so you can speak about it after delivery of the products. Many analysts, even

companies, have made mistakes by misunderstanding automated output and including bad data.[1]

Put the automatically generated information in context
The automated report needs to be part of telling the story of the product. Without context, these automated reports are just data.

Provide links to the automated analysis for reference and updates
For example, some samples may have a low-detection rate on VirusTotal early on, but as vendors start adding signatures, these detection rates will change. That context is important, so make it easy for intelligence product consumers to check that information for themselves.

By taking these three actions, you can ensure that your use of automated analysis improves intelligence products instead of muddying the water and confusing your consumers.

Actionability

Intelligence products need to be actionable. A product is *actionable* when it provides the right information, in the right format, for the consumer to take action or make a better decision than they would have without the product. An otherwise excellent intelligence product becomes useless if the consumer can't use the information it contains to improve their network defense posture. (In the F3EAD nomenclature, if a product doesn't improve a team's ability to Find, Fix, or Finish an adversary, the report is missing a key component.) In the end, every intelligence product's goal should be to lead to a meaningful decision or action.

Here are some do's for actionability:

- Provide information on adversary tactics, techniques, and procedures that makes it easier for the consumer to detect or respond to an adversary they're likely to face.
- Ensure products that contain easy-to-use IOCs and signatures that make it easier for a consumer to add detection or hunt for malicious activity. Open formats used by multiple vendors such as Snort and Yara are especially helpful.
- Answer specific questions from the consumer that are relevant to their needs (see "The RFI Process" on page 193).

The following are don'ts for actionability:

---

1 8.8.8.8 and windowsupdate.microsoft.com are great examples, commonly cited as malicious even by vendors. They commonly show up in dynamic analysis since malicious code will often reach out to them to verify it has internet access as an anti-forensic technique.

- Avoid overly broad descriptions of activity without meaningful details that would allow a network defense team to use it. For example, don't reference an attacker's phishing campaign without including information about the sender's email addresses, subject lines, attachments, or malicious links.
- Don't use tools or methods to hinder copying information out of intelligence products. For example, many vendors flatten their reports from text into images so that consumers can't copy and paste information from them. This is especially frustrating for lists of hashes, domains, and IPs.
- Skip distribution of contextual information via vendor-specific formats that are useful only in that vendor's products, or sharing information that can be used only for host detection with a consumer that has only network tools.
- Don't overclassify information so it can't be used. This can occur in both government-classified and TLP environments (see the following "Avoid TLP: Black" sidebar).

Avoid TLP: Black

We've discussed the Traffic Light Protocol for protecting sensitive intelligence. In addition to the official Red, Amber, Green, and White designations, some analysts reference information as TLP: Black. This unofficial designation is meant to convey the highest sensitivity, so high it should not be acted on in any way and is shared only to contextualize activity. TLP: Black has a clandestine, spy sort of feel to it, but because TLP: Black intelligence is by definition unactionable, it's seldom useful. Avoid using TLP: Black if at all possible.

Actionability is a nuanced thing that varies greatly based on the consumer and their intelligenece program maturity. In some cases, a product can be perfectly well crafted, but if the consumer is already highly aware of the threat, that product may not be highly actionable. Conversely, that same product could be highly actionable when shared with another team that's just discovered the threat. Ultimately, improving actionability requires listening to stakeholders and understanding the following consumer characteristics:

Needs
    What problems do they have, and what questions are they trying to answer?

Technology
    What tools do they have available?

Maturity
    What is the skill level of their team and ability to act effectively?

Methodologies
How do they approach team tasks?

After we understand all of these characteristics, we can tailor products to help them act effectively.

The Writing Process

Many people think good writing is the result of being a good writer. Although one aspect of being a great writer may be innate ability, for most of us writing is a slowly learned and patiently practiced skill. Writing for DFIR, intelligence, or any rigor-backed analytic needs requires not only a sense of style, but also a particular process. This section covers a generalized process to intelligence product development (expert intelligence-generating organizations should create their own detailed guides, such as Mercyhurst University's Institute for Intelligence Studies *Analyst's Style Manual* (*http://bit.ly/2gQjJUI*)).

Writing has three major phases: plan, draft, and edit. Let's dive into these now.

Plan

Intelligence writing always starts with a plan. Though it's easy to just start putting pen to paper (or fingers to keys), this path doesn't result in the best output. Intelligence products are thoughtful, well reasoned, and structured deliberately to provide the most value possible to stakeholders. To that end, remember to focus on the key aspects of intelligence products during the planning phase:

Audience
Who are you writing for? What are their goals and needs? Intelligence needs to be understood to be used effectively.

Authors
Who is doing the writing, and what are their skill sets? Intelligence requires deep understanding to contextualize, which means informed authors.

Actionability
What actions should the intelligence receivers be able to take after? Intelligence should always drive decision making (and usually change).

All three of these concepts help plan what needs to be in the product and what format it should take. Keep these in mind throughout the various phases of creating intelligence products, from the draft to delivery to the consumer.

Draft

While creating intelligence products, the drafting process is different for everyone. Nearly everyone has their own approach and processes. Regardless of the approach, however, most people find that the most difficult part is getting the first few words on paper. For example, it took your humble authors about 45 minutes to type the first sentence of this section on drafts, and it wasn't even that great of a sentence. Most authors agree that the best way to start a first draft is just to begin with getting something written down, and then moving on from there. If you do not already have your own approach to drafting, here are several strategies for starting the process. You can use just one of these approaches or several—whatever works for you.

Start with the direction statement

A *direction statement* is a one-sentence summary of the entire product and makes an ideal place to start an intelligence product. By starting with the direction, it's easy to make sure that the resulting product answers the original stakeholder request. Put the direction statement at the start and then begin building out evidence that speaks to the direction, calling out facts and assessments. In some cases, it may make sense to leave the direction statement as a distinct element of the product, but don't feel obligated. This is just a starting point.

Using Narrative in Intelligence Writing

Human beings are storytellers, and we like hearing stories. It's a format we're used to and find comfortable. We like characters, finding out what they're like, and hearing stories about what they do and how they relate to other characters. This narrative format is natural for both intelligence producers and consumers. Rather than fight this instinct, embrace it. Stories are simple to remember and have greater impact than simple statements. People relate to stories, so use narrative.

Start with facts

Another method is to start with a list of facts that have been identified in the investigation. This technique is especially useful when the product creators have comprehensive notes. Focus less on format and prose, and instead try to get all facts, times, indicators, and any concrete pieces of information on the page. When the facts are all available, they become easier to rearrange, adjust, and contextualize with prose.

Start with an outline or bullet points

Creating an outline is a good way to start getting your thoughts on paper with some structure. At this point, it is not important to fill out the content for each section of the outline; just put down the main subjects that will be covered in the report.

If it is too soon in the process to understand the structure or order of your findings, start with bullet points instead. This can cover a wide variety of topics, including facts (more on that next) analysis, considerations, and anecdotes. Once the information is written down, the best way to arrange it often emerges organically.

Edit

No draft should be the final product. Creating a truly great product, even from a great draft, requires great editing. For shorter products, editing may take nearly as long as drafting.

Editing is rarely a single-person job. Editing is hard, and the human mind has multiple glitches that can cause problems while editing. The worst by far is the human mind's ability to edit while reading, adding missing words or ignoring misplaced words—in short, mentally replacing what's on the page with what you meant to say instead. The more familiarity you have with the content, the more inclined you may be to make these mistakes. You can use various techniques, including the following, to avoid these kinds of mistakes:

Don't trust yourself
> The most obvious technique is having another analyst (in bigger shops, even a dedicated editor) read your product. A second set of eyes can often see things that the original writer cannot. Having a formal process for working with an editor is highly useful.

Walk away
> One way to make text fresh, even text you've written yourself, is to take some time away from it. Walk away from your desk, get a cup of coffee (or your beverage of choice), and take 15 minutes to clear your mind. When you come back and reread the text, you'll have fresh eyes and hopefully a fresh perspective.

Read it out loud
> When you read things silently, your mind lets you skip small and less significant words. This is useful for reading quickly, but bad for proofreading. One solution is reading out loud. It may feel a bit crazy, but you'll be amazed how often you identify mistakes in the small words you skip over otherwise.

Automate
> Many tools are meant to help writers. Spellcheckers and grammar checkers are common and built into most word processing systems. In other cases, you can go far beyond that. Tools such as write-good (*https://github.com/btford/write-good*) identify grammatically correct but inefficient or counterproductive constructs including weasel words (words that don't describe much, like *really* or *very*) or using phrases like *So* or *There is/are* at the beginning of sentences. Any tools that automate editing of products will scale for an entire team's intelligence producers.

Editing should go beyond identifying misspelled words or a sentence that ends in a comma instead of a period. Good editing should improve organization, ensure accuracy, make the topic easier to understand, identify inconsistencies, and help the original writer focus on end-consumer needs.

Here are common pitfalls specific to intelligence writing:

Passive voice (http://writingcenter.unc.edu/handouts/passive-voice/)
Using the format *direct object verb subject* is known as passive voice (as is this sentence). Passive voice makes sentences sound complex, but can often be confusing and may soften the action. Intelligence products should use the more straightforward *subject verb direct object* pattern, which conveys action and is easier for readers to understand. For example, "The child liked the ball." instead of "The ball was liked by the child."

Uncommon terms and acronyms
Consider the audience's technical proficiency. Using unknown terms causes the consumer to lose interest. Not sure how technical to go? You should look at the consumer's persona. When in doubt, add a definition or explanation for a term.

Leading or unobjective language
Be careful not to mislead consumers. It's key to identify bias in any subjective language and ensure it's in line with any assessments.

Imprecision about known versus suspected
One of the most dangerous mistakes you can make when creating an intelligence product is confusing known versus suspected. Although consumers want an analyst's suspicions (essentially leveraging their experience and bias), any confusion around what's suspected versus what is fact can have devastating consequences and cause bad decisions by stakeholders.

Editing is also the phase where content is checked both for accuracy and completeness. This is especially important for indicators of compromise or other data that may be used by the consumer directly. In many cases, a dangling participle is less problematic to a security operations team than a mistyped IP address. A good editor won't just identify the mistakes, but will call out gaps in information, confusing descriptions, or places where the content would benefit from a different approach.

Instead of using a text-only approach, consider visualizing data or adding graphics. "A picture is worth a thousand words" is good advice. Wherever possible, replacing information with graphs or images makes the data more engaging, easier to digest, and often more memorable. Creating custom graphics can be a challenge without access to a graphic designer, but in many cases even stock clip art can provide useful insight.

The last aspect that great editors bring isn't about what they add, but what they cut. Intelligence products benefit from brevity, which means a good editor pays as much attention to redundant information and opportunities to streamline the product as they do to what stays in it.

Intelligence Product Formats

After planning is complete, the characteristics we discussed (goals, authors, audience, and actionability) will help define the structure of the document you use. *Structure* is the actual format and layout of the intelligence product, including headings, length, even formats of data. The audience and actionability aspects in particular will naturally match up with specific products.

Making up products on the fly is a dubious proposition. You run the risk of neglecting audience needs or missing out on critical actionable information. Mature intelligence programs have a library of intelligence-product templates for analysts to choose from, as well as guidance on how to choose them.

Developing product templates is an organization-specific task that relies on an understanding of anticipated audiences, needs, and organizational tone. This customization is an ongoing evolution based on feedback from consumers and analysts.

The best way to understand what these products should look like is to walk through our example report templates. These templates illustrate the kinds of products that teams can produce for a variety of stakeholders. In fact, we're sharing these templates so you can use them to start building products for your own stakeholders. All sample products described in this chapter can be found on GitHub (*http://bit.ly/2uix6jC*).

Short-Form Products

Short-form products are intelligence products, generally one to two pages in length, meant to address specific tactical or operational intelligence needs. In many ways, short-form products are directly linked to RFIs. They are often longer responses to similar forms of questions, focused on being timely and quickly actionable. They are often done in direct response to consumer needs or to alert others in the organization to adentdversary actions. Short-form products have distinct goals and are usually not comprehensive, but instead are meant to provide details on specific aspects of an investigation or to meet specific needs around a given event or actor.

Incident and Actor Names

When writing short- and long-form products, analysts often need a way to reference current or past incidents or the actors behind them. This is far easier than just referring things as "that email thing from last year" or "those bad guys who use that tool." Having actor names or memorable incident names fits the concept that human beings like narrative and thus characters and specific events.

Although these names are important, be careful choosing. Code names may make it out into the public, so they should be public friendly. It's also important to use code names that are nonattributable; otherwise, they're marketing terms.

A great example of a good naming convention is the Microsoft Threat Intelligence Center (MSTIC) convention, which uses elements of the periodic table to group malicious activity. These names are distinctive and memorable, and a wide range of options is available.

We're going to review a variety of these products, starting with the event summary.

Event summary

An event summary is a common product that bridges the gap between incident response and threat intelligence. This short-form product is useful for bringing incident responders, SOC analysts, and management up to speed on evolving situations by giving a short one- or two-page breakdown of an ongoing event. This product should be highly time-bound and tied to a specific action. Example 9-1 provides a sample.

Example 9-1. Example event summary format

```
# Event Name

## Summary

> Most products start with a comprehensive summary. This is
> important so consumers can determine relevance quickly and
> because in many cases the summary is the only part of the
> product that many consumers will read.

## Timeline

- 2000-01-01 Event One Description
- 2000-01-02 Event Two Description
- 2000-01-03 Event Three Description

## Impact
```

```
> Describe what resources were impacted and what that means for
> operations.

## Recommendations

- Suggested Mitigation Action 1
- Suggested Mitigation Action 2
- Suggested Remediation Action 1
- Suggested Remediation Action 2

## Ongoing Actions

- What's Being Done Now Action 1
- What's Being Done Now Action 2

## References

- www.example.com/1
- www.example.com/2
- www.example.com/3
```

Check out the appendix for an example event summary based on GLASS WIZARD.

Target package

Whereas an event summary is focused on something that recently took place, often unattributed, a *target package* is a description of an actor, regardless of whether an event from that actor has been observed. Target packages are often useful for summarizing information pulled from vendor reports.

Target packages are one of the most universally useful products and are often of interest to a wide variety of consumers. A good target package won't dive too deep into attribution. This is a fact-based project that shouldn't get too far into estimative analysis. Example 9-2 shows a sample format for a target package.

Example 9-2. Example target package format

```
# Target Name

## Summary

> Most products start with a comprehensive summary. This is
> important so consumers can determine relevance quickly and
> because in many cases the summary is the only part of the
> product that many consumers will read.

| Alternative Name | Source    |
|:-----------------|:----------|
```

```
| Alternate Name 1 | Company 1 |
| Alternate Name 2 | Company 2 |
| Alternate Name 3 | Company 3 |
```

Tactics, Techniques, & Procedures

```
- TTP1
- TTP2
- TTP3
```

Tools

```
| Name    | Description | Notes |
|:--------|:------------|:------|
| Tool 1 |             |       |
| Tool 2 |             |       |
| Tool 3 |             |       |
```

Victim Profile

```
- Victim Type 1
- Victim Type 2
- Victim Type 3
```

Example information on reasoning.

Related Actors

```
| Name          | Type        | Notes |
|:--------------|:------------|:------|
| Actor Name 1 | Group       |       |
| Actor Name 2 | Individual  |       |
```

References

```
- www.example.com/1
- www.example.com/2
- www.example.com/
```

Indicator-of-compromise report

IOC reports are highly tactical products typically aimed at SOCs and responders meant to share the context of indicators. An IOC report can be especially useful when used in conjunction with new detection or alerts (such as newly blacklisted indicators). Given that indicators require context in order to be intelligence, IOC reports can often provide the necessary context.

Keep in mind that references included in IOC reports may be external but are often more valuable if they point to internal sources. For example, it would make sense to reference the related target package for an associate actor, or even an event report from a time those IOCs were observed. Tracking back through multiple products often provides the context that analysts need to understand complex events. Example 9-3 provides a sample IOC report format.

Example 9-3. IOC report format

```
# IOC Report

## Summary

> Most products start with a comprehensive summary. This is
> important so consumers can determine relevance quickly and
> because in many cases the summary is the only part of the
> product that many consumers will read.

## Indicators

| Indicator | Context | Notes |
|:----------|:--------|:------|
| IOC1      |         |       |
| IOC2      |         |       |
| IOC3      |         |       |

## Related TTPs

- TTP1
- TTP2

## References

- www.example.com/1
- www.example.com/2
- www.example.com/3
```

Long-Form Products

Long-form products are multipage, often multianalyst, intelligence products that cover a wide range of needs. Short-form products tend to have a hard timeliness requirement. Long-form products, while they may have a deadline, tend to be much less time-constrained. Whereas a short-form product may be put out in less than 24 hours, long-form products may take weeks or months to deliver. This is due partially to their length, often more than five pages with no solid upper bound, but even more so in the level of effort and content expected. Short-form products are often the output of a small team or even single analyst, whereas long-form products are usually developed by large teams covering a wide variety of skills and capabilities, from reverse engineers to graphic designers.

Long-form products are expected to be a complete view of a given topic. One of the first major long-form products was the Mandiant APT1 report (*http://bit.ly/*

2uHaxrq). This was a campaign analysis report that dove into multiple years of investigation and analysis of the Chinese APT group People's Liberation Army Unit 61398. The APT1 report involved multiple perspectives from a variety of victims, discussed the actor and the actor's common TTPs, explored their infrastructure, and analyzed motivations.

Like any other product, long-form products require considerable customization and effort to use effectively. Given the deeper technical, writing, editorial, and overall effort requirements, long-form products are general used primarily by more mature intelligence teams and even then only sparingly. Because these tend to be long products but have a strategic focus, it's important to remember that strategic consumers, often leadership, may read only bits and pieces that are relevant to them. So it's important to start with a wide-ranging summary covering major points and a comprehensive index to let a stakeholder jump straight to aspects that are useful to them.

Here are three templates for common long-form products (one tactical, one operational, and one strategic).

Malware report

The tactical long-form example product is the malware report. Generally an output from a reverse-engineered analysis, *malware reports* provide a wide range of benefits to multiple teams, from SOC analysts and incident responders who will use this information to identify new or ongoing attacks, to systems architecture folks who use this information to build future defenses.

Make sure to include outputs from automated tools such as sandboxes in these tactical, long-form reports. Although longer-form narrative tells a useful story, hunting through these reports for usable indicators of compromise slows response actions. Example 9-4 shows the format for a malware report.

Example 9-4. Malware report format

```
# Malware Report: Sample

| Key                     | Value         |
|:------------------------|:--------------|
| Reverse Engineer        | Analyst Name  |
| Date                    | 2017          |
| Requester               |               |
| Associated Intrusion Set |              |

## Summary:

> Most products start with a comprehensive summary. This is
> important so consumers can determine relevance quickly and
> because in many cases the summary is the only part of the
```

> product that many consumers will read.

Basic Static Analysis:

- File Name:
- File Type: Portable Executable
- File Size: 0

Hashes:

> Static file hashes useful for pivoting.

Hash Algorithm	Value
MD5	ddce269a1e3d054cae349621c198dd52
SHA1	7893883873a705aec69e2942901f20d7b1e28dec
SHA256	13550350a8681c84c861aac2e5b440161c2b33a3e4f302ac680ca5b686de48de
SHA512	952de772210118f043a4e2225da5f5943609c653a6736940e0fad4e9c7...f41
Ssdeep	<FOO>

Current antivirus detection capabilities:

> Gathered from VirusTotal, these are useful for understanding
organization-wide detection

Vendor	Sample
Vendor 1	Signature.xyz

Interesting Strings:

> Unique static file strings helpful for building detection such
as Yara signatures.

- `foo`
- `bar`
- `baz`

Other Relevant Files or Data:

- `c:/example.dll`
- `sysfile.exe`

Basic Dynamic Analysis:

> Input from an automated sandbox.

Behavioral Characteristics:

> Descriptions of how the malware accomplishes its major goals,
based on kill chain methods.

Delivery Mechanisms:

> How the malware got to the victim system.

Persistence Mechanisms:

> How the malware runs at startup and continues running.

Spreading Mechanisms:

> How the malware migrates between systems.

Exfiltration Mechanisms:

> How the malware uses to move data outside the victim network.

Command-and-Control Mechanisms:

> How the malware is given tasking by the attacker.

Dependencies:

> System-level requirements for the malware to execute.

Supported Operating Systems:
- Operating System 1

Required Files:
- `c:/example.dll`

Second-Stage Downloads:
- `c:/example.dll`

Registry Keys:
- `/HKEY/Example`

Detection:

> Unenriched information from the sample useful for identifying infections.

Network Indicators of Compromise:

> Network strings, domains, URLs, tls certificates, IPv4, IPv6 Addresses, etc.

- 10.10.10.10
- example.com

Filesystem Indicators of Compromise:

> File strings, file paths, signing certificates, registry keys,

```
mutexes, etc.

- `foobar`

## Response Recommendations:

> Incident-response-centric steps for pausing and removing the
malware.

### Mitigation Steps:
- Excepteur sint occaecat cupidatat non proident.
- Sunt in culpa qui officia deserunt mollit anim id est laborum.

### Eradication Steps:
- Excepteur sint occaecat cupidatat non proident.
- Sunt in culpa qui officia deserunt mollit anim id est laborum.

## Related Files:

> Important for establishing relationships between exploits,
droppers, RATs, etc.

- C:/example.dll
```

See the appendix for a report on one of GLASS WIZARD's implants.

Campaign report

The most common operational long-form report is the *campaign report*, an end-to-end breakdown of an entire intrusion campaign. These are useful for identifying analysis gaps (places where your team doesn't fully grasp the adversary action), which may lead to RFIs. These reports are also useful for identify missing response actions. They're also good for bringing new responders, intelligence analysts, or other stakeholders up to speed on long-running investigations. For most teams, campaign reports are the longest products that analysis teams create on a regular basis. Example 9-5 provides a template for a campaign report.

Example 9-5. Campaign report template

```
# Campaign Report: Sample

| Key                      | Value                                          |
|:-------------------------|:-----------------------------------------------|
| Lead Analyst             | Analyst Name                                   |
| Analysis Team            | Analyst Name 1, Analyst Name 2, Analyst Name 3 |
| Date                     | 2017                                           |
| Requester                |                                                |
| Associated Intrusion Set |                                                |

## Summary
```

> A one-paragraph summary of the campaign and the impact.

Description

> A comprehensive, multiparagraph summary of the entire incident,
> including the malicious activity, the actor, and the response
> actions taken by the incident-response team.

Kill Chain

> The campaign maps against the kill chain and breaks out the
diamond model characteristics for each.

Reconnaissance

> How the attacker gathered pre-attack information.

Diamond Model

- __Adversary:__ The attacker or attacker persona
- __Capability:__
  - Capability/TTP 1
  - Capability/TTP 2
- __Infrastructure:__
  - Infrastructure Resource 1
  - Infrastructure Resource 2
- __Victim:__ Target person/system of this stage

Weaponization

> A description about the setup and configuration of the attack.

Diamond Model

- __Adversary:__ The attacker or attacker persona
- __Capability:__
  - Capability/TTP 1
  - Capability/TTP 2
- __Infrastructure:__
  - Infrastructure Resource 1
  - Infrastructure Resource 2
- __Victim:__ Target person/system of this stage

Delivery

> A description of the methods used to introduce the exploit
> into the target/victim environment.

Diamond Model

- __Adversary:__ The attacker or attacker persona

- __Capability:__
  - Capability/TTP 1
  - Capability/TTP 2
- __Infrastructure:__
  - Infrastructure Resource 1
  - Infrastructure Resource 2
- __Victim:__ Target person/system of this stage

Exploitation

> This introduces the method of exploitation, how the adversary
> took control of their target system.

Diamond Model

- __Adversary:__ The attacker or attacker persona
- __Capability:__
  - Capability/TTP 1
  - Capability/TTP 2
- __Infrastructure:__
  - Infrastructure Resource 1
  - Infrastructure Resource 2
- __Victim:__ Target person/system of this stage

Installation

> A description of how the attackers achieved persistence on
> after exploitation.

Diamond Model

- __Adversary:__ The attacker or attacker persona
- __Capability:__
  - Capability/TTP 1
  - Capability/TTP 2
- __Infrastructure:__
  - Infrastructure Resource 1
  - Infrastructure Resource 2
- __Victim:__ Target person/system of this stage

Command & Control

> How the attacker communicates with their compromised resources.

Diamond Model

- __Adversary:__ The attacker or attacker persona
- __Capability:__
  - Capability/TTP 1
  - Capability/TTP 2
- __Infrastructure:__
  - Infrastructure Resource 1

```
  - Infrastructure Resource 2
- __Victim:__ Target person/system of this stage

### Actions On Objectives

> The attacker's ultimate goal and what tools and techniques
> they use to achieve those objectives.

#### Diamond Model

- __Adversary:__ The attacker or attacker persona
- __Capability:__
  - Capability/TTP 1
  - Capability/TTP 2
- __Infrastructure:__
  - Infrastructure Resource 1
  - Infrastructure Resource 2
- __Victim:__ Target person/system of this stage

## Timeline

| Index | DateTime          | Actor  | Action  | Notes |
|:------|:------------------|:-------|:--------|:------|
| 1     | 20170101 12:00+00 | Actor1 | Action1 |       |
| 2     | 20170102 12:00+00 | Actor2 | Action2 |       |
| 3     | 20170103 12:00+00 | Actor3 | Action3 |       |

## Indicators of Compromise

> A collection of all IOCs identified, including enrichment and
pivoting, and useful signatures

### Network Indicators

> Individual Network IOCs

- 10.10.10.10
- example.com
- www.example.com/path

### Host Indicators

> Individual Host IOCs

- /HKEY/foobar
- example.exe
- `foobar`

### Network signatures

> Individual Network Detection Signatures (Snort, etc)
```

__Signature for 10.10.10:__
```

```
alert ip any any -> 10.10.10.10 any (msg: "Bad IP detected";)
```

Host Signatures

> Individual Host Detection Signatures (Yara, etc)

__Example Rule for foobar__

```

```
rule example : example
{
    meta:
        description = "This is just an example"
        thread_level = 3
        in_the_wild = true

    strings:
        $a = "foobar"

    condition:
        $a
}
```

Observations

> It's useful to keep track of even casual observations
and analyst notes.

Datetime	Analyst	Observation
20170101 12:00+00	Analyst 1	Observation One
20170102 12:00+00	Analyst 2	Observation Two
20170103 12:00+00	Analyst 3	Observation Three

Related Products

> Other related intelligence, short- or long-form products.

Internal Products

> Internally generate related intelligence products.

- product1
- product2
- product3

External Products

```
> In many cases external vendor products are useful to hold on to.

- www.example.com/product.pdf
```

Intelligence estimate

Intelligence estimates are a long-form product that comprehensively explores a major strategic issue. This product originated in one of the precursors to the the US Central Intelligence Agency, an agency in the State Department called the Office of National Estimates (ONE). ONE created the National Intelligence Estimate, a yearly State of the Union-esque intelligence product meant to identify and explore major strategic threats to the United States.

A typical Intelligence Estimate–style product is a wide-ranging, largely strategic product aimed at the highest level of stakeholders, providing context necessary for making strategic decisions throughout the year. Not perfect in every case, it was supplemented throughout the year, but an intelligence estimate sets a baseline and provides stakeholders a starting point for understanding a wide variety of issues.

Instead of a sample intelligence estimate, which is a highly tailored document, we recommend looking at some declassified examples from the United States CIA (*http:// bit.ly/2uj8Pd0*).

The RFI Process

A *request for intelligence* (RFI) is a specialized product meant to answer a specific question, often in response to a situational awareness need. A requester submits a very short-form question to the intelligence team. At that point, the intelligence team either answers it directly based on information already collected (if possible) or treats this as a request for collection, kicking off a new intelligence cycle. To keep the process orderly and consistent, it helps to have a template, not only for the response product, but also for the initial request. The RFI process, illustrated in Figure 9-3, needs to stay focused. An RFI can be used for tactical, operational, and strategic requests.

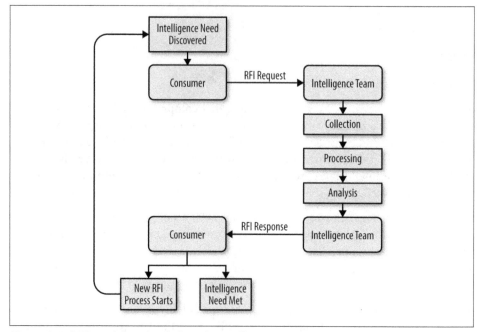

Figure 9-3. RFI workflow (including the intelligence process)

An easy way to get started with an RFI flow is by using email-based requests. Consumers send a request by using the team template to a common mailbox such as *rfi@company.com*, where the intelligence team can pick up requests. Because RFIs come in two parts, the request and the response, this will include two templates.

RFI request

The request from a consumer follows a strict and limited structure, as shown in Example 9-6.

Example 9-6. RFI request template

```
- _FROM:_ Requester
- _TO:_ Intelligence Team
- _Response By:_ 2016-11-12

_Request:_

> The RFI request needs to be a straightforward question with a
> distinct description of what a good answer would look like.

_Request References:_
- www.example.com/request_source_1
- www.example.com/request_source_2
```

The To and From fields should direct the request from the consumer to the intelligence team. The Response By field specifies how quickly the consumer needs the intelligence (an alternative is using severity levels such as high, medium, or low). Next is the Request. This should be a directed question with a concrete answer. Finally, a requester may provide Request References or other background to the question as a starting point for the intelligence team.

RFI response

The response also follows a strict and limited structure, as shown in Example 9-7.

Example 9-7. RFI response template

```
- _FROM:_ Intelligence Team
- _TO:_ Requester
- _TLP:_ red/yellow/green/white
- _Response At:_ 2016-11-13

_Response:_

> The response should be crafted to be complete but succinct,
> directly answering the question in the request.

_Response References:_
- www.example.com/response_source_1
- www.example.com/response_source_2
```

The From and To fields direct the response back to the original requester. The Traffic Light Protocol (TLP) field specifies the sharing rules that the response recipients should follow. It's also key to call out the date the response was sent back to the consumer (Response At) for reference and metrics. Success for the RFI process hinges on intelligence getting back to the Requester with a meaningful Response to their request. This request should address the specific question asked and not stray into secondary issues. Finally, it's useful to include sources of information that the intelligence team used for the RFI as Response References.

RFI flow example

Here's an example of a typical request for intelligence workflow. We'll start with the request from the consumer.

RFI request. A useful RFI request could look like this:

- *From*: Security Operations Center
- *To*: Intelligence Team
- *Response By*: 2017-02-20

What are the useful network IOCs for detecting X-Agent malware?

- *http://bit.ly/2vsOsdE*

RFI Response. And now the response (after going through an intelligence cycle as we described in Chapter 2:

- *From*: Intelligence Team
- *To*: Security Operations Center
- *Response By*: 2017-02-22

Based on public sources, we recommend the following network indicators for detection of the APT28 X-Agent malware:

- Snort `alert tcp $HOME_NET any -> $EXTERNAL_NET $HTTP_PORTS (msg:"Downrage_HTTP_C2"; flow:established,to_server; content:"POST"; http_method; content:"="; content:"=|20|HTTP/1.1"; fast_pattern; dis tance:19; within:10; pcre:"/^\/(?:[a-zA-Z0-9]{2,6}\/){2,5}[a-zA-Z0-9]{1,7}\.[A-Za-z0- 9\+\-\_\.]+\/\?[a-zA-Z0-9]{1,3}=[a-zA-Z0-9+\/]{19}=$/I";)`
- http://23.227.196[.]215/
- http://apple-iclods[.]org/
- http://apple-checker[.]org/
- http://apple-uptoday[.]org/
- http://apple-search[.]info

Further intelligence could be developed with a follow-up request.

nbsp;

- *http://bit.ly/2uiuqEb*
- *http://bit.ly/2uJ9erk*

For another real-world example, check the appendix for another RFI flow based on GLASS WIZARD.

Date and Time Formats

Few things can cause as much consternation and confusion for a security operations team as inconsistent datetime representations. In the US, it's common to use the MM/DD/YYYY format that, while familiar, is often hard to use. European custom is typically DD/MM/YYYY, which is more straightforward. Unfortunately, both of these may cause problems in intelligence products since they're difficult to sort and can often be jarring to read inline. Instead, consider the YYYYMMDD format, which is easy to read, especially in timelines, and easy to sort. Time is also better when it's sortable, so consider using the 24-hour system and use a consistent time zone, preferably UTC; for example, 20170219 22:02+00. This is also easier for scripts and tools to ingest.

Automated Consumption Products

Automated consumption products are group IOCs meant to be used by tools such as alerting or analysis systems (unlike IOC reports, which are meant to be read by human analysts). Used in conjunction with *written products* (which provide useful context), automated consumption products make it much faster to start using threat data effectively and improve accuracy. Automated consumption products fall into four categories:

- Unstructured/semistructured IOCs
- Network signatures with Snort
- Filesystem signatures with Yara
- Automated IOC formats

In the following sections, we'll explore all types of automated consumption products.

Unstructured/semistructured IOCs

Generalized indicators of compromise are groups of indicators (a piece of data plus context), typically in basic text-based lists, which make them easy to integrate into other tools or formats. When sharing information for automated consumption by scripts and tools, the most important consideration is what tools or scripts will be ingesting the product. A variety of complex standards such as OpenIOC (*http://open ioc.com/*) and STIX (*https://stixproject.github.io/*) are incredibly expressive but limited to the tools that implement those standards. If your consumers can't use these formats, they are often more trouble than they're worth. We'll discuss them at the end of this section.

Even after the advent of these security-centric standards, most IOC sharing is still done using lists in text files or semistructured with CSV. While lacking in context, these formats are easy to consume, easy to read by people (as well as computers), and easy to write scripts against.

GLASS WIZARD unstructured IOCs. Generalized IOCs can be incredibly simple. Here's an example of hashes from GLASS WIZARD (*http://www.novetta.com/wp-content/uploads/2014/11/Hashes.txt*):

```
Family, sha256
ZoxFamily,
0375b4216334c85a4b29441a3d37e61d7797c2e1cb94b14cf6292449fb25c7b2
ZoxFamily,
48f0bbc3b679aac6b1a71c06f19bb182123e74df8bb0b6b04ebe99100c57a41e
...
Plugx,fb38fd028b82525033dec578477d8d5d2fd05ad2880e4a83c6b376fa2471085c
Plugx,ff8dbdb962595ba179a7664e70e30e9b607f8d460be73583af59f39b4bb8a36e
...
Gh0st,ff19d0e8de66c63bcf695269c12abd99426cc7688c88ec3c8450a39360a98caa
Poison
Ivy,ffc3aa870bca2da9f9946cf162cb6b1f77ba9db1b46092580bd151d5ed72075f
...
ZxshellModule,
6dc352693e9d4c51fccd499ede49b55d0a9d01719a15b27502ed757347121747
...
```

This format is incredibly simplistic, but easily scriptable for use with other tools. These lists of IOCs are most often shared as plain text, Markdown, or Excel/CSVs.

Network signatures with Snort

In general, when we reference network signatures, we mean Snort signatures. *Snort* was one of the earliest intrusion-detection systems and uses a text-based, open signature format. Snort has a verbose and effective signature language that has been adopted by many other vendors, implemented in a wide variety of tools, and thus is the standard for describing network traffic.

Snort signatures are shared as simple text files, making them easy to ingest with a wide variety of tools and easy to manage using scripts. Example 9-8 shows a sample Snort signature.

Example 9-8. Sample Snort signature

```
alert tcp any any -> 10.10.10.10 any (msg:"Sample Snort Rule";
sid:1000001; rev:1;)
```

GLASS WIZARD network signatures. There are signatures for GLASS WIZARD. Specifically, here is a Snort Community signature (*https://www.snort.org/rule_docs/1-30948*) for GLASS WIZARD's Hikit malware:

```
alert tcp $HOME_NET any -> $EXTERNAL_NET any (msg:"MALWARE-BACKDOOR
Win.Backdoor.Hikit outbound banner response";
flow:to_client,established;
content:"|5D 00 20 00|h|00|i|00|k|00|i|00|t|00|>|00|";
fast_pattern:only; metadata:impact_flag red, policy balanced-ips
drop, policy security-ips drop, ruleset community, service http,
service ssl; reference:url,www.virustotal.com/en/file/aa4b2b448a5e24\
6888304be51ef9a65a11a53bab7899bc1b56e4fc20e1b1fd9f/analysis/;
classtype:trojan-activity; sid:30948; rev:2;)
```

If you need a reminder of how Snort signatures work, refer to Chapter 5. Here are some key pieces:

```
alert tcp $HOME_NET any -> $EXTERNAL_NET any
```

The Hikit malware used by GLASS WIZARD sits on a server in the victim's network demilitarized zone (DMZ), where the attacker then connects to it from the outside. (This is an unusual architecture, because most remote-access Trojans *phone home* from inside the victim network to a command-and-control node outside.) To model this, the Hikit Snort signature uses $variables, which make it easy to set network ranges for different network locations. ($HOME_NET is typically an organization's range, and $EXTERNAL_NET is basically everything else.) As a result, the Hikit signature should trigger only when the server (the system inside $HOME_NET, usually the victim's DMZ) is sending a message back to the client (the attacker's system outside somewhere in $EXTERNAL_NET).

As important as what this clause specifies is what it doesn't: ports. If ports were hardcoded in, changing the server port could be trivial for the attacker, depending on the malware. Because client ports are almost always random ephemeral ports (picked at random from higher port numbers (*http://bit.ly/2uiBCAc*)), specifying universally correct ports would be difficult. If the attacker guessed the port, the attacker could easily avoid detection. Given the specificity of the content bit string and directionalty, this wildcard for the port will not likely cause too many false positives. Specifying ports can be important for signatures impacting specific services, such as attacks on SMB (445/TCP for those of you playing along at home):

```
flow:to_client,established;
```

These flow clause characteristics help model a similar directionality as the To/From in the alert clause. The key is this clause adds established, meaning this signature shouldn't trigger on the first few packets of a connection. This improves accuracy and prevents someone from generating packets with the Hikit bit string shown here:

```
content:"|5D 00 20 00|h|00|i|00|k|00|i|00|t|00|>|00|";
```

The second key piece of this signature is the byte signature of the communication (this byte signature is where the malware got its colloquial name). This combination of bytes is always observed in the command-and-control communication of the Hikit malware (at least the sample it was based on, which is specified with the reference to VirusTotal).

Combined, these three characteristics (directionality, flow specification, and the content) create a comprehensive signature for the Hikit malware.

Filesystem signatures with Yara

When describing file content, information analysts rely on Yara. Staying true to its tagline, *The pattern matching swiss knife for malware researchers (and everyone else)*, Yara makes it easy to describe a wide variety of patterns useful for identifying malware—not just individual files (as with hashes), but entire families. Yara signatures are an ideal way to share this data because they're usable with any tools that implement the open source Yara detection libraries. This means consumers can use Yara with a wide variety of command-line tools, automation tools, host and network detection tools, and even hunting for samples on VirusTotal Intelligence.

Yara signatures are also shared as simple text files, like Snort signatures, making them similarly easy to ingest with a wide variety of tools and easy to manage using scripts. Example 9-9 shows a sample Yara signature.

Example 9-9. Sample Yara signature

```
rule sample_signature : banker
{
    meta:
        description = "This is just an example"

    strings:
        $a = "foo"
        $b = "bar"
        $c = {62 61 7a}

    condition:
        $a or $b or $c
}
```

Automated IOC Formats

Fully automated and comprehensive formats such as OpenIOC (*http://open ioc.com/*) and STIX (*https://stixproject.github.io/*) are useful only for teams that use tools built for them (or are capable of of building tools to use these standards). These can be used as general intelligence consumption but may require translation to more accessible formats. In the past, one thing that has limited the adoption of these formats outside of vendors is that both OpenIOC and STIX version 1 were based on Extensible Markup Language (XML). XML was a data format for many years, but as REST interfaces have overtaken SOAP, so has JavaScript Object Notation (JSON) overtaken XML.

In keeping with the times, the STIX format is being updated to JSON. Example 9-10 shows a C2 indicator based on Oasis's GitHub (*http://bit.ly/2uQUM1A*).

Example 9-10. STIXv2 Command and Control IOC (based on FireEye's Deputy Dog report (http://bit.ly/2vxKsLb))

```
{
  "type": "bundle",
  "id": "bundle--93f38795-4dc7-46ea-8ce1-f30cc78d0a6b",
  "spec_version": "2.0",
  "objects": [
    {
      "type": "indicator",
      "id": "indicator--36b94be3-659f-4b8a-9a4d-90c2b69d9c4d",
      "created": "2017-01-28T00:00:00.000000Z",
      "modified": "2017-01-28T00:00:00.000000Z",
      "name": "IP Address for known Deputy Dog C2 channel",
      "labels": [
        "malicious-activity"
      ],
      "pattern": "[ipv4-addr:value = '180.150.228.102']",
      "valid_from": "2013-09-05T00:00:00.000000Z"
    }
  ]
}
```

STIX is especially valuable when sharing indicators with a wide variety of consumers and the authors don't know what tools or formats those consumers use. This can be especially useful in public reporting, such as the US-CERT's Grizzley Steppe report (*https://www.us-cert.gov/security-publications/GRIZZLY-STEPPE-Russian-Malicious-Cyber-Activity*). In this case, wanting to make indicators widely effective, US-CERT released both a written report (a similar format to our campaign reports) along with indicators in multiple formats including in STIXv1. The use of STIX was appropriate because as a TLP:White general public report, it was impossible for the authors to know what formats the consumers would want. STIX provides a middle ground that any threat intelligence team should be able to use, and some teams could make use of quickly.

Establishing a Rhythm

Intelligence teams have to establish their own rhythm for releasing intelligence products. Some products benefit from regular release, such as situational awareness reports and intelligence estimates, while others make more sense released in an ad hoc nature based on ongoing events such as RFIs.

Regularly released products are useful for keeping stakeholder interest and establishing lines of communication. That said, it's important to work with stakeholders to calibrate frequency, length, and content of regular products. Too often, and the analysis team runs the risk of having nothing of consequence to put in the products, giving little value to the consumers, wasting their time, and eventually causing them to lose interest. Conversely, if intelligence products get released too infrequently, no forward momentum is established and too much time has to be spent reorienting the consumer each time a new product is released.

Distribution

Once a product is written and edited, it's ready for distribution to consumers. Like all other aspects of the dissemination process, distribution must be usable by the target audience and at the same time must effectively display the product content.

Ease of distribution must be balanced with intelligence product protection. Government classification systems are one example of intelligence product protection. While establishing an elaborate system may seem useful, in many cases it's far more trouble than it's worth.

Within analysis teams, portals are effective for distributing intelligence products. Wikis or CRMs such as Microsoft SharePoint provide a centralized point for creating, updating, and sharing information. They're commonly searchable, which is useful for gaining context around indicators. Intelligence teams can set up CRMs offline, such as in an isolated noncompany SOC or intel team network.

Depending on sensitivity, products for leadership can be distributed in multiple ways. Common channels such as email are useful for less-sensitive products, especially regularly distributed products. Most executives won't go to extensive lengths to view intelligence products, so email and printed hard copies are most effective. Presentation decks are also useful.

Feedback

The last stage of the intelligence-writing process, and the most often overlooked, is the feedback stage. During feedback, the intelligence consumer shares what would make future products more useful. This largely breaks down into two categories:

Technical feedback
> The first and most important piece of feedback from a consumer is whether the original direction was met and whether the stakeholders got the information they needed. In many cases, there aren't simple yes or no answers to these questions; the intelligence team may instead need to conduct another round of the intelligence cycle. Generating more specific requirements and providing a new direction is its own form of success.

Format feedback
> Another form of feedback is whether the products were useful for the stakeholders. In many cases, the intelligence itself is useful but the product type could be better, either for the original consumer or a new consumer. For example, a campaign report is useful for the SOC team, but the SOC team lead could ask for a new, shorter-form version aimed at executives.

Intelligence teams greatly benefit from establishing open lines of communication and getting regular feedback from their consumers. Regular feedback guides changes to processes, formats, conventions, and even how to staff the intelligence team.

Getting feedback can be a difficult problem. The simplest method? Reach out to intelligence consumers and solicit feedback. Want to go the extra mile? Combine gathering feedback on intelligence products with improving consumer personas. These interviews can improve a wide variety of intelligence products, and once the floodgate of feedback is open, it's easy to gather information about a variety of topics, including improving intelligence products.

Regular Products

One of the keys to establishing a rhythm for creating intelligence products is having regular intelligence product output. Many successful intelligence programs use regular products to great effect. Here are the reasons regular products make an impact:

- Regular intelligence products inform consumers on important topics such as imminent threats, situational awareness items including security news, and activity of the intelligence and incident-response teams.
- Regular intelligence products keep the intelligence team at the front of consumers' minds, reminding them of the option to make requests (whether RFIs or formal) and be on the lookout for future products.

- By producing regular products, the intelligence team keeps security priorities on the radar of the consumers, even when they're not necessarily related to the incident response.

Establishing a cadence for intelligence products depends greatly on the incident-response team's operational tempo, the intelligence team's bandwidth to create regular intelligence products, and consumer needs.

One way to get started is with a weekly threat report. This basic one-page product should focus on ongoing investigations and incidents and situational awareness in the form of security news. This type of product is valuable to a wide variety of consumers, from SOC analysts through C-level stakeholders. It keeps them informed, keeps everyone aware of the status of urgent matters (either internal or external), and acts as a conversation starter for intelligence and incident response.

Conclusion

Analysts need great products to share their intelligence effectively. Effective dissemination requires taking the time to create products that are accurate, audience focused, and actionable by focusing on the presumed consumer, understanding how they plan to use the information, and planning accordingly.

Great intelligence products generally have the following characteristics:

- Accuracy
- Audience focused
- Actionable

In addition, analysts should ask themselves the following five questions during the writing process to ensure that the intelligence products that they develop will be well received and will meet the needs of their intelligence customers:

- What is the goal?
- Who is the audience?
- What is the proper length of product?
- What level of intelligence? (Tactical, operational, strategic?)
- What tone and type of language can you use? (Technical or nontechnical?)

Your answers to these questions all inform the final product. Learning to pair the goals and audience together is a skill, not a formula. It takes time to develop an understanding of how to approach this. Building processes on how to plan, draft, and edit content will dramatically speed up the entire process.

Ultimately, the entire dissemination process relies on developing a continous feedback loop between analysts, writers, editors, and consumers. Only through this cycle can the process develop, the products improve, and the intelligence program mature.

## PART III

The Way Forward

Intelligence-driven incident response doesn't end when the final incident report has been delivered; it will become a part of your overall security process. Part 3 covers big-picture aspects of IDIR that are outside individual incident-response investigations. These features include strategic intelligence to continually learn and improve processes, as well as implementation of an intelligence team to support security operations as a whole.

CHAPTER 10

Strategic Intelligence

"Our products have become so specific, so tactical even, that our thinking has become tactical. We're losing our strategic edge because we're so focused on today's issues."

—John G. Heidenrich

Every once in while, an incident responder will start an investigation with a prickling sensation in the back of his mind. Some call it a premonition, some call it deja vu, but as the investigation unwinds, it will inevitably hit him: he has done this before. This. Exact. Same. Investigation.

Whether it was a month ago or a year ago, incident responders find themselves dealing with the same situation manifesting itself in the same way. The same vulnerabilities, the same lateral movement, maybe even the exact same stolen or reused passwords. At this point, many find themselves shaking their fists at the sky, asking how this could have happened. Didn't we learn from the last time? Didn't we fix the problems? And unfortunately, the answer is often no. When the last incident was resolved, there were other things to worry about, other problems requiring the attention of everyone from the IT manager to the CIO, and since the problem had been "resolved," there was no more time to spend thinking about it. Lessons were not learned, and although some small changes may have been made, there was no lasting impact on the security of the organization because new, urgent problems took priority.

There is a misconception about strategic intelligence that has resulted in it being overlooked. (This phenomenon is not unique to the cybersecurity or incident-response realm; it has been witnessed across intelligence disciplines for decades.) The misconception is that there is simply no time to conduct strategic intelligence. There is so much happening on a daily—and in the world of incident response, sometimes an hourly—basis, that many people feel overwhelmed by trying to keep up at the tactical level. Strategic intelligence, often viewed as a "nice to have" rather than a "need to have," gets relegated to the pile of things to do when time allows, and time rarely allows. However, strategic intelligence is critical to our ability to do our jobs, and although it does take time away from the daily emergencies, it can position us to better deal with those emergencies, and therefore it should not be overlooked. This chapter covers what strategic intelligence is and why it is critical to the intelligence-driven incident-response process.

What Is Strategic Intelligence?

Strategic intelligence gets its name not only from the subjects that it covers, typically a high-level analysis of information with long-term implications, but also from its audience. Strategic intelligence is geared toward decision makers with the ability and authority to act, because this type of intelligence should shape policies and strategies moving forward. This doesn't mean, however, that leadership is the only group that can benefit from these insights. Strategic intelligence is extremely useful to all levels of personnel because it can help them understand the surrounding context of the issues that they deal with at their levels. Ideally, helping individuals understand why certain policies were created, or why an emphasis is being placed on a particular area will help them to fulfill their role more effectively.

In his paper, "The State of Strategic Analysis (*http://bit.ly/2uVLDod*)," John Heidenrich wrote that "a strategy is not really a plan but the logic driving a plan." When that logic is present and clearly communicated, analysts can approach problems in a way that supports the overarching goals behind a strategic effort rather than treating each individual situation as its own entity.

Strategic intelligence supports intelligence-driven response processes by helping analysts prioritize responses, identify when an intrusion is particularly significant to their organization, and ensure that the lessons learned from each incident are analyzed and acted upon. Without strategic intelligence, intelligence-driven incident response can still provide insight and support to the incident-response process; but with strategic intelligence, it can drastically improve an organization's ability to understand and posture themselves to prevent, identify, and respond to subsequent intrusions.

Sherman Kent: Father of American Intelligence Analysis

Sherman Kent is known as the godfather of intelligence and quite literally wrote the book on intelligence analysis. He was so instrumental to the intelligence discipline that the CIA's school to train new intelligence analysts is called the Sherman Kent School for Intelligence Analysis.

Kent received a doctorate in history from Yale University and taught on the faculty until World War II, when he joined a new division of the Office of Strategic Services (OSS) called the Research and Analysis Branch (R&A). There, Kent used his experience as a historian, combined with an ability to lead, to bring together economists, scientists, and military members to conduct some of the most influential analysis of the war. Kent and the R&A analysts were not planning operations or tactical skirmishes; they were analyzing the underpinnings of the enemy and operating environment. They analyzed the cultures and the resources available (food, finances, and transportation) to help the United States determine what actions would have the most significant impact to the national strategy. They generated strategic intelligence that helped not just a single mission, but the entire war effort.

In many cases, one of the most significant differences between strategic and tactical or current intelligence is the modeling process. In tactical and current intelligence, analysts use the models that they have available, whether that model is an actor dossier or an internal network map, to solve the problem at hand. In strategic analysis, those models are often being updated or developed for the first time.

Developing Target Models

Target models are representations of an area of focus. Target models can describe things such as a government structure, a process, or a logical network. Developing these models can be time-consuming, and the larger or more complex a target is, the more complex the model will be. Models are also rarely static; they must be updated periodically. In the case of a network map, for example, it must be updated frequently to remain current. With organizational structures, it can be necessary to update them whenever there is a reorganization or when key leaders change or leave, which can occur almost as frequently as network changes. Developing models is an investment.

If developing models is so time-consuming, why bother developing them at all? Models are critical to developing a common understanding of a situation, and this common understanding is what enables people to learn to respond to situations in a consistent way to work toward a common goal. In a business, that common goal is usually increased revenue, and network defense supports that goal by preventing breaches that result in loss of intellectual property, brand damage, and incident-response expenses. In the government or the military, the goal is to support the national strategy and ensure national security. Without understanding what those things mean, however, it can be difficult to respond in a way that supports those objectives. Developing models is one key area of strategic intelligence that will influence decision making as well as operational and tactical analysis. Taking the time to develop and update models will almost always be time well spent.

Hierarchical models

Some sets of information, such as organizational structure, fit best as *hierarchical models*. These models use a parent-child relationships to illustrate the chain of command, or leadership structure, of a target. This can help an analyst identify all the components of a target that need to be further analyzed. It can also help identify any choke points or bottlenecks that could be significant. This information can be gathered from many sources, and needs to be updated periodically as personnel or organizational structures change. Figure 10-1 shows an example of a hierarchical model.

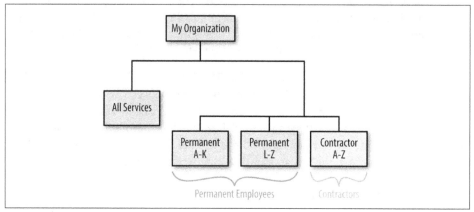

Figure 10-1. Hierarchical model

Hierarchical models are traditionally used to show personnel or roles, but one unique application of a hierarchical model is to use it to identify the data that is important to an organization. A hierarchical model for data includes the broad categories of data, such as financial information, customer information, and sensitive company information. Any information that is valuable to the organization and that an attacker may try to access or impact should be identified, including impacting accessibility, as we have seen in many ransomware cases over the past few years.

After the main categories have been identified, the next step is to identify all of the subcategories of information. Financial information may break down further into credit card information, payroll information for employees, and futures projections for the company. All of this data likely sits in different places within the organization, with different teams responsible for maintaining and securing. Owner information for each data type should also be built into the model. This type of model will help organizations understand the data they are protecting and where it resides, and can be used to identify which data types are most targeted using internal and external information. It can also be overlaid with network models to identify where on the network this data lives.

Network models

Network models are useful when representing the relationships or interactions between individuals or groups. Network models are also used to develop computer network diagrams, both of an organization's own network and often of an attacker's infrastructure. Network models have also been used to show the relationships between attacker groups, as well as the relationships between victims of an intrusion. Network models have to be updated the most frequently of any of the data types discussed here, because they have many moving parts that change quickly and often. Figure 10-2 shows a sample network map.

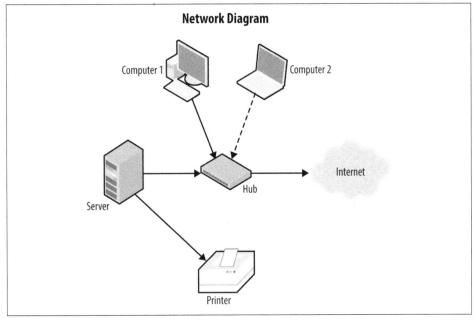

Figure 10-2. Network model example

Process models

Process models illustrate the various actions and decision points that make up a structured process. The structured intelligence analysis model is a type of process model that shows the steps that need to be taken to complete a process. The cyber intrusion kill chain is another kind of process model. In chapters 4, 5, and 6, it was used to capture indicators of a specific incident, but the kill chain can also be used to document the steps that an attacker takes at a more strategic level to assist in the development of the target model.

Timelines

Timelines are linear models that show the time-based relationships between activities. Incident responders are most familiar with attack timelines that show when specific actions were taken during an incident, but many other timelines can be helpful in an incident-response situation. Understanding the timeline from vulnerability discovery to remediation is useful to help a network defender know how long they will remain vulnerable to a particular attack and can help decision makers determine when they will need to act. A timeline indicating when different actor groups were seen using a particular exploit or tool can help an analyst determine the threat from that malware, as well as understand how quickly or slowly tool-reuse propagates after a tool is identified. An example of the timeline of external GLASS WIZARD reporting and internal GLASS WIZARD activity is shown in Figure 10-3.

Figure 10-3. GLASS WIZARD timeline example

Visualizing the temporal aspects of various activities provides analysts with a framework for understanding how those aspects will impact their organization's goals and objectives.

The Strategic Intelligence Cycle

Chapter 2 covered the intelligence cycle pretty extensively, but the primary focus was on tactical and operational-level intelligence—following the cycle in order to respond to a specific and often immediate threat. At the strategic level, the intelligence cycle follows the same process, but each step (from setting requirements to dissemination) looks different than it does when dealing with an immediate threat. Let's examine these differences.

Setting Strategic Requirements

It may seem that setting requirements at the strategic level would be more vague than with tactical intelligence. With tactical intelligence, there is a specific threat to focus on, which helps direct requirements. That is not often the case with strategic intelligence; and when requirements are passed down, they are often something vague like "Tell me what we need to know." Although the scope and the time frame are much larger, the requirements should still be specific.

Strategic requirements often follow the military concept of *commander's intent*. Commander's intent is what allowed large, dispersed units to make decisions about when and how to conduct operations. Using the models that were developed as part of the strategic process, the commander, or the CEO or CISO, can state their goal or objective (a.k.a intent) and trust that all decision makers are on the same page and will take actions that will support that objective without the need to micromanage. For example, if the intent is to ensure that a company is first-to-market with a new product, then making sure that the manufacturing schematics, marketing plans, and other sensitive information are not leaked is a task that would fall under the commander's intent. Developing a model of the attackers who may target that sensitive information is a strategic intelligence requirement that is necessary to support the ability to protect that information.

Strategic requirements, unlike tactical or operational ones, have the luxury of time on their side. Requirements can be planned far in advance, allowing them to be larger or broader in scope, depending on the needs of the organization, and they can also specify timing or periodicity. For example, a strategic requirement may be to update a company's threat model twice a year, or to analyze what new threats may impact a business if they move into a new market or a new geographical region. When setting strategic requirements, it is helpful to identify early on if the requirement is ongoing, when analysis needs to be completed, and how often the findings will need to be reviewed or updated. It is also important to periodically review standing strategic requirements to identify whether they are still relevant and necessary. Strategic requirements, just like tactical and operational ones, can become stale if they are no longer relevant. However, it can take much longer to realize that strategic requirements are stale.

Collection

The type of collection we have focused on so far in this book has been centered around logs and external sources such as threat feeds and information sharing. Although these types of collections still play a part in strategic intelligence, the scope of what you are collecting and from where will greatly increase, which is pretty exciting for those of us who are intelligence nerds at heart. Depending on your requirements—which have been specifically called out, *right*?—you may find yourself pulling information on economic, political, and cultural sources, or any number of other sources. This type of collection will also be more extensive than tactical collection, where any information older than a few days or even hours may be obsolete. With strategic intelligence, you may be searching for information that goes back years in order to capture trends or look for changes. The following sections describe useful types of strategic information to collect.

Geopolitical sources

Geopolitical intelligence provides information on what is going on in the world, including conflicts, alliances, tensions, and other factors related to international relations in a particular region. There was a time when many people, maybe even some of the people reading (or writing) this book, disregarded geopolitics when it came to incident response. It is possible to hack a network from anywhere, so why would it matter if conflicts existed in certain areas of the world? Well, it turns out that there are many reasons geopolitics are important for incident response. Although it is possible to access networks from anywhere in the world, it doesn't mean that regional conflicts or international tension have no impact on intrusion targeting and planning. Numerous times over the past decade, understanding geopolitical intelligence has been critical to understanding and responding to cyber attacks. Here are some examples:

- In 2008, the ongoing conflict between Russia and Georgia escalated with a series of DDoS attacks against the Georgian state government, specifically targeting the website of the president along with sites dedicated to communications and finance. Shortly after these attacks began, kinetic operations commenced, making this the first official case of joint cyber-kinetic offensive operations.
- In 2011, public outcry arose against the beating and eventual death of a homeless man in Fullerton, California, by police officers. As the investigation and hearings against the officers were conducted, both the city and the police department were targeted with DDoS attacks against websites and other attempted attacks targeting city assets. Attackers were successful at bringing the police department's website down on at least one occasion.

What is going on in the world, whether it is in our own backyards or across the globe, matters to strategic cyber threat intelligence. Understanding political climates, conflicts, triggers, and tactics of adversaries can assist in strategic planning.

Although it is normal to focus outward on international threats, some aspects of geopolitics are local and should be considered as well. Good sources of geopolitical intelligence are peer-reviewed articles, white papers, and assessments. For this type of intelligence, is it often useful to look for historical information as well as current information about a situation. Understanding trends and patterns is particularly useful with geopolitical intelligence, where history often seems to repeat itself.

Is News Intelligence?

It is possible to get a lot of information related to current events from the news, and it can be easy to interpret those as geopolitical intelligence. However, the information provided may not be a complete assessment of a situation and should be used with caution. Current events and the news should be used to understand what threats an analyst should look into more, but from there the analyst can begin to research the events and their implications by using peer-reviewed sources such as academic journals and white papers.

Economic sources

Economic intelligence is incredibly important to network defense. Economics, the study of the production, consumption, and transfer of wealth, is not just useful for situational awareness, but for understanding the motivations of many threat actors. The vast majority of intrusions are economically motivated, whether that involves stealing credit cards for direct monetization or stealing intellectual property for strategic economic gain, and economic intelligence sources can provide insight into an adversary's motivations.

Economic intelligence sources vary, and can include information on how stolen information is monetized, the types of information that criminals target, the types of information that are being targeted for industrial espionage, and economics associated with nation states that are likely to target you or have targeted you in the past. Even with a broad understanding of economics, this type of information can help organizations understand the strategic threats that they are facing. A specialized knowledge can provide an even greater level of insight, though it is harder to find someone specializing in economics on a network security team.

Historical sources

Historical sources, such as analysis of a nation's tactics or priorities from a previous conflict, are another often overlooked aspect of intelligence analysis when it comes to responding to cyber threats. The internet is new, relatively speaking, so how could historical sources possibly support cyber threat intelligence? If we consider the cyber realm to be an extension of the physical world, any activities that take place in the physical world will likely end up manifesting in the cyber realm as well. Because of this, history becomes important. If we can understand how adversaries targeted organizations before the internet existed, we can begin to pick up on ways that they will attempt to achieve the same goals by using new tactics and new mediums.

This is one of the reasons that military doctrines ranging from Sun Tzu's *Art of War* to Carl von Cluasewitz's *On War* are so often quoted in cyber-security presentations. Just because they were written long before modern incident response does not mean that they are not relevant to the prevention and detection of attacks in this new domain.

Con men were operating long before email was invented, and many of the tactics they used were similar to modern phishing scams, which just use a new avenue for their schemes. One tactic to help integrate historical sources into strategic intelligence analysis is to look at the most common threats that an organization sees, whether that is phishing emails targeting employees or targeted intrusions aimed at obtaining corporate information, and then to look for how those attacks have been carried out in the past. The goal of this type of analysis is to identify any lessons learned or patterns that can help the organization better understand the threats and better posture itself to defend against those threats.

Business sources

Strategic intelligence, when used to support business operations, relies heavily on an understanding of the defending organization's business. Many security professionals struggle with supporting strategic-level business decisions because they do not take the time to understand the problems that the business is facing or what information is critical to operations. Without understanding the business, it is nearly impossible for intelligence analysts or incident responders to produce strategic intelligence that will help leaders make the best decisions for their organization's security.

Like all things in security, business operations and priorities are not static, so it is important to continually update and gather new information as it becomes available. *Business sources* include information on the markets an organization operates in, competitors, challenges to the business, new regions or markets that the business is planning to expand into, key personnel changes, and other aspects of business operations that have been identified as significant.

 In addition to these sources of information (geopolitical, economic, historical, and business), which are more strategically focused than other collection sources discussed in earlier chapters, it is also important to incorporate information from previous incidents into strategic analysis. Doing so allows the analyst to present a holistic picture of what is being seen in the network combined with additional insight into historical, political, and economic trends that may influence the threats that an organization faces. All of this information will be pulled together in the strategic analysis phase.

Analysis

Analysis at the strategic level follows the same process described in Chapter 8. Requirements are clearly stated, collection and processing occur, and hypotheses are developed and tested by researching and reviewing evidence that supports or refutes them. Strategic intelligence teams, however, must analyze a larger and more diverse data set, and therefore a larger team with diverse backgrounds and experiences should be utilized. You should keep these points in mind when conducting strategic-level analysis:

- The evidence to be considered will come not just from network information, as is often the case with incident response, but from many sources that the analysts may or may not have subject matter expertise or substantial knowledge of. In those cases, understanding the source of the information is especially relevant because the analysts will often end up taking the information at face value. Look for information that comes from peer-reviewed, reputable sources. If a particular piece of evidence is deemed to be a key during a process such as analysis of competing hypotheses, it is best to try to find more than one source that is reporting the same information.

- Biases can run rampant in strategic intelligence, where there is often a smaller amount of tactical evidence and more evidence that is open to interpretation.

Processes for strategic intelligence

Some specific processes are more conducive to strategic-level intelligence, and others are far less effective at this level. For example, the target-centric model, which is an asset to an analyst investigating an intrusion or working at the operational and campaign level, is not as useful at the strategic level because as we discussed, many of the target models are being developed during the analysis.

Several analytic models and processes stand out as particularly useful for strategic intelligence, including SWOT analysis, brainstorming, and murder boarding.

SWOT analysis. *Strength*, *Weakness*, *Opportunity*, and *Threat* (SWOT), is a model that is commonly used in risk management. SWOT takes into consideration internal aspects (strengths and weaknesses) as well as external aspects (opportunities and threats). It also lends itself to strategic intelligence specifically around network security and defense, because in many cases it will identify big-picture problems and concerns that will need to be addressed. It requires that an organization have a solid understanding of its core competencies and where they excel, be honest and up front about the issues that they face, and understand the external threats that are facing them. The basic outline for SWOT analysis is pictured in Figure 10-4.

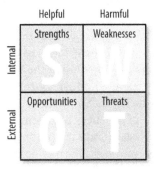

Figure 10-4. SWOT analysis (http://www.discoveryresearchgroup.com/swot)

For example, if documentation indicates that 90% of successful intrusions into the network come from phishing emails, this demonstrates a weakness of the organization that needs to be addressed. Identifying strengths can help determine steps that can be taken to mitigate those weaknesses.

SWOT analysis is useful not only for determining an organization's own strengths and weaknesses. It can also be used to analyze a foreign government, a criminal organization, or an attack group. To conduct this analysis, it is important to pull heavily from the research that was done in the collection phase. An important part of using this type of SWOT analysis is to look for places where an adversary's strengths line up with your organization's weaknesses. Those are places that need to be addressed.

Brainstorming. Strategic intelligence analysis should not be the work of one individual. As we mentioned, it is helpful to have multiple analysts with different backgrounds focusing on identifying the issues that will have a significant impact on an organization moving forward. An analysis on past intelligence failures (an analysis of analysis, one might say) has found that many times an intelligence failure is the result of group think, which discourages creativity and thinking outside of the box. General James Mattis said there is no place for group think, especially when it comes to national policy (*http://washex.am/2trKeBt*): "The national security decision-making process, as you know, you need different ideas to be strongly argued. You don't want the tyranny of consensus of group-think."

Brainstorming, especially with a group that comes from different disciplines, is a good way to counter group think by encouraging new and creative approaches to problems. Brainstorming can be used on its own or with nearly any other analytic method. Although it sounds as if it is unstructured, the CIA's Tradecraft primer notes that brainstorming should be structured in order to be most effective. One of the most critical components of successful brainstorming is to allot enough time at the beginning of the process to enable the group to explore a wide variety of possibilities. When a group is time-constrained or feels rushed, they are more likely to select a smaller group of hypotheses that sounds realistic rather than exploring a larger set of possibilities that may generate new insight into an issue. It is also a good idea to ensure that at least one person is participating in the brainstorming who has a different role or approach than the team. Although getting together a group of incident responders to brainstorm will likely bring more than one point of view, it is still likely to be constrained to the typical experiences of an incident responder. By bringing in an outsider, whether that is a systems administrator, security architect, or someone from human resources, having new and different perspectives in the group will also discourage group thinking and force the rest of the team to consider new angles.

Brainstorming should result in the identification of a new set of hypotheses, and at that point the team can focus on identifying specific evidence from the collected information to support or refute the hypothesis, and then use an analytic method such as ACH to complete the analysis. It is just fine if it is not possible for the entire group to see the analysis to completion. One of the most important aspects of brainstorming is having the group there to identify new hypotheses, call out our unfounded assumptions, and identify bias at the beginning of the analytic process. If one or more analysts takes the lead on completing the analysis, it is still critical that they consult or check in with the group from time to time.

Murder boarding. The term *murder board* was originally coined to describe a process used to help a candidate prepare for oral presentations. During a murder board, an analyst presents his findings to a review board, which then questions not only the findings, but the analytic processes used to come to that conclusion. Through this process, it is possible to identify any biases that are present in the analysis, any key assumptions that were not validated, and any analytic leaps that were not founded in evidence. Even if the analysis is sound and no obvious errors exist, a murder board helps an analyst vocalize the process used and explain the methods and findings, something that many intelligence analysts struggle with. When questioned about how a certain conclusion was reached, especially at the strategic level, that has more variables and pieces to tie together, an analyst will often default back to using vague terminology or anecdotes to explain how they conducted the analysis, and that type of explanation often does not inspire confidence in decision makers. Being prepared to describe not just the conclusion, but the analytic process itself, is a skill that takes time and practice to develop.

Rob Dartnall, an analyst from Great Britain, reminded us of the importance of the murder board, especially when it comes to strategic intelligence where the stakes are high, in his presentation "Conventional Intelligence Analysis in Cyber Threat Intelligence (*https://www.youtube.com/watch?v=jzHw8lkocXA*)."

When analysis that you have done is about to lead directly to important and potentially drastic actions, it is imperative that not only is your analysis sound, but that you are prepared to defend it under scrutiny.

Check Your Egos at the Door

Strategic intelligence analysis is no place for egos. The goal of this type of analysis is to provide intelligence to decision makers so that they can act, which also means identifying the level of confidence an analyst has and any intelligence gaps, and updating the assessment when new information is identified that changes the findings. When egos get involved, it becomes difficult to objectively assess things like confidence, and it is difficult to go back to stakeholders and acknowledge when mistakes were made or when information changes. Processes such as murder boards help remove ego from the equation. It is important to note, however, that the presenter's ego isn't the only one that needs to be checked. Individuals participating in a murder board and asking questions should also be careful not to let their egos get in the way and cloud their judgment. It can be tempting to try to "prove the presenter wrong" for the sake of ego, which can lead to the board member's own biases running rampant.

Dissemination

Dissemination is only slightly different at the strategic level, and those differences are due to the scope and nature of strategic intelligence. The recommendations that are being made have the potential to significantly impact a businesses's operations moving forward, and therefore, unless there are specific time requirements, accuracy and thoroughness take precedence over speed.

Many of the same principles that we discussed in Chapter 9 are directly applicable to dissemination at the strategic level, but there are some unique aspects, too. Specifically:

- The audience is key at this level, and so it is important to identify who the audience will be before beginning the process of writing or creating the final deliverable. If multiple audiences would like to receive information in different ways, it is a good idea to make sure that the information is presented to each audience in the way that will be most useful to them. Make sure that the different versions of intelligence products or reports tell the same story, however. The last thing you want is for different leaders within an organization to have a different interpretation of the analysis and its meaning.
- In strategic intelligence, it is important to specifically call out any intelligence gaps or trigger events that would result in a change to the analysis. It can be difficult to tell leadership that the analytic findings have room for doubt, but setting these expectations will make it easier to communicate changes as they occur.

Conclusion

We consider strategic intelligence to be the logic behind the plan, and it is no wonder that many incident responders struggle with finding the time to conduct this level of analysis. In many organizations, incident responders would be hard-pressed to find a plan at all, much less understand the logic behind the plan. Strategic intelligence, when properly analyzed and adopted by leadership, can not only inform leadership of the long-term threats to an organization, but can also provide incident responders with policies and procedures that will support their ability to meet the needs of their organization.

Strategic intelligence for incident response not only enables you to make smart decisions about the visibility of your networks, but also feeds directly into the requirements for tactical and operational levels of analysis. It will help you to know the following:

- Which threats are most significant so that incident response can prioritize and focus on those threats
- Which types of information are important to capture, and what warrants a brief to the CISO or other executives
- Which situations can be handled at the local levels

Any and all actions that take place can be tied back to strategic requirements. As you understand the logic behind the requirements you will be able to adapt and respond when situations change without having to revisit the entire process. Strategic intelligence takes time, but when it is done correctly, it can set up entire programs for success long into the future. It is well worth the time and effort.

## CHAPTER 11

Building an Intelligence Program

"Great things in business are never done by one person. They're done by a team of people."

—Steve Jobs

Working with an intelligence team can be a game changer for many security operations programs. However, there needs to be system in place to get everyone on the same page, both within the intelligence team and with the customers that the team will be supporting. A structured intelligence program will provide the benefit of a robust intelligence support capability while avoiding many of the struggles teams go through when they are thrown together rather than purposely built. This chapter covers the various elements to consider when building an intelligence team or function at your organization.

Are You Ready?

One question that frequently gets asked is, "What are the prerequisites for forming an intelligence team?" Many things need to be done before a formalized intelligence function will be beneficial. We are not of the mindset that an intelligence program is the last thing that should be created at an organization, but we do view the intelligence function as the glue that holds many other security functions together. If you do not have those existing functions, you will just end up standing around, holding a bottle of glue.

Here are some fundamental questions to ask before beginning to develop an intelligence program, which will require funding, time, and effort:

Is there a security function at the organization?
   This seems like an easy question, but it is surprising how many organizations start thinking about developing a threat-intelligence capability with a one-person

security team or even a one-person team responsible for both IT operations and security. Although an intelligence-driven approach would probably benefit the poor individual responsible for keeping everything from catching on fire, the intelligence team would take budget away from additional security-focused personnel and tools, meaning that the intelligence team would likely *become* the security team rather than focusing on intelligence work.

Is there network visibility?

Intelligence programs rely on access to information, both internal and external, with internal being some of the most critical information needed to conduct intelligence analysis. When there is no visibility, whether that is because of technical limitations or privacy or legal concerns, then the intelligence team's effectiveness will be limited. If visibility is a technical issue, the best approach is to focus on gaining that visibility prior to establishing an intelligence program. If there are legal or privacy concerns, it is probably best to discuss those concerns with legal counsel to determine what can be done, and whether an intelligence program is a good fit at all. At times, intelligence can help overcome some of these types of hurdles for an organization, including providing additional insight into external threats to compensate for the lack of visibility, but these types of situations are the exception rather than the rule.

Are there multiple teams or functions to support?

As we mentioned, intelligence can be thought of as the glue that holds together multiple functions. Intelligence gained from incident response can help with prevention and detection, assist with vulnerability management and security architecture, and inform strategic planning. That is a lot of work for a single individual. When multiple facets of intelligence work need to be done in an organization, that is a good sign that it is time to set up an intelligence program with multiple team members. If the plan is for intelligence to support a single aspect such as primarily supporting incident response, it is probably best to start with an intelligence-focused role on that individual team.

Is there room in the budget?

The answer to this question is usually no, followed up with, "But if we need it, we will make it work." Either of these answers is a good sign that now is *not* the best time to start an intelligence program. Intelligence is almost always a cost center rather than a profit center, which means that it will not generate additional revenue to sustain its operations. Getting the appropriate level of funding can be difficult. Intelligence programs do not need to be budget breakers, but the one thing that will almost always be a high-ticket item is personnel. If you are just developing a program, it is important to find the right person, whether internally or hiring externally, to get the program started on the right foot. A much better answer to this question would be "Yes, we have some room because this has been identified as an important step in maturing our security program." OK, we know that an answer like that doesn't come around often, but if it does, that is a good sign that you are ready for an intelligence program.

 At the far end of the spectrum of determining budget is the answer, "We were just horribly hacked and now we have to show what we are doing differently ASAP so that it never happens again. Go buy things. All the things." Even though the knee-jerk reaction to a significant breach often comes with substantial budget, it is important to know that a breach is not the best reason to start an intelligence program, and if key prerequisites (network visibility, guidance and requirements, and budget) are not met, then what looks like a good opportunity now could turn into questions about ROI a few years down the road. If your organization is in this situation, be sure to take a pragmatic approach to the program, follow the guidelines described in the next section to determine goals and audience, and ensure that you are capturing meaningful metrics to ensure that the intelligence program will not fall victim to the first round of budget cuts after your organization has recovered from the initial knee-jerk reaction to the breach.

After you have determined whether a formalized intelligence program is the best option, many other aspects of the program still need to be defined before hiring and product generation begins. Developing a new program requires a lot of work up front in order to make sure that it is successful in the long term. It is important to clearly define your program so that everyone is on the same page about what you are trying to create.

Planning the Program

Three types of planning go into the development of a solid program: conceptual planning, functional planning, and detailed planning:

1. *Conceptual planning* sets the framework that the program should work within. Stakeholders contribute the most to conceptual planning, but it is important for them to understand what intelligence can offer them, especially if they are unfamiliar with intelligence work.
2. *Functional planning* involves input from both stakeholders and intelligence professionals to identify requirements to complete goals, logistics such as budget and staffing needs, constraints, dependencies, and any legal concerns. Functional planning provides structure and realism to the sometimes abstract conceptual planning phase.

3. *Detailed planning* is then conducted by the intelligence team, which will determine how the goals identified by the stakeholders will be met within the functional limits.

All three phases of planning are important to ensure that all aspects have been considered, from budgeting to the metrics that will be reported to stakeholders.

Defining Stakeholders

It is crucial for the intelligence team to understand its stakeholders so that the analysis it conducts and the reports it provides are useful and understandable to its stakeholders. Those stakeholders should be clearly defined. Defining stakeholders should take place during the early phases of conceptual planning, because the stakeholders will contribute to the rest of the process.

Here are a few common stakeholders:

Intelligence response team
> Incident response is an ideal stakeholder because incident response will not only benefit from intelligence support of operations, but also provides additional information to the intelligence team that will feed into other functions as well.

Security operations center/team
> Intelligence teams can provide SOCs with information on emerging threats, whether they are general threats or threats targeting an industry, or even specifically to the organization. Intelligence can also provide technical indicators for alerts, enrichment information to provide context on alerts, and information to help with prioritizing alerts. The security operations center team can also provide information to the intelligence team on attempted attacks that never reach the point of a full-blown incident. Even if the incident-response team is not involved, there is still a great deal of information that an intelligence analyst can gain from failed attempts.

Vulnerability management teams
> Vulnerability management teams often deal with vulnerabilities numbering in the hundreds, if not thousands. Intelligence teams can help prioritize patching based on the most significant threat to the organization. Many vendors will provide information on the severity and the impact of the vulnerability, but an additional level of analysis still needs to be done to identify the threat that the vulnerability presents to a particular organization. An intelligence team is ideally situated to assist with this analysis. The intelligence team can also work with the vulnerability management team and the security operations team in tandem to ensure that the security team can monitor for exploits that are targeting unpatched vulnerabilities while an organization is in the process of remediation.

Chief information security officers

The CISO is responsible for understanding and managing the risk to an organization's information, and intelligence can provide insight to help both understand and manage that risk. As a stakeholder, a CISO will likely have the broadest intelligence requirements, both tactical and strategic in nature. It is important to understand what a CISO expects from an intelligence program and how that information relates to other teams within security operations.

End Users

End users are most often an indirect stakeholder for intelligence. Often an intelligence program will support end-user security training by providing information on recent or evolving threats and helping users understand the impact of those threats and how they should respond. If end-user education or awareness is something that the intelligence program will support, it is important to identify what team will be responsible for this relationship, because it is impossible for the intelligence team to directly communicate with each end user in an organization.

After stakeholders have been identified, it is important to document them. The format shown in Figure 11-1 is an example of a way to document stakeholder identification. It includes basic information, including the name of the stakeholder, the point of contact (who should be informed that they are responsible for this relationship), and a brief description of what the intelligence program will provide to the stakeholder.

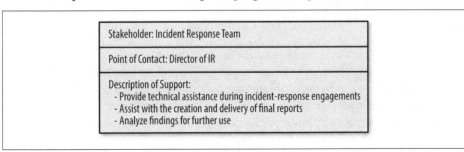

Stakeholder: Incident Response Team

Point of Contact: Director of IR

Description of Support:
- Provide technical assistance during incident-response engagements
- Assist with the creation and delivery of final reports
- Analyze findings for further use

Figure 11-1. Sample stakeholder documentation

Defining Goals

After stakeholders have been defined, it is time to identify the goals of the program with respect to each stakeholder. This is a more in-depth process that involves discussing the needs of the stakeholders and the ways the intelligence program can meet these needs in a concrete way. This dialogue is necessary because the stakeholders know best the types of support they need, and the intelligence program representatives know best whether a particular goal is achievable.

During goal setting, you should not define how a goal will be met or what tools or personnel will be used to meet the goal. At this stage, the intelligence team may not be staffed or have acquired tools, and defining these details puts arbitrary boundaries on the team's processes.

Defining Success Criteria

Defining concrete goals gets the stakeholders and the intelligence team on the same page by using the same definition of *success*. In the stakeholder documentation template in Figure 11-1, different people likely will have different definitions of of *support*. One of the definitions may be to provide technical assistance during incident-response engagements. To one person, that may translate to providing technical IOCs, and to another person, that may mean that the intelligence team will conduct log analysis to identify anomalous behaviors. Those different definitions drastically change the nature of the support; one is external facing, and the other is internal facing. This is a good example of how setting concrete goals should clarify the support that is provided. In this case, although providing technical support is an overall requirement, the goals could clarify that this technical support could include (1) identifying external intelligence, including IOCs, to assist with the investigation, or (2) assisting incident-response teams with analyzing anomalous behaviors in logs—or both, depending on requirements.

Here are some key questions that can help an organization start the conversation:

- What current problems are the stakeholders dealing with?
- What are the ways that an intelligence program can help with those problems?
- What are the ideal outcomes of intelligence support to the stakeholder?
- If there are multiple outcomes, how should they be prioritized?
- How will the support be initiated? Is it continuous or on-demand?
- Are there any dependencies for support?

After success criteria has been determined, the process can move to identifying potential ways to achieve success. There is rarely just one way to achieve a goal, and the best choice is often determined by the resources required by each option.

Identifying Requirements and Constraints

Requirements and constraints fall into the functional portion of planning. Once success criteria has been outlined and ideal outcomes identified, it is important to also identify the things that are needed to accomplish the tasks that have been set out. These things usually fall into two buckets: requirements—things needed to accomplish the goals, and constraints—things that hinder the ability to accomplish goals.

One way to identify requirements and constraints is to conduct a walk-through or a tabletop exercise of the problem, stepping through the various ways that the problem can be addressed with a potential solution. The goal of this exercise is not to solve the problem, but to identify the things needed to achieve the goal (requirements) as well as to identify potential issues or problems that need to be addressed (constraints). These should be documented for each potential solution, and the results can be used to identify the best course of action. This should be done at a high level still, and should not focus on the particular details of a requirement. For example, a walk-through of a potential process may determine that an automated solution would be necessary to provide results at the scale required, but at this stage it is not important to determine what that solution is, just to identify it as a requirement. Success criteria and requirements and constraints should be added to the stakeholder documentation to continue building a comprehensive picture of the intelligence program, as shown in Figure 11-2.

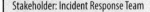

Stakeholder: Incident Response Team

Point of Contact: Director of IR

Description of Support:
- Provide technical assistance during incident-response engagements
- Assist with the creation and delivery of final reports
- Analyze findings for further use

Success Criteria
- All incidents are reviewed by an intelligence analyst
- Incidents deemed significant are worked in tandem with an IR analyst and intelligence analyst
- Intelligence analysts contribute contextual information on threats to IR reports.
- Finding from engagements are used to create alerts for the SOC and include contextual information

Requirements
- Criteria for determining "significant" incidents
- Staffing to support average number of significant incidents
- Analysis platform for IR and Intelligence to coordinate
- Communications channel with SOC

Figure 11-2. Advanced stakeholder documentation

Think Long Term

Some people in this industry, ourselves included, often bite off more than they can chew. Whether it is because of pride, dedication to the mission, or a firm belief that a human can operate on less than four hour of sleep a night, we sometimes take on tasks we shouldn't. Even when we identify that there are constraints that have not been addressed, that doesn't always stop us.

Though it is tempting to take on exciting tasks even when there are obvious constraints, make sure to think through the long-term impacts of that decision and whether it is sustainable. Identify whether things that can be done to ensure that the constraints are at least identified and earmarked for future attention, even if they cannot be addressed immediately. Sometimes it is necessary and appropriate to say yes to a task that is not completely resourced, but it should be done in a way that will not allow it to have a negative impact on operations for years to come.

Defining Metrics

Good metrics tell a story, and they are best received when they tell a story about something that the stakeholders care about. Many intelligence programs start operating without thinking about how they will routinely communicate progress to stakeholders, especially in a quantitative rather than a qualitative manner. The planning stage of a program is the best time to determine the metrics that will be gathered and reported. This activity falls into the detailed planning phase, but it relies heavily on both the conceptual and functional planning phases.

Metrics should speak directly to the conceptual issues that stakeholders identified during planning. When you start defining your intelligence program, one of the first questions that should have been asked was what the stakeholder gaps or requirements were that needed intelligence support to fulfill. It may not be possible to determine the exact metrics that will be captured initially, but even identifying what success looks like and how it can be measured will help set up the program to report on progress. If stakeholders have specific results that they would like to be informed of, these can be built into the process at the beginning, and functional planning can ensure that the necessary resources are being captured and accounted for. If teams wait until they have been operating for a year or more before trying to identify whether the program is meeting its goals, they might not only lack the data to show success, but also lose sight of what success looks like for the program.

Different stakeholders will have different goals and therefore different definitions of success, which will be demonstrated through different metrics. Capturing what success means and how it can be measured for each stakeholder will make it much easier to stay focused on the tasks at hand and identify success as the program moves forward.

Stakeholder Personas

Some people may think it is a little odd to have dossiers of fellow employees laying around, but we are intelligence professionals, and that is just what we do. Stakeholder personas are incredibly valuable to an intelligence program because they ensure that intelligence analysts are able to focus on the specific needs of the individual stakeholders throughout their work. Understanding your intelligence customers is key to providing them the right information at the right time in a way that they can best receive and act on the information.

Stakeholder personas can be developed for a group of stakeholders, such as a team of SOC analysts or threat hunters, but the best approach is to develop a persona for the individual point of contact within a stakeholder group. Maintaining a persona on an individual means that it will have to be updated when the role changes or when someone new assumes that role. It is important to develop a persona for the individual because that individual is responsible for the relationship between the intelligence team and the stakeholder team and will carry a great deal of weight as far as how the support relationship progresses. Different individuals likely will have different ways of interacting with the intelligence team and different preferences for receiving and sharing information. The better an intelligence team understands the personas that they support, the better value they will be able to provide them through their intelligence work.

When developing a persona for either a group or an individual, you need to take several important things into account. For an individual, it is important to capture information specific to the person, such as background, the things they are passionate about, the triggers they have related to their roles, and the way they typically operate.

Stakeholder personas are similar to the personas developed for dissemination, which we covered in Chapter 9. In fact, similar templates can be used with only a few minor adjustments to include things such as triggers and the specifics of the requirements between the stakeholder and the intelligence team. We also recommend documenting the individual's coffee or tea order—you never know when that will come in handy.

Tactical Use Cases

Use cases are a staple of program development, and intelligence programs are no different. If you are fortunate enough to work in an organization that already has intelligence use cases identified and documented, you are ahead of the game, as that is something many teams struggle with. Even if the use cases are intuitive and well understood without much documentation, putting something in writing is good practice, to ensure that everyone stays on the same page and to provide a concrete reference for new team members.

Tactical use cases involve intelligence that is useful on a day-to-day basis. This type of intelligence will change rapidly but can also be some of the most directly applicable intelligence in a security program. The following sections cover some of the most common tactical use cases for an intelligence team.

SOC Support

SOC support is one of the primary customers of an intelligence program. Within SOC support are three primary and unique use cases:

Alerting and signature development

Intelligence analysts provide intelligence, both internal and external, to generate rules or signatures for alerting. Based on the program requirements, this may involve searching out intelligence to generate signatures and sharing them with the SOC, or creating alerts or rules based on that intelligence.

Triage

Intelligence provides context to SOC analysts to assist with the triage and prioritization of alerts that are generated. Intelligence can help the SOC understand the significance of an alert, which can then be triaged based on its severity and impact. Intelligence can also tell an analyst the steps that should be taken to identify whether the alert is a false positive by providing examples of true positive and false positives for comparison or by providing secondary indicators to look for. Triage intelligence often includes handling guidelines as well so that analysts have instructions on how to respond to a threat.

Situational awareness

Intelligence can provide situational awareness to SOC analysts to help them understand emerging and significant threats to their organization, both of which can help with generating rules for alerts and performing triage on those alerts. SOC analysts, while often more focused on the tactical, day-to-day application of threat intelligence, still benefit from a strategic understanding of threats faced by their organization. Providing situational awareness may involve a daily or weekly brief or may be on demand when a significant threat warrants additional information. *Tactical* does not always have to mean *reactionary*, and intelligence can provide situational awareness to the SOC to help them understand and prevent threats from ever impacting their networks.

Indicator Management

Another tactical level use case for intelligence is indicator management. We have touched on indicators in multiple places throughout this book, and the bottom line is that indicators can be useful intelligence tools when they are properly generated, actioned, and maintained. Indicators are used heavily in rule generation, threat detection, and information sharing. They can also be used in operational and strategic-level analysis to help create a holistic picture of a threat. Managing indicators is not a trivial task. The more indicators that are being maintained, the more difficult it becomes. This section covers several aspects of indicator management, including managing a threat-intelligence platform, identifying and documenting context for tactical indicators, and integrating threat-intelligence feeds:

Threat-intelligence platform management

In many cases, the intelligence team is responsible for managing a threat-intelligence platform, sometimes known as a TIP, which usually consists of a database for storing indicators and a user interface for assigning context and relationships between the indicators. Threat-intelligence platforms should be queryable to assist in analysis, and many also provide ways to export indicators to security appliances.

 A threat-intelligence platform makes managing indicators easier, but it is important to have a clear idea of why you are storing indicators in the first place. This understanding will ensure not only that you are managing them properly, but also that the team does not fall into the trap of gathering indicators for the sake of having more indicators. Collections are good; hoarding is not.

Updating indicators

Indicators are not static. They may, as with most network-based indicators, be malicious for a time and then disappear or become benign. Or they may, as with many host-based indicators, remain malicious even as the context around them changes or evolves. In many cases, malware that is originally linked to one attack or group is adopted by different actors or used in new campaigns. Tracking that information and linking new uses or tactics to existing indicators while weeding out or deactivating indicators that are no longer valid will ensure a steady stream of reliable, high-confidence indicators for tactical uses. Always remember that these indicators should be used; they should not just sit in a repository being carefully curated and maintained.

Third-party intelligence and feeds management

Threat feeds and third-party intelligence are another source of indicators that must be managed by an intelligence team in order to be useful to an organization. In many cases, these feeds are fed into a threat-intelligence platform. However, in some instances, they are directly tied into a security system such as a security incident and event management (SIEM) system. In most cases, a direct feed is not ideal, because it can be difficult to know what information is being shared across automated feeds. However, the practice is so widespread that many organizations believe that threat feeds are the cornerstone of threat intelligence. Threat feeds and intelligence from external sources must be carefully vetted and applied cautiously. A better method is to use third-party intelligence and feeds as an enrichment source. They can provide context around internally generated indicators and can be used to maintain and update existing indicators and rules.

It is important to understand the sources of these threat feeds so that you can easily identify how to use the information. Third-party feeds derived from honeypots will be useful in different situations than feeds of community-sourced incident-response data.

Operational Use Cases

Operational use cases for an intelligence program focus on understanding campaigns and trends in attacks, either against your own organization or against other organizations similar to yours. The sooner a campaign can be identified or a series of intrusions tied together, the more likely it is that the activity can be identified before the attackers are successful in achieving their goals.

Campaign Tracking

A *campaign* is a series of actions or attacks that support a common goal or objective. The island-hopping campaign in World War II is a good illustration of the concept. The United States wanted to defeat Japan, and therefore needed land from which to carry out attacks against the Japanese mainland. The island-hopping campaign was a series of attacks that targeted the less-defended Pacific Islands. After an island was taken, the military would build landing strips and fortify defenses and then use the newly established base to launch further attacks to gain the strategic advantage. Even though they may have employed different forces to carry out the attacks or used varying tactics based on terrain and fortification, the goal of the campaign was the same, and the various actions taken were all aimed at achieving that same goal.

This is the way that many adversaries operate: they have a goal or a target in mind, but achieving it is not always as easy as simply attacking the primary target. Often many steps are involved, and many organizations may be targeted by the same group in an island-hopping fashion, or an attacker may carry out a string of attacks against one or two organizations over a long period of time. It all depends on the goal of the campaign, so when it comes to campaign tracking, understanding the goal will provide far more insight than tracking only the various discrete indicators. Campaign tracking has various aspects, including identifying the campaign goals, identifying tools and tactics being used, and responding to the activity. We dive into those aspects here:

Identify the campaign focus
Many campaigns are focused on a particular industry, and identifying and understanding campaigns that target other organizations in your industry can provide early warning that something may target you soon, or may have already targeted you and threat hunting may be required. Identifying the industries that are targeted involves industry-based sharing communities such as ISACs, commercial intelligence, or open source intelligence.

Identifying tools and tactics

Once a campaign has been identified or is suspected to be part of a larger operation, the next step (after identifying the goal or intent of the operation) is to identify tools and tactics that are being employed in order to prevent and detect their use. Network-based indicators associated with an ongoing campaign are often useful for monitoring for threats. However, remember that they will not remain malicious forever, and their usefulness will eventually pass. Attacker tactics and behaviors are better places to focus, as long as you have the ability to monitor for them.

Response support

It is important to not only understand what campaigns are active, but also what should be done after an intrusion, whether successful or failed, is identified in an organization. Campaign reports often provide information on the threat actor group behind the attacks, including tactics and tools, and sometimes even how the actors respond if they are detected or lose access to a network. All of these pieces of information can support SOC operations as well as incident response if necessary, and can be used to provide updates and situational awareness to the CISO or other executives.

Strategic Use Cases

Strategic intelligence should always have a place in an intelligence program, regardless of how small that part is. As we discussed in Chapter 10, strategic intelligence enables an organization to truly learn from its previous incidents and begin to change long-term, large-scale behaviors and policies in order to combat those experiences. To be most effective, strategic use cases require support and buy-in from executive leadership, because many of the actions that need to be taken in response to strategic-level intelligence need to be made at the executive level. Strategic intelligence will always be useful for providing situational awareness, but it will not be as effective if the right stakeholders are not involved. The primary strategic use cases are architecture support and risk assessments.

Architecture Support

Strategic intelligence can provide information not only on the ways an organization should respond to intrusions or attacks, but also on the ways it can posture itself to minimize attack surface and better detect these attacks. This information is primarily based on two things: internal incident-response information and campaign analysis. Using these two primary sources, several things can be done to help focus on the right protections for a network:

Improve defensibility

Intelligence teams can work with IT and security operations to improve the defensibility of a network by understanding how adversaries have attacked or attempted to attack it in the past. Although attackers are clever, they will often repeat the same tactics as long as they work. If a network is designed or configured in a way that provides an easy attack vector, they will continue to use that vector until they are successful or the opportunity is removed. Identifying these tactics can help identify an attacker's next logical move, and can help structure network defenses to protect against these threats.

Focus defenses on threats

Networks will always have vulnerabilities. It is simply a part of operating systems and programs that are created by humans. Not all vulnerabilities are created equally, however, and some deserve more attention than others. A threat-based approach can help identify which vulnerabilities to focus on. Outside of patch management, intelligence can also support vulnerability management at a higher level by providing insight into the threats posed by potential network architecture changes. For example, if an organization was debating a bring-your-own-device policy, or planning to introduce smart TVs into conference rooms across the organization, intelligence can help identify the threats to those devices and make recommendations before the policies are rolled out.

Risk Assessment/Strategic Situational Awareness

One of the primary roles of a CISO is to understand and manage the risks to an organization's information. Understanding threats is a critical part of risk assessment, and intelligence can provide information on the threats facing an organization. Here are some key steps to perform to support risk assessments and strategic situational awareness:

Identify when risk changes

Risk does not stay the same, and external as well as internal factors may change the risk level to an organization. Intelligence teams, by working with multiple stakeholders within an organization, can provide information to the CISO when there is the potential that the risk to an organization changes.

Identify mitigations

Another aspect of risk management that can be supported by intelligence is identifying mitigations to reduce risk. Often security professionals assume that when there is a significant threat, the organization will not accept the risk, but at the end of the day, many organizations have businesses to run and must find ways to mitigate risks so that business can continue. Shutting down operations or halting the deployment of a new program that will increase efficiency is simply not an option. Mitigations become important to business continuity. These mitigations take many shapes, and an intelligence team can help a CISO identify what can be done to bring risk down to an acceptable level.

Organizations rarely focus all of their attention on one level of intelligence, whether it is strategic, operations, or tactical. Most organizations have a multilevel program. Moving between levels of intelligence itself requires planning and consideration as well, which we will discuss in the next section.

Strategic to Tactical or Tactical to Strategic?

You can organize a multilevel intelligence program in two ways. Intelligence can either take a *top-down approach* (strategic to tactical) or a *bottom-up approach* (tactical to strategic). With a top-down approach, strategic intelligence at higher levels guides policies and strategy, and determines what tactical-level indicators the team should focus on and how they should be used in day-to-day operations. With a bottom-up approach, intelligence is primarily focused on tactical operations, and significant information is pushed up to the strategic level. Both approaches have advantages and disadvantages based on the stakeholders involved and the needs of the organization.

Top-down planning is the standard approach of traditional military planning. In military operations, planning is a key responsibility of the commander. The commander is responsible for knowing the overarching goals, what is important to sustained operations, and the status and disposition of forces. In situations where the leadership has a clear understanding of what they want to accomplish and how intelligence can support those plans, you can expect to see more of a top-down approach. Strategic intelligence support is important with the top-down approach because it keeps the leadership up-to-date on the threat landscape, which they integrate into their overall understanding of how to protect their networks.

Many organizations do not have a robust strategic intelligence function to provide overarching guidance, but still believe in the value of intelligence to support operations. In those situations, a bottom-up, or tactical-to-strategic approach may work best. Operations focus on the tactical levels, such as supporting the SOC or incident-response teams, but the intelligence team will push significant information or trends up to executives when they deem it is important. With the bottom-up approach, there is no guarantee that leadership will respond to information as expected, and even if things run smoothly at the tactical level, there may always be a degree of uncertainty at higher levels. Bottom-up planning can be difficult to implement unless the strategic level of leadership has bought into the concept and has simply decided that, for the time being, operations are best left at the tactical level.

Critical Information Needs

Whether an organization is employing a top-down or a bottom-up approach, one concept can remain consistent: the critical information needs of executives. Critical information includes things that leadership has determined that they need to know about ASAP. It often includes things such as successful intrusions that result in loss of protected information, intrusions into sensitive portions of the network, information on breaches or compromises at partner networks. Some of these information needs will be compliance based, and some will be driven by business needs, but whatever the case, it is important to understand the priorities and the time frame in which executives expect to be informed of one of these situations.

Hiring an Intelligence Team

Now comes the fun part! Planning has been painstakingly carried out, the stakeholders for the intelligence program have been identified, goals have been set, and requirements identified. Now is the time to find the individuals who will do the work. Based on budget and the requirements, this may mean hiring a single individual or a team, but the important part is to find the right people based on all of the objectives that have been identified during the planning process. The skill sets and experience levels will vary based on the primary stakeholders and goals, but one key tenet is almost always true when assembling an intelligence team: diversity.

Diversity in experiences and backgrounds is important to developing a well-rounded team capable of tackling a variety of issues. Diverse skill sets will strengthen the overall team. Based on stakeholder's needs, an intelligence team can include intelligence professionals with cultural, geopolitical, and even language knowledge. It can also include those with a background in business intelligence or a knowledge of the organization's operations. It may also include incident handlers, penetration testers, programmers and tool developers, and management. With such a variety of potential team members, it is critical that hiring the team is the last step in the process of building an intelligence program, because until stakeholders and goals are identified, it is difficult to know the correct team composition.

Demonstrating Intelligence Program Value

Once the program has been implemented and the team begins operations, they will inevitably have to demonstrate the value of the program. If the program was properly planned and resources were allotted, you should already have an idea of what will show value to stakeholders. While it may be important to report daily or weekly statistics or metrics on the work that is being done, what will really show value is being able to convey the impact of the intelligence program. How has the program supported stakeholders? What is the organization able to do or focus on that they could not have without intelligence support? What risks was the organization able to take based on a better understanding of the threats facing them? Be sure to answer these questions as explicitly as possible when reporting on your program's activities.

It is also important to capture and discuss the lessons learned when things did not always go as expected. Identifying what worked and what didn't, and why, can provide information to help others avoid making the same mistakes. Intelligence teams will not always get everything right the first time, but learning from missteps is an important part of maturing a program.

Conclusion

The move from selective support of incident-response engagements to a full-fledged intelligence team is a big jump. This book focused on how to become proficient and add value as an individual supporting incident response, but once your organization sees how much value a single incident-response person can provide, key stakeholders may realize how valuable it would be to have an entire team of IR professionals. Intelligence is the glue that can bind together multiple diverse teams operating at different levels with different priorities. Although they may not work together directly that often, that doesn't mean that there aren't many benefits of having those teams support each other, and an intelligence program can enable those interactions.

Moving toward a formalized intelligence program, especially one that is properly planned and resourced, can help organizations continue to build upon the foundation and processes introduced in intelligence-driven incident response and move even further toward intelligence-driven security.

Intelligence Products

Here are some example products based on the GLASS WIZARD threat.

Short-Form Products

As described in Chapter 9 Short Form products are one or two page tactical products meant for quick release and consumption.

IOC Report: Hydraq Indicators

This is a short form IOC report detailing indicators of the Hydraq malware used by the GLASS WIZARD actor.

Summary

Hydraq is one of the pieces of malware used by GLASS WIZARD on important targets. The following indicators may be useful for identifying malicious activity.

Table A-1. Indicators

Indicator	Context	Notes
Rasmon.dll	Filename	
Securmon.dll	Filename	
A0029670.dll	Filename	
AppMgmt.dll	Filename	
HKEY_LOCAL_MACHINE\SYSTEM\CurrentControlSet\Services\RaS[% random 4 chars %]	Malware reg key	Space removed before random chars
%System%/acelpvc.dll	Secondary file	Not a definitive indicator
%System%/VedioDriver.dll	Secondary file	Not a definitive indicator
RaS[FOUR RANDOM CHARACTERS]	Service name	May have false positives as a result

Indicator	Context	Notes
yahooo.8866.org	C2 domain	
sl1.homelinux.org	C2 domain	
360.homeunix.com	C2 domain	
li107-40.members.linode.com	C2 domain	
ftp2.homeunix.com	C2 domain	
update.ourhobby.com	C2 domain	
blog1.servebeer.com	C2 domain	

Notes

- Inactive domains are set to loopback (127.0.0.2).
- Symantec also had information about network traffic indicators.

Related TTPs

- Delivery is believed to be via spear phishing.

References

- McAfee virus profile: *Roarur.dll* (*https://home.mcafee.com/virusinfo/viruspro file.aspx?key=253416*)
- Symantec blog (*https://www.symantec.com/connect/blogs/trojanhydraq-incident*)

Event Summary Report: GLASS WIZARD Spear Phishing Email— Resume Campaign

Summary

Starting on February 22, we have observed a targeted phishing campaign aimed at four (4) system administrators within our organization. The attacker sent a fake introduction email requesting consideration for junior system administrator positions with a malicious link leading to a site attacking Internet Explorer vulnerability CVE-2014-0322. This campaign may be attempting to gain access for future attacks.

Timeline

- 2015-02-22 10:47: Earliest observed email delivered.
- 2015-02-22 11:02: Email opened by User1, no click-through.
- 2015-02-22 11:14: Email opened by User2, clicked through, not vulnerable (Firefox user).
- 2015-02-22 13:10: Email opened by User3, clicked through, exploited.

- 2015-02-22 13:15: User3 recognizes oddness on exploit site, reaches out to SOC.
- 2015-02-22 13:26: SOC begins investigating.
- 2015-02-22 14:54: SOC identifies previously unseen process running on user system.
- 2015-02-22 14:58: Incident declared
- Current state

Impact

Unknown at this time; investigation in progress.

Recommendations

- Remove network connectivity for infected host.
- Identify command and control.
- Sinkhole the DNS records.
- Block IPs at external firewalls.
- Remediate host.
- Perform triage malware analysis.

Ongoing Actions

- Hunt for secondary infections and C2 activity.
- Contact vendors about ongoing protection.
- Patch related hosts.

References

- Cisco blog (*https://blogs.cisco.com/security/talos/threat-spotlight-group-72*)

Target Package: GLASS WIZARD

This is a target package (see Chapter 9) for the GLASS WIZARD actor.

Summary

GLASS WIZARD is a threat actor known for targeting organizations inline with China's strategic goals. GLASS WIZARD is known for using a wide variety of tools, moving from generic multiuser tools like Poison and PlugX to unique, actor-specific malware such as WINNTI and Hydraq. The actor has TTPs that indicate a high level of adaptability and even a large organization.

Alternative Name	Source
AXIOM	Novetta

Tactics, Techniques, & Procedures

- Uses a tiered approach to malware, starting with commodity tools and saving custom capabilities for harder targets.
- Leverages common network admin tools to move laterally between systems.
- Utilizes strategic compromises (such as stealing certificates) to enable future attacks.

Table A-2. Tools

Name	Description	Notes
Poison Ivy	Remote-access Trojan	Commodity kit
PlugX	Remote-acess Trojan	Commodity kit
Gh0st	Remote-access Trojan	
WINNTI	Remote-access Trojan	Closely held but shared
Derusbi	Unknown	
Hydraq	Unknown	
Hikit	Server-side remote-access Trojan	Specific to Axiom
Zox	Remote-access Trojan	Malware family, specific to Axiom

Victim Profile

The following characteristics are based on information from third-party reporting:

- Human intelligence information sources
- Technology organizations
- Nongovernmental organizations (NGOs)
- Strategic compromises to steal useful resources (e.g., Bit9 signing certificates)

Table A-3. Related Actors

Name	Type	Notes
WINNTI	Actor group	High levels of overlap, possibly closely related
Elderwood	Actor group	From Symantec reporting

Related References

- Novetta Executive Summary (*http://bit.ly/2u9wjkJ*)

Long-Form Products: Hikit Malware

More detailed, multipage reports are referred to as long form products. These are products typically developed by teams of analysts and cover particularly wide or deep content.

Here is a (very basic) malware report based on one of GLASS WIZARDs most notorious pieces of malware, Hikit.[1]

Key	Value
Reverse engineer	Novetta Malware Analysis Team (*http://bit.ly/2weOoBp*)
Date	2014/11/01?
Requester	Intelligence team
Associated intrusion set	GLASS WIZARD

Summary

Hikit is a later-stage remote-access Trojan (RAT) used by GLASS WIZARD on compromised high-value targets. What makes Hikit unique is that unlike early-stage implants (such as Poison Ivy) that are used on victim organization client systems (employee endpoints), Hikit is deployed on internet-facing services. Instead of using a callback beacon, as is used in Poison Ivy, the attacker accesses Hikit as a server via a trigger, and then uses it for a variety of uses including proxying into the victim network.

Basic Static Analysis

- Filename: *oci.dll*
- File type: portable executable—Win32 Dynamic-Link Library
- File size: 262,656 bytes

Table A-4. Hashes

Hash algorithm	Value
MD5	d3fb2b78fd7815878a70eac35f2945df
SHA1	8d6292bd0abaaf3cf8c162d8c6bf7ec16a5ffba7
SHA256	aa4b2b448a5e246888304be51ef9a65a11a53bab7899bc1b56e4fc20e1b1fd9f
SHA512	
Ssdeep	6144:xH8/y2gN1qJ2uvknuXsK+yW14LSb5kFiE:6/y9N1ruvkiEyW14LSb5kB

---

1 This malware report was created using resources from Novetta (*http://www.novetta.com/wp-content/uploads/2014/11/HiKit.pdf*), Contagio (*http://bit.ly/2uQvG2q*), Hybrid Analysis (*http://bit.ly/2vSGIB4*), and VirusTotal (*http://bit.ly/2tv2p9o*).

Table A-5. Current antivirus detection capabilities

Vendor	Sample
Avast	Win32:Hikit-B [Rtk]
ClamAV	Win.Trojan.HiKit-16
CrowdStrike	-
ESET-NOD32	Win32/Hikit.A
F-Secure	Gen:Variant.Graftor.40878
Kaspersky	Trojan.Win32.Hiki.a
Malwarebytes	-
McAfee	GenericR-DFC!D3FB2B78FD78
Microsoft	Backdoor:Win32/Hikiti.M!dha
Qihoo-360	Trojan.Generic
Sophos	Troj/PWS-BZI
Symantec	Backdoor.Hikit
TrendMicro	BKDR_HIKIT.A

Interesting strings

- `Nihonbashi Kodenmachou10-61`
- `7fw.ndi`
- `W7fwMP`
- `CatalogFile= w7fw.cat`
- `ClassGUID = {4D36E974-E325-11CE-BFC1-08002BE10318}`
- `ClassGUID = {4d36e972-e325-11ce-bfc1-08002be10318}`
- `CopyFiles = W7fw.Files.Sys`
- `DelFiles = W7fw.Files.Sys`
- `DiskDescription = "Microsoft W7fw Driver Disk"`
- `W7fwmp`
- `W7fw_HELP`
- `Norwegian-Nynorsk`
- `W7fw.Files.Sys = 12`
- `W7fw.sys`
- `W7fwMP_Desc = "W7fw Miniport"`
- `W7fwService_Desc = "W7fw Service"`
- `W7fw_Desc = "W7fw Driver"`
- `h:\JmVodServer\hikit\bin32\RServer.pdb`
- `h:\JmVodServer\hikit\bin32\w7fw.pdb`
- `h:\JmVodServer\hikit\bin32\w7fw_2k.pdb`
- `h:\JmVodServer\hikit\bin64\w7fw_x64.pdb`

Other relevant files or data

- *RServer.pdb*
- *w7fw.pdb*
- *w7fw_2k.pdb*
- *w7fw_x64.pdb*
- *W7fw.sys*
- Driver file, currently unknown to us.

Basic Dynamic Analysis

N/A. Using information from third-party report.

Behavioral Characteristics

- Acts as a remote-access Trojan including:
  — shell: allows remote shell access to the victim system
  — file: gives direct filesystem access
  — connect: establishes a port-forwarded connection
  — socks5: forwards proxy traffic
  — exit: ends channel
- Receives HTTP request from outside host (malware acts as service) by intercepting network traffic

Delivery Mechanisms

- Second-stage tool, delivered via adversary upload to target host.

Persistence Mechanisms

- Runs as a service on the compromised host.

Spreading mechanisms

- Manual. Attacker may proxy through an infected host in spreading.

Exfiltration mechanisms

- File exfiltration may take place via `file` command.

Command-and-control mechanisms

- Attacker accesses the victim host via direct network connection (host must be internet facing).
- Attacker uses the */password* path.

Dependencies

Environment & files neccessary for Hikit to run.

Supported operating systems.

- Microsoft Windows operating system (versions unknown)
- Imports from the following system files:
  — *ADVAPI32.dll*
  — *KERNEL32.dll*
  — *ole32.dll*
  — *SETUPAPI.dll*
  — *SHLWAPI.dll*
  — *USER32.dll*
  — *WS2_32.dll*

Required Files.

- Driver file that allows network access: *%TEMP%\w7fw.sys*

Second Stage Downloads

- N/A (this is a second-stage kit)

Registry Keys

- Unknown

Detection

Information for detecting Hikit.

Network Indicators of Compromise.

- N/A at this time (this is a server component)

Filesystem indicators of compromise.

- "YNK Japan Inc." code-signing certificate

- See "Interesting strings" on page 246 and Table A-4.

Response Recommendations

Recommended actions for mitigating and remediating Hikit infections.

Mitigation steps.

- Disrupt internet-facing network access for an infected system.
- Secondary: block internal network access to prevent the attacker from using an internal proxy.

Eradication steps.

- Because tool is installed by adversary manually, a full rebuild of infected system is recommended.

Related files

- *%TEMP%\w7fw.sys*
- *%TEMP%\w7fw.cat*
- *%TEMP%\w7fw.inf*
- *%TEMP%\w7fw_m.inf*
- *%TEMP%{08acad5e-59a5-7b8c-1031-3262f4253768}\SETEA6F.tmp*
- *%TEMP%{08acad5e-59a5-7b8c-1031-3262f4253768}\SETEDAF.tmp*

Requests for Intelligence: GLASS WIZARD

Requests for Information are a meta-product where a stakeholder requests specific information from an intelligence generating team. Here's an example of an RFI flow that took place during our investigation into the GLASS WIZARD investigation:

- *From:* Forensics team
- *To:* Intelligence team
- *Response by:* ASAP

We're investigating multiple hard drives associated with GLASS WIZARD activity at the request of the SOC. We're requesting any filesystem indicators for the WINNTI malware. We intend to use these for system triage.

References:

- N/A

GLASS WIZARD RFI Response

- *From:* Intelligence team
- *To:* Forensics team
- *TLP:* yellow
- *Response at:* 2016-11-13

GLASS WIZARD (GL) uses a wide variety of malware based on target, including Hydraq, Poison Ivy, Derusbi, Fexel, and others. As a result, WINNTI indicators provided may not be 100% comprehensive.

Included are two attachments (*gw_winnti_hashes.txt* and *gw_winnti_yara.txt*).

Axiom report

- Hashes (*http://www.novetta.com/wp-content/uploads/2014/11/Hashes.txt*)
- YARA (*http://bit.ly/2wmhajQ*)

Index

Symbols

5 Ds of defense, 51, 113

A

access
    credential-based access, 114
    denying, 51, 113
    denying lateral movement, 114
ACH (Analysis of Competing Hypotheses), 156
acknowledgments, xvi
actionability do's and don'ts, 174
Actions on Objective phase, 45
actions over target, 84, 86, 108, 111
active data collection, 37
active defense, 50-53, 113-116
activity groups, 50
activity threads, 49
actor-centric targeting, 62-70
actors
    defined, 62
    determining goals of, 69
    identifying behaviors of, 66
    identifying in reports, 181
    known information on, 63
Address Space Layout Randomization (ASLR),
    40
Admiralty Code, 25
advanced persistent threat (APT), 87
adversaries, 49
alerting
    network alerting, 80-85
    system alerting, 85
analysis
    ACH analysis, 156
    contrarian techniques, 159
    disk analysis, 97
    enriching your data, 142-146
    fundamentals of, 137
    graph analysis, 158
    hypothesis development, 146
    in intelligence cycle model, 20
    judgment and conclusions based on, 151
    key assumption evaluation, 147
    malware analysis, 99-101
    memory analysis, 96
    network analysis, 89
    questions to start with, 140
    role in intelligence process, 10
    social network analysis, 158
    in strategic intelligence, 216
    structured analysis, 151-154
    target-centric analysis, 154
Analysis of Competing Hypotheses (ACH), 156
Analysis phase (F3EAD)
    analytic processes and methods, 151-160
    conducting the analysis, 141-151
    determining what to analyze, 139
    diagram of, 137
    fundamentals of analysis, 137
    overview of, 55, 137
Analyst's Style Manual (Mercyhurst Univer-
    sity), 176
anchoring bias, 149
antivirus systems, 32
APT (advanced persistent threat), 87
APT1 report, 184
architecture support, 235

ASLR (Address Space Layout Randomization), 40
assessing attack responses, 33, 125
asset-centric targeting, 70
association matrices, 158
attachments, 81
attacks
    actions on objective phase, 45
    assessing responses to, 33, 125
    command and control phase, 44, 82
    containing, 30
    credential reuse and, 82
    cryptolocker-style attacks, 86
    delivery phase, 42
    denial-of-service (DoS), 44, 87
    distributed denial-of-service (DDoS), 44
    eradicating, 31
    exploitation phase, 43, 85
    identifying, 30
    installation phase, 43, 86
    preparing for, 28, 235
    reconnaissance phase, 37
    recovering from, 32
    targeting phase, 36
    weaponization phase
        determining exploitability, 39
        implant development, 40
        infrastructure development, 41
        locating vulnerabilities, 38
        testing phase, 41
attribution, 62-64, 105
audiences
    developing consumer personas, 170
    executives and leadership figures, 165
    external technical consumers, 169
    importance of understanding, 164
    internal technical consumers, 167
    risks of exposure and, 169, 181
authors, of intelligence products, 173
    (see also writing process)
automated consumption products, 197-202
    automated IOC formats, 201
    filesystem signatures with Yara, 200
    network signatures with Snort, 198
    unstructured/semistructured IOCs, 197
automated report information, 173, 185
availability bias, 149
Axiom Group, 6

B
backdoors, 31, 43, 114
bandwagon effect, 150
behaviors, of attackers, 66
Betz, Christopher, 49
Bianco's Pyramid of Pain, 64-67
biases
    accounting for, 148
    anchoring bias, 149
    availability bias, 149
    bandwagon effect, 150
    confirmation bias, 149
    mirroring, 150
bottom-up approach, 237
Boyd, John, 14
brainstorming, 218
business sources of intelligence, 216

C
C-suite executives, 166
C2 communication, 82
    (see also Command and Control phase)
campaign reports, 188
campaign tracking, 234
CAPEC (Common Attack Pattern Enumeration and Classification), 131
CIA Library, 25, 165
CIA's Tradecraft Primer, 147
CIRT (computer incident response team), 24
CISO (chief information security officer), 21
Clinton campaign email incident, 40
CME (Coordinated Malware Eradication), 5
CNN-centric targeting, 71
code names, 181
cognitive biases, 148
Collaborative Research into Threats (CRITS), 134
COMINT (communications intelligence), 11
Command and Control phase, 44, 82, 107
commander's intent concept, 212
comments and questions, xvi
Common Attack Pattern Enumeration and Classification (CAPEC), 131
computer incident response team (CIRT), 24, 128
computer network defense
    architecture support, 235
    assessing attack responses, 33, 125
    attacker identification, 30

eradicating attacks, 31
 preparation against attack, 28, 235
 recovering from attacks, 32
confirmation bias, 149
consumers, 164
 (see also audience)
containment, 30
contrarian techniques, 159
Coordinated Malware Eradication (CME) , 5
credential reuse, 82
credential-based access, 114
critical information needs, 238
CRITS (Collaborative Research into Threats), 134
CRUD acronym, 86
cryptolocker-style attacks, 86
Cuckoo's Egg, The (Stoll), 2
cyber kill chains (see kill chains)
Cyber Observable eXpression (CybOX), 126
cyber threat intelligence (CTI)
 defined, 2
 history of, 1
 modern day, 2
 role in incident response, xiii, 1-4
CYBINT (cyber intelligence), 12
CybOX/STIX/TAXII, 126

D

D5 model of defense, 51, 113
dangles, 116
data
 converting between standards, 130
 data exfiltration, 84
 email metadata, 81
 enrichment of, 19, 142-146
 flow-based data, 90
 handling by sensitivity level, 132
 hard vs. soft, 37
 vs. intelligence, 10, 65
 managing information, 132
 metadata, 19
 organizing incident data, 116-120
 prioritization of, 19
 sharing, 146, 169
 soft data, 37
 storing threat information, 126-135
 translation of, 19
 visualization of, 20
Data Breach Incident Report (DBIR), 130

data collection
 active vs. passive, 37
 avoiding duplicate data, 133
 in Exploitation phase, 125
 from disk analysis, 98
 from full content analysis, 95
 from malware analysis, 101
 from previous incidents, 125
 from signature-based analysis, 94
 from traffic analysis, 91
 in intelligence cycle model, 17
 key things to capture, 132
 sources and methods, 11-13
 in strategic intelligence, 213
data processing, 18
data standards and formats
 converting between standards, 130
 for indicators, 126-130
 for strategic information, 130
date and time formats, 197
DBIR (Data Breach Incident Report), 130
deception, 52, 115
deep web/dark web data collection, 13
Delivery phase
 alerting on delivery, 81
 common forms of delivery, 81
 in kill chains, 42
 mitigating delivery, 107
denial-of-access attacks, 45
denial-of-service (DoS), 46, 87
denying access, 51, 113
detectability, 41
development practices, 39
devil's advocate technique, 160
DHS's Traffic Light Protocol, 132
diamond model, 49
Digit Forensics and Incident Response (DFIR), 24
direction statements, 177
disk analysis, 97
disrupt and degrade, 51, 114
dissemination (see also intelligence products)
 defined, 163
 in intelligence cycle model, 20
 resources required, 163
 in strategic intelligence, 220
Dissemination phase (F3EAD)
 actionability and, 174
 audience in, 164-172

authors in, 173
establishing a rhythm, 202
intelligence consumer goals, 164
intelligence product formats, 180-202
overview of, 55, 163, 204
writing process, 176-180
distributed denial-of-service (DDoS), 44
DNS (Domain Name System), 143
documentation, 29
DoS (denial-of-service), 46, 87
drones, 45

E

economic intelligence, 215
ELINT (electronic intelligence), 11
email metadata, 81
enrichment of data, 19, 142
eradication, 31
estimative probability, 25, 165
event summaries, 181
exploitability process, 39
exploitation phase, 43, 85, 110
Exploitation phase (F3EAD)
    choosing what to exploit, 124
    gathering information, 125
    overview of, 55, 123
    storing threat information, 126-135

F

F3EAD process
    Analysis phase, 137-161
    diagram of, 53
    Dissemination phase, 163-204
    Exploitation phase, 123-136
    Find phase, 61-78
    Finish phase, 105-122
    Fix phase, 79-103
    key issues addressed by, 53
    overview of, 54-56
    primary components of, 61
    using, 56
Fast Incident Response (FIR), 119
feedback, obtaining, 203
filesystem indicators, 66, 200
filtering of data, 19
Find phase (F3EAD)
    actor-centric targeting, 62-70
    asset-centric targeting, 70
    main goal of, 64

news-centric targeting, 71
organizing targeting activities, 75
overview of, 54, 61
prioritizing targeting, 73
RFI process, 77
targeting based on third-party notifications, 72
FININT (financial intelligence), 12
Finish phase (F3EAD)
    assessing damage, 120
    vs. hacking back, 105
    monitoring life cycle, 121
    organizing incident data, 116-120
    overview of, 54, 105
    stages of, 106-113
    taking action, 113-116
FIR (Fast Incident Response), 119
FISINT (foreign instrumentation signals intelligence), 11
5 Ds of defense, 51, 113
Fix phase (F3EAD)
    hunting, 102
    intrusion detection, 80-89
    intrusion investigation, 89-101
    overview of, 54, 79
    scoping, 101
flow-based data, 90
FM 2-22.3 (NATO System), 25
formalized intelligence programs, 239
    (see also intelligence programs)
full content analysis, 94
functionality of malicious code, 41

G

GEOINT (geospatial intelligence), 12
geopolitical intelligence, 213
GLASS WIZARD scenario
    biases in, 149
    building a kill chain, 67
    CybOx object example, 126
    F3EAD application, 57
    Fix phase, 87
    graph analysis of, 159
    hypothesis development, 147
    key assumption evaluation, 148
    malware report, 245
    mitigating, 108
    network signatures, 199
    rearchitecting, 112

remediating, 112
RFI process, 249
spear phishing email, 242
target package, 243
timeline model, 212
unstructured IOCs, 198
GNU Emacs, 2
goals
defining for intelligence programs, 227
determining attacker's, 69
of intelligence consumers, 164
Google's Looking into the Aquarium report, 169
graph analysis, 158
Grey Spike example kill chain, 47
group IOCs, 197

H

hack backs, 50, 105
hard data, 37
hard leads, 75
hardening, 29
Heuer, Richard, 148
high-level information vs. technical details, 125
historical sources of intelligence, 215
honey pots/honey nets, 13, 115
HUMINT (human-source intelligence), 11
hunting, 102
Hutchins, Eric M., 35
hypotheses
analysis of competing, 156
developing, 146

I

ICS (industrial control systems), 70
IDIR (intelligence-driven incident response)
approach to learning, xiv
benefits of, 5, 7
defined, 5
examples of applied, 5
responsibility for collection, analysis, and dissemination, 139
role of strategic intelligence in, 208
IMINT (imagery intelligence), 12
implant development, 40, 114
incident data, organizing, 116-120
Incident Object Definition and Exchange Format (IODEF), 128
incident response

active defense, 50
defined, 27
diamond model, 49-50
examples of IDIR, 5
F3EAD process, 53-57
incident-response cycle, 28-34
kill chains, 35-48
model selection, 57
role in intelligence, 4
role of threat intelligence in, xiii
scenario: GLASS WIZARD, 57
incident-response cycle, 28-34
Containment phase, 30
diagram of, 28
Eradication phase, 31
goal of, 28
Identification phase, 30
Lessons Learned phase, 33
Preparation phase, 28
Recovery phase, 32
incident-response systems, 119
incidents and investigations data, 13
indexing data, 19
indicator management, 232
indicators of compromise (IOCs), 11, 65, 183, 197, 232, 241
indicators, data standards and formats for, 126-130
industrial control systems (ICS), 70
information (see also data; data collection)
managing, 132
sharing, 146, 169
Information Sharing and Analysis Centers (ISACs), 146
Information Sharing and Analysis Organizations (ISAOs), 146
infrastructure development, 41
installation phase, 43, 86, 110
intelligence (see also cyber threat intelligence; intelligence process; strategic intelligence)
confidence levels of, 25
defined, 4
early applications of, 3
levels of intelligence, 24
role of incident response in, 4
sharing with external consumers, 169
translatable intelligence, 169
intelligence cycle model
analysis step, 20

collection step, 17
diagram of, 17
direction step, 17
dissemination step, 20
feedback step, 21
processing step, 18
using, 21
intelligence estimates, 193
intelligence process (see also cyber threat intelligence)
ligence)
basic premise of, 9
confidence levels of intelligence, 25
data collection, 11-13, 17
data vs. intelligence, 10, 65
levels of intelligence, 24
models used, 14-22
qualities of good intelligence, 23
use of military jargon in, 13, 124, 197
intelligence products
actionability and, 174
audience for, 164-172
authors of, 173
cycle of production, 202
date and time formats, 197
defined, 164
distributing, 202
formats for, 180-202
intelligence consumer goals, 164
long-form product examples, 245-250
overview of, 204
sharing with external consumers, 169
short-form product examples, 241-244
writing process, 176-180
intelligence programs
building collection capability, 18
costs of, 224
defining goals, 227
defining metrics for, 230
defining stakeholders, 226
defining success criteria, 228
demonstrating value of, 238
hiring teams, 238
identifying requirements and constraints,
228
organizing multilevel programs, 237
planning for, 225, 237
prerequisites for creating, 223
use cases, operational, 234
use cases, strategic, 235

use cases, tactical, 231
internal enrichment information, 145
Internet Relay Chat (IRC), 83
intrusion detection
diamond model of, 49
incident-response cycle, 28-34
intrusion detection systems (IDSs), 92
kill chain pattern, 35-48
network alerting, 80
role of models in, 27
system alerting, 85
intrusion investigation
disk analysis, 97
live response, 96
malware analysis, 99-101
memory analysis, 96
network analysis, 89-95
IOCs (indicators of compromise), 11, 65, 183,
197, 232, 241
IODEF (Incident Object Definition and
Exchange Format), 128
IODEF-SCI (IODEF—Structured Cybersecurity
ity Information), 129
IRC (Internet Relay Chat), 83
ISACs (Information Sharing and Analysis Centers), 146
ters), 146
ISAOs (Information Sharing and Analysis
Organizations), 146
Island Hopping campaign , 234

K
kanban boards, 119
Kent, Sherman, 25, 165, 208
key assumptions, evaluating, 147-151
kill chains
Actions on Objective phase, 45
actor-centric targeting and, 67
attacker behaviors and, 66
benefits of, 35
building, 67
Command and Control phase, 44, 82
Delivery phase, 42, 81
diagram of, 35
example: Grey Spike, 47
Exploitation phase, 43
Exploitation Phase, 85
history of, 36
incident cycles and, 46
Installation phase, 43

Installation Phase, 86
Reconnaissance phase, 37
Targeting phase, 36
Weaponization phase, 38-42
Krebs, Brian, 72

L
lateral movement, 114
leads
 developing, 102
 grouping related, 75
 hard vs. soft, 75
 storing/tracking, 76, 116
 testing, 103
Lee, Robert, 71
Lessons Learned phase, 33
links, 81
live response, 96
Lockheed Martin Cyber Kill Chain, 35
long-form products, 184-193
 campaign reports, 188
 examples of, 245-250
 intelligence estimates, 193
 malware reports, 185
 RFI process, 193-197
 vs. short-form, 184
Looking into the Aquarium report (Google),
 169

M
malware
 automated analysis of, 173
 extracting technical details from, 125, 145
 identifying threat actors with, 64
 lacking command and control, 84
 long-form reports, 185, 245
 malware analysis, 99-101
 remediating installation, 110
 self-guided, 45
 Yara filesystem tool for, 200
Malware Information Sharing Platform (MISP),
 133
Managed Incident Lightweight Exchange
 (MILE), 128
Mandiant APT1 report, 184
Mandiant's OpenIOC, 65
MASINT (measurement and signature intelligence), 12
memory indicators, 66, 96

Mercyhurst University's Institute for Intelligence Studies , 176
metadata, 19, 81
metrics, defining, 230
Microsoft Threat Intelligence Center (MSTIC),
 181
Microsoft's Enhanced Mitigation Experience
 Toolkit (EMET), 40
Microsoft's Security Development Lifecycle, 39
MILE (Managed Incident Lightweight
 Exchange), 128
mirroring, 150
MISP (Malware Information Sharing Platform),
 133
mission statements, 164
mitigation
 ideal execution of, 107
 in intelligence programs, 236
 mitigating actions over target, 108
 mitigating command and control, 107
 mitigating delivery, 107
MITRE, 65, 126
models
 active defense, 50
 diamond model, 49-50
 effective use of, 14
 F3EAD process, 53-57
 hierarchical, 209
 incident-response cycle, 28-34
 intelligence cycle, 17-22
 kill chain, 35-48
 linear, 211
 network models, 210
 OODA loop, 14
 overview of, 14
 process models, 211
 selecting, 57
 target models, 209
 timelines, 211
moonlighting, 70
movemail function, 2
MSTIC (Microsoft Threat Intelligence Center),
 181
murder boards, 219

N
name deconfliction, 18
National Security Agency (NSA), 2
NATO System (FM 2-22.3), 25

NATO's Computer Incident Response Capability (NCIRC), 133
NCPH Group, 64
network alerting
    activities identified by, 80
    alerting on actions over target, 84
    alerting on command and control, 82
    alerting on delivery, 81
    alerting on reconnaissance, 80
network analysis
    applying intelligence to full content analysis, 95
    applying intelligence to signature-based analysis, 94
    applying intelligence to traffic analysis, 91
    full content analysis, 94
    gathering data from full content analysis, 95
    gathering data from signature-based analysis, 94
    gathering data from traffic analysis, 91
    signature-based analysis, 92, 198
    traffic analysis, 90
network indicators, 66
network models, 210
network persistence, 44
network signatures, 198
news-centric targeting, 71
NIST 800-61 Computer Security Incident Handling Guide, 28
normalization of data, 19

O

OASIS Suite, 126
Office of National Estimates (ONE), 193
OODA (observe, orient, decide, act) loop model, 14
    Act phase, 15
    Attacker-Defender OODA loops, 16
    Decide phase, 15
    Defender- Defender OODA loops, 16
    Observe phase, 15
    Orient phase, 15
open systems interconnection (OSI), 94
OpenIOC, 65, 130
Operation Aurora, 6
Operation SMN, 5
operational intelligence, 24
OPM breach incident, 138
OSINT (open source intelligence), 12

OSXCollector, 96

P

PaaS (platform-as-a-service), 83
passive data collection, 37
Passive DNS Replication, 143
patching, 110
payload delivery, 40, 42, 81
People's Liberation Army Unit 61398, 184
personas, developing, 62, 170, 230
phishing, 42, 242
platform-as-a-service (PaaS), 83
PlugX , 64
port scans, 38, 80
practicing plans, 29
preparation for attacks, 28
previous incidents, gathering data from, 125
prioritization of data, 19
privilege escalation, 39
probability estimates, 25, 165
process models, 211
processing data, 18
Pyramid of Pain, 64-67

Q

questions and comments, xvi

R

ransomware, 45
Real-time Inter-network Defense (RID), 129
rearchitecting, 112
recon (Reconnaissance phase), 37-38, 80
recovery, 32
red team analysis, 160
Redline memory analysis tool, 96
reformatting systems, 111
remediation
    goal of, 109
    remediating actions over target, 111
    remediating exploitation, 110
    remediating installation, 110
remote-access Trojan (RAT), 44, 108
report writing (see writing process)
RFI (requests for information), 77, 193-197, 249
RID (Real-time Inter-network Defense), 129
risk assessment, 236

S

SaaS (software-as-a-service), 83
scanning ports, 38, 80
scoping, 101
scorched-earth approach, 31
security operations center (SOC), 24, 232
self-guided malware families, 45
sensitivity levels of data, 132
sessions, revoking, 108
shared resources, misuse of, 83
short-form products, 180-184
    event summaries, 181
    examples of, 241-244
    IOC reports, 183
    target packages, 182
SIGINT (signals intelligence), 11
signature-based analysis, 92, 198, 232
situational awareness, 232, 236
SMN (some marketing name), 5
Snort IDS signature, 92, 198
SOC (security operations center), 24, 232
social network analysis, 158
social-engineering lures, 110
SOD (Spreadsheet of Doom), 118
soft data, 37
soft leads, 75
software development practices, 39
software-as-a-service (SaaS), 83
spear phishing, 42, 242
Spreadsheet of Doom (SOD), 118
SQL injection, 42
stakeholders
    defining, 226
    demonstrating value to, 238
    personas for, 230
stated goals, 164
STIX (Structured Threat Information Expression), 65, 126, 201
Stoll, Cliff, 1
strategic intelligence (see also intelligence)
    analysis of, 216
    brainstorming and, 218
    data standards and formats for, 130
    defined, 208
    developing target models, 209
    disseminating, 220
    as ego-free process, 219
    extracting strategic-level details, 125
    importance of, 207, 220
    in intelligence programs, 235
    military vs. CTI view of, 25
    murder boards and, 219
    processes for, 217
    setting requirements and goals, 212
    sources of data, 213
    strategic intelligence cycle, 212-220
    SWOT analysis, 217
strategic web compromise, 43
structured analysis, 151-154
Structured Threat Information Expression (STIX), 65, 126, 201
Stuxnet incident, 39, 45
success, defining criteria for, 228
SWOT analysis, 217
system alerting
    alerting on actions over target, 86
    alerting on exploitation, 85
    alerting on installation, 86
    target operating systems and tools, 85
system persistence, 44
system reformatting, 111

T

tabletop exercises, 229
tactical intelligence, 24
tactical-level details, 125
tactics, techniques, and procedures (TTPs), 36, 62
target models
    developing, 209
    hierarchical, 209
    network models, 210
    process models, 211
    timelines, 211
target-centric analysis, 154
targeting
    actor-centric targeting, 62-70
    asset-centric targeting, 70
    news-centric targeting, 71
    organizing targeting activities, 75
    prioritizing targeting, 73
    RFI process, 77
    target packages, 63, 182, 243
    targeting based on third-party notifications, 72
Targeting phase, 36
TAXII (Trusted Automated eXchange of Indicator Information), 126

teams, hiring, 238
TECHINT (technical intelligence), 12
technical details vs. high-level information, 125
telemetry systems, 29
testing malicious code, 41
third-party notifications, 72
threat data (see data; data collection)
threat intelligence (see also cyber threat intelligence; intelligence process)
    defined, 2
    vs. IOCs, 11
    need for, 3
threat-based approach, 236
threat-intelligence platforms (TIP), 133, 233
ticketing systems, 119
time and date formats, 197
timelines, 211
top-down approach, 237
Tradecraft Primer (CIA), 147
traffic analysis, 90
Traffic Light Protocol (TLP), 132, 175
translatable intelligence, 169
translation of data, 19
Triage Intelligence, 232
Trusted Automated eXchange of Indicator Information (TAXII), 126
TTPs (tactics, techniques, and procedures), 36, 62
typographical conventions, xv

U

United States' Office of Personnel Management (OPM), 138
unknown unknown situations, 31

V

Verizon Data Breach Incident Report (DBIR), 130
virus removal tools, 32
visualization of data, 20

Vocabulary for Event Recording and Incident Sharing (VERIS), 130
Volatility toolkit, 97
vulnerabilities, locating, 38, 236

W

walk-through exercises, 229
watering hole attacks, 43
Weaponization phase, 38-42
weekly threat reports, 204
"what if" analysis, 160
White Sands Missile Range, 2
WHOIS protocol, 142
Wireshark, 94
Words of Estimative Probability (CIA), 25, 165
writing process
    automated consumption products, 197-202
    campaign reports, 188
    common intelligence writing pitfalls, 179
    date and time formats, 197
    direction statements, 177
    draft creation, 177
    editing stage, 178
    establishing a rhythm, 202
    event summaries, 181
    identifying actors, 181
    intelligence estimates, 193
    IOC reports, 183
    malware reports, 185
    narrative format and, 177
    obtaining feedback, 203
    planning stage, 176
    product examples, 241-250
    RFI (requests for information), 193-197
    target packages, 182
    understanding the audience, 164-172

Y

Yara, 200
Your Everyday Threat Intelligence (YETI), 134

About the Authors

Scott J. Roberts is an incident handler, intelligence analyst, writer, and developer who protects companies from computer network espionage and attack. Scott believes in sharing techniques and tools for identifying, tracking, and responding to advanced computer network attackers. He has released and contributed to multiple open source incident response, intrusion detection, and cyber threat intelligence tools. Scott is an instructor for SANS Forensics 578 Cyber Threat Intelligence course. He currently works for GitHub as the manager of Security Operations: SIRT. Scott studied Information Science & Technology and researched information security at Penn State University.

Rebekah Brown has spent more than a decade working in the intelligence community; her previous roles include NSA network warfare analyst, operations chief of a United States Marine Corps cyber unit, and a US Cyber Command training and exercise lead. Rebekah has helped develop threat-intelligence and security-awareness programs at the federal, state, and local level, as well as at a Fortune 500 company. Today, Rebekah leads the Rapid7 threat-intelligence programs at Rapid7, where her responsibilities include program architecture, management, analysis, and operations. Rebekah lives with her three kids in Portland, Oregon, where she grew up, and spends her free time hiking and hacking and reading *Harry Potter*.

Colophon

The animal on the cover of *Intelligence-Driven Incident Response* is a Fan-tailed raven (*Corvus rhipidurus*). It is a member of the crow family and is the smallest of the raven species. These birds are native to countries of the Arabian Peninsula and those across the pond (the Red Sea) in Northeast Africa. These days, they can also be found further west and south in the Sahara, Kenya, and Niger with nests on rock ledges, cliffs, or trees.

The fan-tailed raven is completely black in plummage, beak, and feet, with overall shades of purple, gray, or brown in certain light. Both males and females average about 18 inches in length, with wingspans of 40 to 47 inches. With its rounded tail, broad wings, and long primary remiges, this bird resembles a vulture when in flight.

The diet of the fan-tailed raven is omnivorous and consists of insects and other invertebrates, berries, grain, and food scavenged near human populations. They will also pick out grain from other animal feces, ride goats and camels for a parasitic meal, or eat nestlings and eggs from nests of smaller birds.

Like a parrot or other talking bird, the fan-tailed raven is capable of vocal mimicry of humans, but only seems to do so if in captivity.

Many of the animals on O'Reilly covers are endangered; all of them are important to the world. To learn more about how you can help, go to *animals.oreilly.com*.

The cover image is from *Riverside Natural History*. The cover fonts are URW Typewriter and Guardian Sans. The text font is Adobe Minion Pro; the heading font is Adobe Myriad Condensed; and the code font is Dalton Maag's Ubuntu Mono.

Learn from experts.
Find the answers you need.

Sign up for a **10-day free trial** to get **unlimited access** to all of the content on Safari, including Learning Paths, interactive tutorials, and curated playlists that draw from thousands of ebooks and training videos on a wide range of topics, including data, design, DevOps, management, business—and much more.

Start your free trial at:
oreilly.com/safari

(No credit card required.)

CPSIA information can be obtained
at www.ICGtesting.com
Printed in the USA
BVHW081057040320
574062BV00008B/149

9 781491 934944